Hizbullah and the Politics of Remembrance

Writing the Lebanese Nation

AF215141

Born out of the Israeli occupation of the South of Lebanon, the political armed group Hizbullah is a powerful player within both Lebanon and the wider Middle East. Understanding how Hizbullah has, since the 1980s, developed its own reading of the nature of the Lebanese state, national identity, and historical narrative is central to grasping the political trajectory of the country. By examining the ideological production of Hizbullah, especially its underground newspaper *al-'Ahd*, Bashir Saade offers an account of the intellectual continuity between the early phases of Hizbullah's emergence onto the political stage and its present-day organization. Saade argues here that this early intellectual activity, involving an elaborate understanding of the past and history, had a long-lasting impact on later cultural production, one in which the notion and practice of resistance has been central in developing national imaginaries.

Bashir Saade is a Teaching Fellow in Politics and International Relations at Edinburgh University. Previously a Lecturer at the American University of Beirut, he holds a Ph.D. in War Studies from King's College, University of London. He focuses on the subject of culture and how language and symbols affect political processes. Saade's current research aims at proposing new perspectives on understanding the relations between Islamic movements and states.

Cambridge Middle East Studies

Cambridge Middle East Studies has been established to publish books on the nineteenth- to twenty-first-century Middle East and North Africa. The series offers new and original interpretations of aspects of Middle Eastern societies and their histories. To achieve disciplinary diversity, books are solicited from authors writing in a wide range of fields including history, sociology, anthropology, political science, and political economy. The emphasis is on producing books affording an original approach along theoretical and empirical lines. The series is intended for students and academics, but the more accessible and wide-ranging studies will also appeal to the interested general reader.

Other titles in the series can be found after the index.

Hizbullah and the Politics of Remembrance

Writing the Lebanese Nation

Bashir Saade

University of Edinburgh

CAMBRIDGE
UNIVERSITY PRESS

University Printing House, Cambridge CB2 8BS, United Kingdom

One Liberty Plaza, 20th Floor, New York, NY 10006, USA

477 Williamstown Road, Port Melbourne, VIC 3207, Australia

314-321, 3rd Floor, Plot 3, Splendor Forum, Jasola District Centre, New Delhi-110025, India

79 Anson Road, #06-04/06, Singapore 079906

Cambridge University Press is part of the University of Cambridge.

It furthers the University's mission by disseminating knowledge in the pursuit of education, learning and research at the highest international levels of excellence.

www.cambridge.org
Information on this title: www.cambridge.org/9781107499386

First published 2016
First paperback edition 2018

A catalogue record for this publication is available from the British Library

Library of Congress Cataloging in Publication data
Saade, Bashir, 1980–
Hizbullah and the politics of remembrance : writing the Lebanese nation / Bashir Saade, University of Edinburgh.
New York : Cambridge University Press, 2016. |
Series: Cambridge Middle East studies ; 47 | Includes bibliographical references and index.
LCCN 2016020881 | ISBN 9781107101814 (hardback)
LCSH: Hizballah (Lebanon) | Lebanon – Politics and government –
1990– | Islam and politics – Lebanon. | Islam and state – Lebanon. |
BISAC: POLITICAL SCIENCE / Government / International.
LCC JQ1828.A98 H626424 2016 | DDC 324.25692/082–dc23
LC record available at https://lccn.loc.gov/2016020881

ISBN 978-1-107-10181-4 Hardback
ISBN 978-1-107-49938-6 Paperback

For Leo and Nour, who give meaning to all things.

Contents

Figures

Acknowledgments

This book, based on seven years of research, has been a long time coming. Since then the world has changed, our region has definitely changed, and I have changed. Despite all these changes certain constants have remained, and they are at the heart of the concerns of this book.

It is impossible to thank by name all those who were directly or indirectly involved in this project or who supported me along the way, but I will try my best and hope that if you are not mentioned you will forgive me . . .

First, I am highly indebted to the patience of Yezid Sayigh and Vivienne Jabri for providing interesting comments and listening to my ideas and argument that change as fast as the weather in the UK. I also want to thank Madawi Al Rasheed and Reinoud Leenders for encouraging me to publish my work.

I also would like to thank Aurélie Daher and Adham Saouli for the long and still unfinished discussions we had on Hizbullah. Sharing our research findings and our passion to understand has been a true blessing of comradeship. I am indebted to Amal Saad-Ghorayeb for being a devoted yet critical ear and a great inspiration and to Ibrahim Moussawi for his priceless support in providing needed documents and media material as well as access to various party members for interviews. His trust and friendship has been a great push forward, especially in times of difficulty.

For more than two years, turning the library of the German Orient Institut in Beirut into a de facto office as I scanned through their impressive integral archive of al-'Ahd made this project possible. More especially I would like to thank the outstanding librarians (Martiniano Roncaglia, and the late Dr. Wolf-Dieter) who diligently collected each issue of the underground newspaper from the beginning of 1984 in the midst of the civil war. I am also infinitely grateful for the assistance, support, and friendship of OIB's chief librarian Marcel Behrens, as well as for the help of Ali Wehbe.

Some friends have been key to my sanity and for encouraging me to finish. Among them are Bilal Orfali, Ahed Sboul, Charles Harb, Alain

George, Maha Taki, Maha Ismail, and Jihad Touma. I would also like to thank Ayman Ayoub for giving his time to travel around the beautiful South of Lebanon, and making me discover its multifaceted sides.

This adventure would not have been possible without the initial inspiration of Yahya Sadowski, who made me believe that academia was my vocation early on during my undergraduate studies at the American University of Beirut. In the same way, I will also always remember Georges Bitar, whose humor and intellectual subtlety were a model to emulate. I also wish to thank Ali Ghandour, whose unending love and grace was a support throughout my studies and beyond.

The support of my family who did not stop believing in me was a huge encouragement, especially my mother and sister. My wife Annabel has been indispensable; her companionship, eternal uplifting smile, and positive spirits have had the most therapeutic effects, and her intellectual help was crucial to the finalization of this draft.

This study is a tribute to all those who dedicated their lives in their fight to regain their lands in South Lebanon. Even if it proposes to study critically the phenomenon that is Hizbullah it respects the core legacy it aimed to defend. In fact, I hope the ethics I try to follow to look at this phenomenon in the most transparent and academic way can attempt to match the ethics of those who decided to choose resistance.

Introduction

In February 2009, the Hizbullah-affiliated Waad organization issued a new song called "Tammuz" in memory of Imad Mughniyya, a top Hizbullah cadre assassinated on 12 February 2008 in Damascus. The video clip pushed to unprecedented levels a genre that uses certain nationalist symbols that the party's media policy began to employ intensively following the Israeli withdrawal from South Lebanon in 2000. Among other scenes, the video showed an old woman sitting calmly and sewing a Lebanese flag as a young boy carried a ball of thread and an old man helped them by holding the slowly assembling flag. This image was preceded and succeeded by images of soldiers and children solemnly walking and raising the Lebanese and Hizbullah flags.

In the mid-1980s, when Hizbullah did not even have a flag and had a much less developed organizational structure, al-'Ahd, the underground weekly newspaper of this newly forming organization, occasionally published pictures of the aftermath of battles, with resistance fighters posing on conquered territory. The only flag visible in these scenes was that of the Iranian "Islamic revolution."[1] These visions of the beginnings of Hizbullah have had a tremendous influence on different perceptions of the party as well as on the party's image of itself. The Lebanese civil wars that took place from 1975 to 1990 had accustomed readers to the notion that new groups emerged only when they had a foreign "sponsor." The flag, pictures of Iranian Supreme Leader Ruhollah Khomeini, and various Iranian Islamic revolutionary slogans, including Khomeini's key call to liberate Jerusalem, testified to a new political entity on the Lebanese arena, but fixed, so to speak, the terms of speeches that helped frame that organization.

The decade that followed the end of the civil wars in Lebanon witnessed a process of official political reconciliation between the different protagonists. This period, dubbed the "reconstruction era,"[2] solidified

---

[1] See for example the front page of al-'Ahd 131 (27/12/1986).
[2] This was owing to the politics of then prime minister Rafic Hariri and his project to rebuild the main infrastructural elements of the country as well as the downtown area of Beirut.

the legitimacy of the resistance as a national or simply political project sanctified by the state of Lebanon, and enabled Hizbullah to become a complex web of institutions and organizations. Apart from the main and essential military section named the "Islamic resistance," and along with having a parliamentary coalition, and since 2005 being part of the cabinet, Hizbullah performed a number of functions more akin to mainstream party work, developing an impressive array of institutions that provide all types of social benefits. This is paralleled by media production, a prolific publishing industry, and the organization of countless events, commemorations, seminars, conferences, public speeches, and rallies of all sorts.

Today, most of the revolutionary slogans are still present alongside newer ones. Hizbullah's current secretary general, Sayyid Hassan Nasrallah, in a 2008 speech to that effect, promised that today's generation would see the liberation of Jerusalem.[3] Although he did not mention by whom or how Jerusalem would be liberated, Khomeini's slogan has been repeated countless times over the years in all types of rallies and ceremonies. For example, as with other commemorations throughout the year, Jerusalem Day is celebrated every year at the end of the month of Ramaḍān, with banners invading the streets of the southern suburbs of Beirut and the main highways to the south of Lebanon or the Bekaa, and rallies taking place during that day in all those regions, during which Nasrallah most importantly, but other officials as well, give speeches. Looking back at this periodic display of symbols and ideas, Hizbullah has very much stuck to these early slogans, not abandoning a single one of them. Indeed, it may be said that Hizbullah deliberately had not departed from any that had circulated since the founding of the organization. Yet, something had changed. What was the order of that change? Where was it located?

A concern over the allegiance or affiliation of Hizbullah and this fear of its intentions both within and outside of Lebanon informed the production of a prolific literature set to "frame" Hizbullah. This was among the prevailing questions one could ask: Is Hizbullah a Lebanese political organization? Or at least, does it have a Lebanese agenda? Hizbullah's display of symbolic production has been interpreted in various ways by political actors, media, and academics at large. It has informed the creation of categories of analysis in order to classify the phenomenon of Hizbullah. As part of a market of symbols and ideas, these attempts were closely interlinked with Hizbullah's efforts as an organization to export specific images of itself to the world at large.

---

[3] Hassan Nasrallah, speech on Jerusalem Day, 26/9/2008.

Tracking the agenda of Hizbullah, and the various meanings available to the organization, caused the views of scholars to diverge in several directions. Some tended to think of Hizbullah as having changed its political agenda, whether gradually or not, and undergoing what has been dubbed a "Lebanonization" process: taking part in the legislative process, expanding relations with other political parties, and, lately, holding ministerial portfolios. These scholars thought of the party as becoming "Lebanese" in the sense of conforming to the "rules of the game" of the different political players: The "revolutionary" Hizbullah of the 1980s was associated with a pan-Islamic political drive, oblivious of the presence of local issues, whereas the "pragmatic" or "realist" Hizbullah became a symbol of national coexistence. This shift has been widely debated, not just by Western or Lebanese scholars, but also by intellectuals close to the party, as well as by party members.[4]

A second trend of thinking saw Hizbullah as adopting various strategies in order to push forth the same agenda it had had since its early inception. Its proponents write about the Iranian link or alliance as proof that Hizbullah will always have an "external" agenda. They claim that the party diligently follows its plan to install an Islamic republic in Lebanon, as its main writings and declarations have claimed since its founding, or at least that it has, at best, a remote interest in state building, mainly using the existing confessional system in order to expand its "state within a state."[5] So the absence of change in slogans here is taken as proof that Hizbullah owes no allegiance to the politically and morally sanctioning entity called Lebanon, which dictates the way "things should be said."[6]

Far from being clearly distinct, however, these two ways of thinking the politics of Hizbullah actually meet in many ways. Arguing that Hizbullah as an organization uses the confessional system either "pragmatically" or "wholeheartedly" presupposes in both cases a clear analytical distinction between the beliefs, discourse and practices of the party and a "cultural sphere" that has some kind of symbolic importance that can be denominated as the confessional system, the Lebanese state, or the nation. It assumes that Hizbullah has a clear-cut, self-conscious set of interests and chooses to engage in this or that political practice. Above all

---

[4] In the larger academic sphere see for example Joseph Alagha, *The Shifts in Hizbullah's Ideology: Religious Ideology, Political Ideology and Political Program* (Leiden: ISIM/ Amsterdam University Press, 2006); Masood Asadollahi, *al-Islāmiyyūn fī mujtamāʿ taʿaddudī* (Beirut: Arab Scientific Publishers, 2004), and Fayyad's papers (examined in chapter 4).

[5] See for example Walid Sharara, *Dawlat Hizbullāh: Lubnān mujtamāʿan Islāmīyyan* (Beirut: Dar al-Nahar, 1998).

[6] Pierre Bourdieu, *Ce que parler veut dire: l'économie des échanges linguistiques* (Paris: Fayard, 1982).

it assumes that, for example, the notions that make up understandings of the Lebanese confessional system are not actually altered by the way Hizbullah conceptualizes itself, a point on which this study differs.

A Note on the Literature

This book attaches special importance to the writings on Hizbullah not only to acknowledge what has been covered but also because it departs signifi-cantly from what has been written so far. Scholarship on Hizbullah, espe-cially Western, has responded to the demands of its policy makers. This is not a fully exhaustive account of the literature on Hizbullah, but it focuses on particular conceptual highlights that inform the overall literature, thus I apologize in advance for those who do not find their works featured here.

Thus, Hizbullah started as a problem that only "political scientists" were interested in, mostly those focused on "security questions," and "security" here refers to Western security. This drove scholars to engage in a kind of "intelligence-gathering" work, and to focus on the hypothetical structure of the organization, as well as finding out the identities of the people who made up the organization. The basic question underlying this approach was: Who was killing Western troops (referring to the blowing up of the American Marines' barracks in October 1983)? Who was taking Americans (and other foreigners) hostage? And who was conducting suicide operations against Israeli troops? Were all these operations by the same organization? Knowing more about the group(s) meant simply gathering "intelligence." As an illustration, during the 1980s one concern (among others) was whether Mohammad Hussein Fadlallah, a leading Shi'i cleric who supported the resistance against the Israelis through his speeches and constant presence at martyrs' commemorations, was in fact part of the organization. However, in this process, the writings of Martin Kramer[7], and later on Magnus Ranstorp, who was mostly concerned with such questions of security, relied heavily on information produced by Israeli intelligence services.[8]

---

[7] See Martin Kramer, "Hezbollah: The Calculus of Jihad," in *Fundamentalisms of the State: Remaking Polities, Economies and Militance* (Chicago: University of Chicago Press, 1993); Martin Kramer, "Redeeming Jerusalem: The Pan-Islamic Premise of Hizballah," in *The Iranian Revolution and the Muslim World* (Boulder: Westview Press, 1990); Martin Kramer, "The Moral Logic of Hizbullah," in *Origins of Terrorism: Psychologies, Ideologies, Theologies, States of Mind* (Cambridge: Cambridge University Press, 1990); Martin Kramer, "The Oracle of Hezbollah, Sayyid Muhammad Hussein Fadlallah," in *Spokesmen for the Despised: Fundamentalist Leaders of the Middle East* (Chicago: University of Chicago Press, 1997).

[8] Magnus Ranstorp, *Hizb'Allah in Lebanon: The Politics of the Western Hostage Crisis* (New York: St. Martin's Press, 1997); Magnus Ranstorp, "Hizbollah's Command

Up until 1997, when Hala Jaber published her book *Hezbollah: Born with a Vengeance*, the most important subject was still the taking of Western hostages and the early part of Hizbullah's (or affiliated groups') history. Although by that time, Hizbullah-affiliated intellectuals had already published several biographies of the movement in Arabic, none would be consulted by English-speaking scholars.[9] Jaber's journalistic account included unprecedented testimonies shedding light on the early phase of hostage-taking and related activities of the 1980s from the viewpoint of the party members. In this justificatory vein, two other papers written in 1998 and 1999 by Augustus Richard Norton aimed at showing the pragmatism of Hizbullah to a Western audience.[10] But the prevailing climate of inquiry at the time was still around security questions: Ranstorp published his first study on Hizbullah as part of general studies on "Terrorism."[11] Ranstorp also argued that the "Lebanonization process" was part of an overall strategy followed by Hizbullah to implement long-term plans for controlling the state. This went hand in hand with Waddah Sharara's long and intricate study that the gradual Islamization and clericalization of Lebanese Shi'i community was the result of an "Iranization" process of which Hizbullah was the proxy.[12]

It was not until 2002, almost twenty years after the appearance of Hizbullah, that a book would attempt to address the issue of ideology more directly: Amal Saad-Ghorayeb's *Hizbullah: Politics and Religion*. Saad-Ghorayeb's book was a full-blown theoretical discussion of the ideology of the party based on interviews with senior party officials: Mohammad Fneish, Mohammad Raad, Nawaf Moussawi[13]. Thus far, Saad-Ghorayeb's book has been a notable exception, dealing with the phenomenon of Hizbullah in the most direct way – that is, eschewing the moral argument of whether the movement is "revolutionary" or "pragmatic," "Lebanese" or "Iranian." The merit (and the limitations) of Saad-Ghorayeb was to take at face value the various ideas party members

---

Leadership: Its Structure, Decision-making and Relationship with Iranian Clergy and Institution," *Terrorism and Political Violence* 6:3 (1994); Magnus Ranstorp, "Terrorism in the Name of Religion," *Journal of International Affairs* 50:1 (1996); Magnus Ranstorp, "The Strategy and Tactics of Hizballah's Current 'Lebanonization Process'," *Mediterranean Politics* 3:1 (1998).

[9] See Hassan Fadlallah's works, for example *al-Khayar al-akhar* (Beirut: Dar al-Hadi, 1994).

[10] Augustus Richard Norton, "Hizballah of Lebanon: Extremist Ideals vs. Mundane Politics" (New York: Council on Foreign Relations, 1999); Augustus Richard Norton, "Hizballah: From Radicalism to Pragmatism," *Middle East Policy* 5 (1998).

[11] Ranstorp, *Hizb'Allah in Lebanon*.

[12] Sharara, *Dawlat Hizbullāh*.

[13] Amal Saad-Ghorayeb, *Hizbullah: Politics and Religion* (London: Pluto Press, 2002).

agreed to discuss with her, thanks to her privileged access to senior members of the organization.

To be fair, these earlier works were mostly concerned with "classical political science" questions, which involved attempts to capture a "formal" ideology of the party or its worldview, its political strategies and choices, and its various military practices and how they evolved over time. Studying change in this case meant looking at overarching ideological shifts, choices and strategies, political priorities that depended on the particular context that the organization faced. The quintessence of such approaches is Alagha's *Shifts in Hizbullah's Ideology*, which groups together concerns with political strategy and ideological visions, and Nizar Hamzeh's *In the Path of Hizbullah*, which aimed at breaking new ground in terms of information on the organization of Hizbullah, published in 2006 and 2004 respectively.[14] Whereas Hamzeh argued that Hizbullah implemented a "gradualist pragmatist" politics that involved engaging with the Lebanese political system, Alagha was more keen on arguing (albeit confusingly) that Hizbullah has drastically changed from a pre-1992 revolutionary politics to a coexistence-motivated "Lebanese" agenda. Even though there was a slight difference between the two arguments, it did not stop some scholars arguing about Hizbullah's political strategy using both works.

This strategy of writing about the party remains prevalent. Most recent books published about Hizbullah, such as Lina Khatib, Dina Matar and Atef Alshaer's study of the "politics and communication" of the party, fall into the same methodological trap, which assumes a particular understanding of "political strategy" or ideology, doctrines, etc. from which it has been working meticulously since its inception, even if these understandings are never fully explained and illustrated.[15] This study aims to shed light on this precise question: How to understand the ideological in Hizbullah.

There are several interlinked problems with traditional political science approaches. The first is the implicit theorization of the existence of a "Hizbullah mind." This tends to essentialize what is being studied, by assuming that there is something (a substance in philosophical terms, a truth, etc.) hidden inside the actor or the organization, something more or less static that possibly escapes social and historical context. A prominent example of that is Alagha's thesis of an alleged overall shift

---

[14] Alagha, *The Shifts in Hizbullah's Ideology*; Nizar Hamzeh, *In the Path of Hizballah* (Syracuse: Syracuse University Press, 2004). Hamzeh had previously written an article joining Norton's concern with the contrast between the ideal and pragmatic politics of Hizbullah. See Nizar Hamzeh, "Lebanon's Hizbullah: From Islamic Revolution to Parliamentary Accommodation," *Third World Quarterly* 21:5 (1997).

[15] See Lina Khatib, "Hizbullah's Political Strategy," in Lina Khatib, Dina Matar and Atef Alshaer, *The Hizbullah Phenomenon: Politics and Communication* (London and New York: Hurst & Co. and Oxford University Press, 2014).

in Hizbullah's ideology, as if a coherent one had existed in the first place.[16] But a completely different one is Sharara's insistence that Hizbullah is an Iranian satellite on Lebanese soil.[17]

Subtler but still similar in effect is the reification of certain concepts which are taken out of their actual everyday and polyvalent uses: examples are infamously used terms such as *jihād* and less well-known ones such as *wilāyat al-faqīh*. These terms seem to have a built-in epistemological life of their own, somehow outside not just the variations given to them by the different ideologues who articulate them, but also the practices of the organization. This is linked to a conceptualization of culture as made up of static symbols somehow floating above social actors. Kramer's formulation is quite revealing in this regard when he states that "the calculus of politics is not driven by a universal logic.[18] It is conditioned by cultural values. Hizbullah did not simply seek power; it sought power in order to implement Islamic law." But what is a universal logic of politics? Aren't representations of politics always culturally laden in the sense of being determined by meaning-making practices? And what are these Islamic laws that seem to stick out from any other kind of rules and regulations that pervade the different forms of human action? It seems that Kramer assumes that there is a universal mode of conduct that is superior in importance to something called a "cultural" or "Islamic" mode. Kramer continues: "submission to Islamic law freed Hizbullah from non-Islamic moral constraints. Hizbullah felt no need to justify its acts by other codes. Its struggle was a jihad, a form of sacred warfare regulated solely by Islamic law." Here again, there is something very frustrating about these statements: Is warfare labeled sacred just because it is regulated by Islamic law? How are these different from other laws? And when people go to war or engage in militant activities, can their actions be explained by having internalized uniformly this monolithic package of rules and regulations?

In reality, the "*jihād* concept" – just like any other notion or term – cannot be extracted from the many different interpretations given by the various social actors engaged in that intellectual production. More importantly, the struggle to define this term is at the heart of the political process. What Kramer says about *jihād* will find an echo in Hizbullah's own theoretical formulations. In sum, looking for formal definitions of

---

[16] In 2011 Alagha replaced his concept of ideological shift with identity construction, although still referring to the same dynamic. See Joseph Alagha, *Hizbullah's Identity Construction* (Amsterdam: Amsterdam University Press, 2011).

[17] Most of Sharara's work is plagued by this implicit idea. See Sharara, *Dawlat Hizbullāh*. Despite all the complexity of the media analysis deployed by Khatib, Matar, and Alshaer, the conclusion there seems to be similar.

[18] Kramer, "Hezbullah."

what *jihād* stands for and how it is related to an epistemological body of rules and regulations does explain what Hizbullah officials, clerics, and intellectuals want to show to the world, but does not describe the actual social process taking place.[19]

This leads us to the second problem: the adoption of what in Bourdieu's terms can be called a "phenomenological approach."[20] This consists of collecting what the party verbalizes as its perception of reality and elevating it to a description of actual political reality; the latter is then regarded as a self-explanatory "understanding" of Hizbullah. This intellectual practice, symptomatic of political science approaches to culture, takes what is being said at face value and treats it as a concrete analytical reality stripped of the social context in which these meanings are produced.[21] This is less easily escapable than it would appear, as it involves a drastic reconsideration of what is meant by "ideology," as argued in this thesis. For example, according to Saad-Ghorayeb, the Huntingtonian "clash of civilizations" thesis holds because Hizbullah party members she interviewed do say that the party is engaged in a "civilizational struggle with the West."[22] However, this is still taking for granted what the Hizbullah actor says without grounding it in its social context, or at least in the reason that drives him to say this. This makes it seem as if everything a Hizbullah-affiliated intellectual says is structured, coherent, and fits into the overall puzzle that constitutes its ideology or worldview.

The Politics of Remembering and Readdressing the Notion of Ideology

The present inquiry starts from the simple intuition that Hizbullah's own representations of politics inevitably changed prevailing representations of Lebanese politics, and have been significantly changed by them. In "political science" jargon, the term that this study evokes is the one of "interest." I adopt a constructivist approach that rejects the idea that representations are just "epiphenomenal" and have no power on more material variables.[23] A constructivist approach understands that concepts

---

[19] Hamzeh also attempts to do that in his chapter on "Islamic Juristical Ideology." See Hamzeh, *In the Path of Hizballah*, 36–39.

[20] See Pierre Bourdieu, *Esquisse d'une théorie de la pratique, précédé de trois études d'ethnologie Kabyle* (Paris: Éditions du Seuil, 1972).

[21] As argued in Lisa Wedeen, "Conceptualizing Culture: Possibilities for Political Science," *American Political Science Review* 96:4 (2002).

[22] Although she rejects the idea that this civilizational "struggle" can be called a "clash." See Saad-Ghorayeb, *Hizbullah: Politics and Religion*, 88–89.

[23] For a formulation of this methodological trend in international relations, see M. Finnemore and K. Sikkink, "Taking Stock: The Constructivist Research

and notions are constantly renegotiated and change in tandem with social reality. Even if Hizbullah-related actors move pragmatically, make "rational" decisions, may have an elaborate political plan, and show, voice, and produce clear intent through their various political practices, these intents are "framed" through prevailing signs and symbols, which in turn shape and thus inform political action. These signs and symbols have a polyvalent use, are changing, and replete with meanings constantly making up different understandings of Lebanese imaginaries, perceptions of population, and representations of the state, writing of histories, and so on, that in turn inform – and thus have a direct bearing on – political and social action. But taking ideas seriously does not discount how embedded they are in material variables, or how they actually produce action on the ground and are in turn produced by it. The point is to understand the dialectical process that inextricably links ideas and materiality.

Thus, I found that scholarly, media, and political interest in a specific "nationality" of Hizbullah or the nature of its affiliation are interesting points of departure to observe a phenomenon that links ideas to materiality or political action on the ground. Looking for an answer to the affiliation of the party led me to delve deeper into the symbolic production of its affiliated intellectuals, party members, journalists, scholars, and other related producers of texts. But as I searched for concrete outspoken theoretical formulations that endorsed visions of the nation or condemned it in other ways, I noticed that theoretical constructions were ceding the space to another process which involved specific writings on history or what I grouped under the general practice of "claiming the past."

How do Hizbullah-affiliated intellectuals produce texts, and thus meaning, shaped by prevailing political practices? These processes of identification by Hizbullah involve a constant rewriting of the past that directly affects the various political actions of the party. The only way Hizbullah, and for that matter most political organizations in general, can set different political objectives is through a constant reappraisal of the past. It is only through this process that Hizbullah writes the theoretical background, the political agenda, and the visions of the party. But these "visions" or "agendas" are never complete at different points in time. Every attempt at fixing them will involve delving into the past through some archiving practice.

This activity of reclaiming the past can only take place through a specific "textual practice," a particular use of available texts and the

Program in International Relations and Comparative Politics," *Annual Review of Political Science* 4:1 (2001).

creation of new ones written either by Hizbullah-affiliated intellectuals or by others. The past is not comprehended or represented just as a set of historical narratives, but also as a succession of texts used, dropped, and reappropriated in different ways. This takes place through the ways Hizbullah-affiliated intellectuals decide to engage in a process of archiving, of marking down, and constantly reusing that symbolic material in order to make sense of reality.

Because of this practice, I argue that the past is translated into successive ideological templates that are used and reused to project a unified doctrine. Instead of having a coherent overarching ideology, the reality of time and that of the interpretability of texts forces writers and speakers affiliated to Hizbullah to constantly engage in an archival process that inscribes the past in the form of text in order to make sense of their present. In other terms, this "presence" of ideological material in the media and other discursive repositories, or projection of an overall ideology, is always contested in so far as the party always needs to jump back in the past, either through commemorations (recalling martyrs or a more general human legacy) or through confronting historical narratives of its political environment, or still, reclaiming the history of its territory, in order to make sense of its political presence or vision.

This is why the production of meaning happens with the backdrop of other symbolic productions that are more or less established or legitimized. Politics in this sense represents the study of the prevailing form of certain understandings, categorizations, and writings that contribute to the strengthening or weakening of a movement by legitimizing or putting it on the wrong side of "logic" or sense. The struggle to fix meaning and to project a coherent "identity" or "ideology" is a political process, as it involves being pitted against certain sanctioning and legitimizing entities such as the state and the myriad institutions related to it. For example, it is not just the fight against the appellation of "terrorist" with which Hizbullah has struggled fiercely almost since its emergence as an organization,[24] but all the other terms of speech – such as modernity, secularism, citizenship, pluralism, liberalism, and so on – all the other signifiers that intellectuals affiliated with Hizbullah had to deal with at one point or another that occur in media, academic settings, or any other information-producing site. In effect, as Hizbullah-affiliated intellectuals elaborate different ideological constructions they are also constrained by cultural imperatives that cannot be "consciously" put into question.

---

[24] See Mona Harb and Reynoud Leenders, "Know thy Enemy: Hizbullah, 'Terrorism' and the Politics of Perception," *Third World Quarterly* 26:1 (2005).

One after the other, intellectuals and ideologues define a political cause, a movement, a political program, while being constrained by the hegemonic, the unquestionable, the unconscious, or the form. For example, Hizbullah ideologues feel compelled to address the question of "terrorism," to show by this or that discursive elaboration, and through action, that the party is not a terrorist organization just because overwhelming numbers of dominant institutions use these terms to classify organizations or political movements and thus produce policy propositions based on these classifications. These institutions include dominant international actors such as the United States administration, or other powerful states, the international community, and more local entities in Lebanon such as the state and the different powerful political parties such as Christian political parties (especially during the civil war). Although there is an actual power struggle taking place involving the monopoly of meaning, dominant discourse is not a coherent set of symbols, and various components enter and exit depending on different ideological elaborations. But these institutions set the terms of speech that are slowly disseminated and replicated by all types of social institutions and agents.[25]

Hizbullah-affiliated intellectuals engaged in four interrelated writing strategies that involved a particular use of the past. First, claiming a specific human legacy became the backbone of Hizbullah's resistance memory. Second, engaging with prevailing writings of history enabled Hizbullah-affiliated intellectuals to propose representations of "the other." One way to do this was to inscribe the other into a tradition of reading the past. Third, claiming territory paves the way to addressing questions of state and a political regime's legitimacy by positing the resistance project as necessary to nation building. Fourth, theorizing what Hizbullah is as a political formation involved mostly a writing of the legacy of the Resistance. These four acts of claiming intersect one another. They are the themes that divide this book into chapters. Inevitably, archiving the past in such a way strengthened the symbolic power of the weapons of the resistance as the backbone of the *raison d'être* of Hizbullah.

Hizbullah started as a slowly agglomerating nexus of militant groups working against the Israeli army occupying Lebanese territories after 1982. Some of these groups existed before the occupation, partly enmeshed in Palestinian or leftist militant formations, and others through Islamic charities and associations. Hizbullah's very local (territorial)

---

[25] For an elaboration of the dissemination of power see Michel Foucault, *L'ordre du discours* (Paris: Gallimard, 1971).

agenda is couched in a regional revolutionary atmosphere through the rise of Shi'ite clerics (mainly from Iraq, Iran, and Lebanon) and rendered feasible after the political takeover of the Ayatollah Ruhollah Khomeini in Iran. Militant clerical developments in Lebanon are not new though. Starting with Musa al-Sadr in the 1960s, and subsequently with Mohammad Hussein Fadlallah in the 1970s, Islamic institutions carved out their presence in political and social environments. These developments were accompanied by a gradual increase in clerical graduates[26] who went to study in the Shi'ite religious schools of Iraq or Iran and came back to practice some form of social or political action in Lebanon. Rula Jurdi Abisaab convincingly argues that these clerics resemble Gramscian organic intellectuals: a class of people who are consciously involved in the social issues of their communities[27] and who contribute significantly to a change in that structure.[28]

These intellectual and militant currents did not emerge in a vacuum then, but, to the contrary, at a time when ideological struggles were at their peak. Communist and other leftist "revolutionary" discourses were the most widespread ideological forces, to which what would later become Hizbullah was to adopt an ambivalent and contradictory stance mostly framed under the prism of Resistance action, as will be seen in Chapter 4. The Syrian Nationalist Party, the Baath, and other more specifically Arab political formations all had a bearing on the discursive practices of Hizbullah. Islamic tropes in its various discursive elaborations were partly shaped indirectly by reading what they reacted to. This process of non-identification represents what Hizbullah became or "what it was trying not to be," what type of "presence" it reacted to. It is in this vein that Hizbullah-affiliated intellectuals could be thought of as "subalterns" who start actually to "speak," to use Gayatri Chakravorty Spivak's expression,[29] and introducing difference from previous dominant narratives of social reality.

One of the peculiar elements that distinguished Hizbullah from other militant organizations of the time derived from Iranian logistical help,

---

[26] For a sociological description of clerical mobilization see Sharara, *Dawlat Hizbullāh*.

[27] Rula Jurdi Abisaab, "The Cleric as Organic Intellectual: Revolutionary Shi'ism in the Lebanese Hawzas," in H. E. Chehabi (ed.), *Distant Relations: Iran and Lebanon in the Last 500 Years* (London and New York: Centre for Lebanese Studies and I. B. Tauris, 2006).

[28] This can be contrasted to the dismissive tone in Kramer's account that Hizbullah-related clerics were angry students who could not complete their studies in Iraq and Iran and had to let out their frustration in one way or another. This is also found all throughout Sharara's work. See Kramer, "Hezbollah: The Calculus of Jihad"; Sharara, *Dawlat Hizbullāh*.

[29] Gayatri Chakravorty Spivak, "Can the Subaltern Speak?" in *Marxism and the Interpretation of Culture* (Urbana: University of Illinois Press, 1988).

military training, and organization building. One important such practice, from the point of view of this thesis, was its obsessive focus on archiving its practices through the collection of all forms of materials and artifacts. As documented by Walid Houri and Rima Saber, Hizbullah has been filming its operations and other forms of activities since the early 1980s, a practice inherited from the Iranians.[30] But borrowing techniques from Iranians does not fully explain this general concern with tracing down, inscribing, and recording the experience of what came to be known as the resistance. The resistance was a project of being-in-a-process in all its practical extensions: Being in the battlefield gained significance through the collection of enemy artifacts, the recording of battles, their dates, unfolding, mapping, and the listing of martyrs, to name but a few. Legitimizing that project through all these dimensions in the face of the sanctioning (Lebanese) state was mandatory in order to have political significance, build alliances, etc.

In a sense, this book aims to explain how an organization such as Hizbullah understands itself and projects a coherent political program. It tries to answer the simple question: "what is Hizbullah"? I look at how the words and writings of its members and affiliated intellectuals relate to their actions and the actions of other political actors on the ground. Hizbullah's understanding of itself is inevitably linked to its central project, which is the military resistance. But this project arises because of urgent community concerns and so irremediably involves a political project. For example, as will be argued in Chapter 6, Hizbullah never wanted a political party but ended up having to adopt one. Because it arose from community-related urges and developed the leverage to mobilize resources and people and so became able to address such "public" questions, Hizbullah was irrevocably set to confront and relate to the state that it spent most of its time escaping. But this relation between Hizbulah and the state had been lurking in the background ever since the founding of the party. This is why, as I show throughout this book, Hizbullah's ideological formulations are mostly geared at proposing different nationalist imaginaries. Hizbullah does contribute to some form of pan-nationalist imaginary through its remembering practices of Islamic commemorations and articulating the project of resistance as going beyond the boundaries of the state.

In her study on the Shi'i population of Lebanon Shaery-Eisenlohr argues that what she terms "ethnic entrepreneurs" from this religious community have developed their own vision of the Lebanese nation, couched in religious rhetoric and convictions, just like any other sect in

---

[30] Walid Houri and Rima Saber, "Filming Resistance: A Hezbollah Strategy," *Radical History Review* 106 (2010).

Lebanon has done.[31] This book builds to a certain extent on this idea, especially on Shaery-Eisenlohr's acknowledgment that all parties and political groups in Lebanon contribute to the construction of nationalistic visions.

Here, I argue that the imperative of the resistance as a legitimate project actually blurs the boundaries between national and Islamic imaginaries. Through various remembering practices Hizbullah-affiliated intellectuals are engaged in constantly rearticulating what is meant by the Islamic or the national. For example, the "Islamic" signifier is waged to defend difference in resistance practices between Hizbullah and other parties. It is used to question the "nationalism" or "patriotism" of other parties, thus articulating different representations of the national imaginary. The "Islamic" is also invoked to question the legitimacy of certain power and institutional relations such as the confessional system in Lebanon, or the domination of a political group of the rest of the constituency. All along, the "Islamic" keeps a regional perspective intact, using the liberation of Jerusalem slogan, for example, in order to solidify the project of resistance locally and regionally, by signaling loyalties to certain states such as Iran or to imagined communities such as Muslims at large.

Chapters' Outline and Sources

Hizbullah's emergence as a political actor was closely followed by the publication of its weekly newspaper, al-'Ahd. As early as 1984 and up until 2000, when its name was changed to al-Intiqād, al-'Ahd never stopped printing while presenting an array of viewpoints, analyses, and information emanating both from the various Hizbullah-affiliated intellectuals and from an eclectic group of writers coming from different social backgrounds. Chapter 1 will explain why this book focuses to a great extent on these early formulations as a witness for later cultural productions by proposing ways to understand the notion of ideology. An examination of al-'Ahd over the years revealed writing styles and recurrences that inspired the thematic division of this book, as will be seen below. Focusing on the early production of texts by the party shows the reader how these formulations are slowly brought together, structured, modified, dropped, or selected in order to create developing ideological constructions. Al-'Ahd as an intellectual site is a reflection of these templates that would come to pervade the different cultural practices of

---

[31] See R. Shaery-Eisenlohr, *Shi'ite Lebanon: Transnational Religion and the Making of National Identities* (New York: Columbia University Press, 2008).

Hizbullah's affiliated intellectuals: speeches, official declarations, mani-festos, TV talk-shows, interviews, and so on.

Thus, in addition to al-'Ahd, I also look at history books, especially those focused on Lebanese or Shi'i history, poetry and other artistic practices, talk shows and documentaries produced by the Hizbullah-sponsored TV station al-Manar. There are also interesting objects to study such as calendars and diaries where all kind of texts can be found on different dates, signaling events, quotes, and religious (or other types of) sayings. Other materials include the books published by affiliates of the party, narrating the story of Hizbullah, such as the one of the deputy secretary general, Sheikh Naim Qassem,[32] or those of an MP, Hassan Fadlallah,[33] describing political causes in their own terms. Although generally retranscribed in most of these press outlets (not least al-'Ahd), the speeches of famous political figures like those of the current secretary general of Hizbullah, Sayyid Hassan Nasrallah, have an important per-formative function and are treated in this study as crucial to understand-ing how certain ideas and writing styles are disseminated.[34]

Chapters are structured with the aim of catching a glimpse of the various ideological constructions of Hizbullah. Among other things, remembering includes the following: claiming a human legacy; addres-sing history as written by the other; and reclaiming one's own history through representations of territory. Chapter 1 will explain in more detail what I mean by writing strategies, ideology as template, and the various textual practices with which I will be concerned. Chapter 2 goes through Hizbullah's remembering of, in a sense, "its own people." Chapter 3 describes different attempts at understanding the political other through assessing and writing their respective versions of history. Chapter 4 dis-cusses Hizbullah's own writing of its experience "on the ground" through its understanding of territory and representations of the state or its "alter-ego": political legitimacy. Chapter 5 closes with an investigation of the relationship between Hizbullah and the social environment from which it emerged.

---

[32] See Naim Qassem, *Hizbullah: The Story from Within* (London: Saqi, 2005).

[33] See for example Fadlallah, *al-Khayar al-akhar*; Hassan Fadlallah, *Harb al iradat* (Beirut: Dar al-Hadi, 1997).

[34] Most of Nasrallah's speeches (along with those of other prominent Hizbullah figures) are available at www.moqawama.org.

1 Mapping the Ground of Hizbullah's Ideological Production

Newly emerging political organizations all face the challenge of explaining the causes of their existence and actions. This is partly because they do emerge from "real" causes, such as occupation in the case of Hizbullah, which trigger the mobilization of people into more organized groups. Parties, groups, or military formations depend on constant interaction with a social constituency to produce, either by writing or through speech, one or several texts that outline what has been called summarily – especially when looking at political mass-mobilization groups of the nineteenth and twentieth centuries – an ideology. One of the trademarks of modern political formations was an almost obsessive concern with framing ideologies that were deemed to express their political agenda or "vision" in their respective environments.

Ideology became the buzzword for the *raison d'être* of modern political movements and an opportunity to differentiate themselves from the rest of the political environment. Hizbullah is no exception to this process, although in this case the obsessive certainty of scholars, media, and other producers of knowledge that Hizbullah has an overarching, homogeneous, and well-thought-out "ideology" could not be further from the truth.[1] This may partly spring from a misunderstanding of the processes at the heart of "the ideological." And indeed, although Hizbullah has a highly prolific ideological production, its performative dimension is not really understood. This chapter sets out to map the cultural repertoire of Hizbullah after outlining the relevance of ideology to political action.

To avoid going into an exhaustive discussion of the meaning of the term ideology, suffice it to say that scholars currently seem to agree that it refers to a "belief system," a way of understanding the world, or even "systems of political thinking"[2] although exactly what these terms stand for and how they relate to different social and political processes remain a source

---

[1] Michael Freeden puts it well when he writes that "the school of ideology as dogma, as a closed and abstract 'ism', is wishful thinking, a streamlined generalization which is itself a highly ideological product of the cold war" (Michael Freeden, *Ideologies and Political Theory* [Oxford: Clarendon Press, 1998], 23).

[2] Ibid., 3.

of debate[3]. Some even proposed dropping the use of the term altogether,[4] while others have pointed out that the "ideological" does designate something more than just random ideas and beliefs.[5] Although I don't pretend to propose another definition of ideology, I do attempt in the following to shed light on one aspect of ideological production: its conduciveness to the transmission of ethics and the invention and continuity of traditions of political action.

It may be said that the ideological involves intellectual rationales of analyzing reality that help either control or are constrained by social reality. These rationales of thinking invariably deploy what could be called strategies of writing that come to form a tradition of discourse. One important aspect of ideology is the coherence produced by a set of ideas or beliefs.[6] If political organizations face a given reality they struggle to make sense of it using different types of cultural production. The erection of a web – to use a term that loosens the rigid tone inherent to the word "structure" – of ideas, symbols, arguments, types of rationale: in brief, the ideological, seems to be at the heart of political struggle.

Now studying a specific medium risks creating an obsession with it. Recent studies of ideology have developed sophisticated understandings of the inner workings of discourse and rhetoric, given that the objects of study are texts and other cultural traces.[7] Yet it is also important to realize that at stake here is what the ideological points to as a trace of something more "real." Ideological production involves a particular set of social and political actions such as the formation, development, and continuity of organizations and institutions. The study of cultural material and its focus on discourse tends to overly focus on the signifying structures erected by social scientists[8] and neglects to address the power relations that ideology

---

[3] For an impressive review of the countless times and ways the term ideology is used in the social sciences, see J. Gerring, "Ideology: A Definitional Analysis," *Political Research Quarterly* 50:4 (1997).

[4] Ibid., 960–961.

[5] Ibid., 965.

[6] Ibid., 974.

[7] Freeden's definition for example is solely focused on "the conceptual patterns" that make ideas transform into ideologies: "ideologies are distinctive configurations of political concepts, and that they create specific conceptual patterns from a pool of indeterminate and unlimited combinations": Freeden, *Ideologies and Political Theory*, 4. Although Freeden acknowledges a performative and sociological dimension of ideology (22–23), its study as such seem to revolve around discursive analysis. See ibid.

[8] This is a legacy mostly started by Clifford Geertz's seminal work *The Interpretation of Cultures* (New York: Basic Books, 1973). For an overview of the concept of culture from Parsonian and Geertzian focus on discursive systems to one of practice and beyond see William Sewell, *Logics of History: Social Theory and Social Transformation* (Chicago: University of Chicago Press, 2005), 160–162.

either produces or is produced by.[9] Even if in need of significant revision, the initial Marxist concern seems to have captured more efficiently this non-discursive dimension with its notion of false consciousness, and that of alienation, for example, where the beliefs and ideas of a particular group of people are not only related to a social condition, as the Marxists would have it, but also to a given "spiritual" and "living" situation that constrains the actions of people. Ideology was not just a discursive pattern but a way of living, a living embodiment of a particular social condition. Gramsci's definition of ideology cannot be more pertinent here. It is "the terrain on which men move, acquire consciousness of their position."[10] The Gramscian focus on consciousness rather than on discourse or semantics as such is revealing.

The concern with ideology is over what culture actually "does," and how the former represents a given system of thought, logic, or sense.[11] It is not the internal coherence of cultural production that seems to be interesting, given that cultures are constantly penetrated and porous, contain all kinds of ruptures, contradictions and paradoxes, and are used in highly polyvalent ways. Nor are they long-held "value systems" that seem to be fixed in time.[12] Rather, it is the actual effort put, the various factors that contribute to producing coherence, and its social and political consequence that is the most interesting part of ideology and cultural production.

Culture is a repository of symbols, texts, and other semiotic idioms, what Ann Swidler calls a "tool-kit" that enables strategies of action.[13] Swidler's most interesting contribution to the present work is her differentiation of the relations between ideology and culture in settled and unsettled times. In unsettled times ideology supersedes tradition, and is conducive to action by mobilizing communities on different fronts. According to Swidler, in unsettled times ideology becomes salient through doctrine, symbol, ritual.[14] Although I do not focus on rituals as such, except in Chapter 2, I am nevertheless interested in a ritualistic use of texts and media practices. Swidler is correct to point out that "ideological activism occurs in periods when competing ways of organizing action are developing or contending for dominance."[15]

---

[9] Talal Asad, *Genealogies of Religion: Discipline and Power in Christianity and Islam* (Baltimore and London: Johns Hopkins University Press, 1993).

[10] Antonio Gramsci, *The Prison Notebooks* (London: Lawrence & Wishart, 2005), 377.

[11] Wedeen, "Conceptualizing Culture."

[12] Talcott Parsons, *The Structure of Social Action* (New York and London: Free Press and Collier Macmillan, 1949 [1937]).

[13] Ann Swidler, "Culture in Action: Symbols and Strategies," *American Sociological Review* 51:2 (1986).

[14] Ibid., 276.

[15] Ibid., 279.

One aspect of this "ideological activism," I argue here, is a particular use of history or the past in general that is conducive to the transmission of "ethics" as a way of doing.[16] This facet of ideology's work is often overlooked by students of both ideology, as seen above, and of memory, possibly because of an overemphasis on the hermeneutics of memory and history rather than on its practical work.[17] For example, Michael Freeden argues that students of ideology should focus on "thought–speech–text or thought–text," whereas anthropologists look at "objects, institutions, or customs as the containers of thought or myth."[18] This dichotomy produces an inherent limitation for the political student who wants to understand how ideology produces and is produced by social phenomena and, most importantly, its instrumentality in transmitting ethical action. Even though this book looks mostly at textual production, it is concerned primarily with its material implications.

Writing history and the narrative form convey understandings that theoretical constructions fail to do, in particular lines of conduct. For philosopher David Carr "narration ... is constitutive not only of action and experience but also of the self which acts and experiences."[19] Narration seems to make shortcuts between the experience of reality and self-comprehension without going through theorizing, because theoreticality is already conferred in the narrative. Although I would add to this that ethical transmission is not only geared towards self-identity or self-coherence,[20] but involves a communal and relational dimension[21] that is crucial to political action and, for the interest of the present work, party and organizational formation.

Thus, writing history brings coherence to who is who politically and shapes action and relations between the various protagonists by delineating their differences and affinities. What is sometimes qualified as doctrine, method, or even ideology – the terms used by Hizbullah are *nahj* and *'aqīda* – are substantiated by writing political actions in narrative forms instead of theorizing. For example, Hizbullah is the resistance legacy, Christian politics is mostly Political Maronitism before and during the civil war (Chapter 3), the Zionist enemy is military

---

[16] Here I follow the initial Aristotelian focus of ethics as skills and a quality of doing, also rearticulated by the philosopher Alasdair MacIntyre. See Alasdair MacIntyre, *After Virtue* (Notre Dame: University of Notre Dame Press, 2007).

[17] See, for example, the seminal work of Paul Ricoeur, *Memory, History, Forgetting* (Chicago: University of Chicago Press, 2004). Also Maurice Halbwachs, *On Collective Memory* (Chicago: University of Chicago Press, 1992).

[18] Freeden, *Ideologies and Political Theory*, 50.

[19] This idea is drawn from MacIntyre's arguments. See David Carr, "Narrative and the Real World: An Argument for Continuity," *History and Theory* 25:2 (1986), 126, especially Carr's critique of Ricoeur and the hermeneutical school.

[20] Ibid.

[21] Irfan Ahmad, "The Study of Islam and the Arab Spring: A Conversation with Talal Asad," *Public Culture* 27:2 (2015): 259–279.

occupation of land, and political usurpation (Chapter 4), and so on. But one cannot understand any of these appellations except through a reading of history and acknowledgment of the various events that make up a legacy of doing. *Nahj* represents then a tradition of doing, whether recent or stretching back in time. The main question then, is how a process of ethics transmission is conducive to collective mobilization or communitarian action.

Although organizations seem constantly to strive to rearticulate what they stand for, this proliferation of speech material is mostly the trace of a struggle to develop, preserve, and transmit a particular quality of life that is communitarian, and first and foremost conducive to effective political action. This chapter explains how and why a political organization such as Hizbullah produces meaning, makes sense of its social and political environment, and, in so doing, achieves specific political objectives. I look at the use of texts, writing strategies deployed by intellectuals close to the party, and the general cultural background of the organization. A writing and archiving strategy is central to the politics of remembrance, and mapping its field can shed light on the overall ideological production of the party.

Traditions and Modernity

In a way then, this book focuses on how traditions are used or reinvented through ideology to produce strategies of action. If as Swidler argues ideology supersedes tradition in unsettled times, an understanding of tradition still remains to be clarified. My understanding is slightly narrow and partly involves Asad's concept of Islam as a "discursive tradition."[22] Hizbullah's party members try to emulate and embody sets of practices sanctioned by Muslim clerics who are deemed to be knowledgeable in Islamic piety and ethical practices. This knowledge, which is a type of ideological construction, is partly held discursively as it is traceable through texts and their interpretations, and is also partly inherent in the way the past is used and archived, what I propose to call the politics of remembrance.

The modern age sees an unprecedented proliferation of ideological production, what Timothy Mitchell observes through colonialist practices of "image-making" that constructs a "world-as-picture" that is confused with "the real."[23] These cultural practices are also used by any political organization that strives to control or manage resources, territory, or population. Mitchell himself locates "the stage" of modernity as

---

[22] Talal Asad, "The Idea of an Anthropology of Islam," *Qui Parle*, 17:2 (2009): 1–30.
[23] Timothy Mitchell, "The Stage of Modernity," in *Questions of Modernity* (Minneapolis and London: Minnesota University Press, 1999), 17.

a series of cultural practices taking place in the outskirts of the Western world.[24] The use of "the modern novel, newspaper, census, map, and museum, as well as the many other, more invasive practices that create the punctual time-space of modernity" promises attainment of the real by endlessly attempting to represent it.[25]

The dualism of image and reality, this readiness to render abstract a specific action on the ground, the way it can be framed as constitutive of a cause or a plan, becomes the main and most effective tool for political organization and institutional formation. This modeling partly feeds into the construction of national imaginaries, using the modern technologies of textual production (newspapers and media outlets at large, political declarations, etc). It involves the textual practices outlined above, especially their archiving mechanisms. It is not that humans and institutions did not engage in such cultural practices before the last two centuries. Yet, one peculiar modern phenomenon is the infinite possibility to delve into this intellectual production thanks to the presence of such technological and archival mechanisms (media, academia, and so on).

One way to understand the relation between ideology and tradition is to borrow from Antonio Gramsci's differentiation between the ideological and the hegemonic. Although Gramsci did not explicitly deal with it in his writing, it is most eloquently retrieved by the anthropologists Jean Comaroff and John Comaroff in their book *Of Revolution and Revelation*.[26] The hegemonic constitutes the repertoire of cultural practices that are assumed and inescapable in the framing of political demands or discontent, whereas the ideological opens the possibility of articulating new representations of change. But ideological material is dependent on the larger dominant hegemonic cultural field. Ideologies "give expression" to resisting voices within a specific hegemonic realm. Social change takes place gradually through a dialectical process where ideological constructions, elaborated by intellectuals and political actors, struggle to challenge these deep-seated hegemonic structures. In this case, ideological constructions become hegemonic once certain groups succeed in institutionalizing consequent changes.[27]

Another interesting implication of this conceptualization of the hegemonic field as the idioms, ideas, categories, concepts, and life habits that structure actions and dispositions is that the ideological constructions

---

[24] Ibid., 22.
[25] Ibid., 18.
[26] J. L. Comaroff and J. L. Comaroff, *Of Revelation and Revolution*, vol II: *The Dialectics of Modernity on a South African Frontier* (Chicago: University of Chicago Press, 1997), Introduction.
[27] Ibid., 25–26.

are constantly engaged in the borrowing and use of the hegemonic. In this sense, the hegemonic is the trace, the archived, what is "there" to be used.[28] The rise of print (and later digital) technology triggered unprecedented possibilities for political formations in attempting to confront, relate, or control the state with its own set of symbols. The modern state is the dominant political institution that either can produce the type of power to control resources, territory, and protect community continuity or is a potential for such power, coveted by different groups and organizations. The presence of the state and its projection of community belonging symbolized as nation "interpellates"[29] people into interacting in a "public sphere" that can only exist because of the presence of a particular configuration of power between various institutions and social groups.

Thus the presence of new media and other forms of cultural technology expands the possibility of spreading hegemonic templates. Religion as a reservoir of such conceptualizations experiences a significant revamping. It is in this sense that the discursive tradition that is Islam grapples with the new reality of the nation-state and the rise of modern types of political formations such as parties[30] through the elaboration of its knowledge producers. As will be seen in Chapter 6, Hizbullah's struggle in defining itself as a political party may have to do with its unique experience as a resistance movement and its ongoing negotiation with the state of Lebanon.

Nationalism and Lebanese State Formation

As argued by Benedict Anderson, the press, by publishing periodically within a given territory, imposes on readers a constant awareness of belonging to an imagined community stretching over a clearly delineated territory. Anderson differentiates religious and other premodern forms of belonging from nationalism by arguing that in the latter case the feeling of "simultaneity" created by imaginings of belonging to a community become horizontal and empty of past and future continuity.[31] Anderson argues that this feeling of horizontal simultaneity conducive to the type of imaginaries that nationalism cultivates was greatly facilitated by

---

[28] This is partly why I proposed describing it as a template.

[29] Louis Althusser, "Ideology and Ideological State Apparatuses," in *Lenin and Philosophy, and Other Essays* (New York: Monthly Review Press, 1971); repr. in A. Easthope and K. McGowan (eds.), *A Cultural and Critical Theory Reader* (Buckingham: Open University, 1992).

[30] Gramsci notes the importance of the political party in modern politics, especially in its capacity in transforming society and state: see Gramsci, *The Prison Notebooks*. 152–154.

[31] Benedict Anderson, *Imagined Communities: Reflections on the Origin and Spread of Nationalism* (London and New York: Verso, 1983), 24.

a technological innovation that he calls "print-as-commodity," which is at the root of the emergence of "national consciousness"[32] and the standardization of literate production into vernacular languages.[33] One of Anderson's more important arguments is that nationalism was not ideologically articulated by a ruling elite occupying state institutions, but rather from below, from a developing "popular" society that created its own sense of belonging to an imagined community through the use of the printing press (newspapers, periodicals, and books). Thus, state-sponsored official nationalism developed in reaction to middle-class or popular pressure.[34]

Yet another important point to note here is that such nationalism could develop only because certain state institutional structures were already present, providing the infrastructure conducive to the consolidation of such an imaginary over time. The Middle East as a political region with a colonial legacy has witnessed a particular process of "late state formation,"[35] and the relationship between the development of nationalisms, ideological articulations of the political party and the consolidation of the state still seem to need the attention of scholars.[36] Although this book does not claim to provide a general theory of nationalism in the Middle East, it hopes to shed light on certain aspects of non-state actors' involvement in nation building in the presence of weak and divided states.

In the case of Lebanon, nationalisms were developed by a highly diverse set of groups, some but not all state sponsored, and this development had a strong impact on how groups mobilized and shaped state–society relationships. Depending on the power of the state, certain dominant narratives prevailed. And in most cases where dominant ruling powers had to struggle to manage the demands of different communities and classes of people, national imaginaries helped in framing these demands. Finally, in the case of Arabic-speaking countries the absence of the emergence of specific vernacular languages, a factor Anderson identifies as a must for effective national imaginary dissemination, contributed to keeping different forms of pan-nationalisms alive, whether pro-Greater-Syrian, pan-Arab, and so on[37].

---

[32] Ibid., 37.
[33] Ibid., 67–80.
[34] Ibid., 77 and 83–111.
[35] See here, for example, Nazih Ayubi's *Over-stating the Arab State: Politics and Society in the Middle East* (London: I. B. Tauris, 1996) and Adham Saouli, *The Arab State: Dilemmas of Late Formation* (London: Routledge, 2014).
[36] Some notable examples include, Joseph Massad, *Colonial Effects: The Making of National Identity in Jordan* (New York: Columbia University Press, 2001) and Lisa Wedeen, *Peripheral Visions: Publics, Power, and Performance in Yemen* (Chicago: University of Chicago Press, 2008).
[37] In the case of Lebanon, for example, nothing is more revealing than the failed attempts by a group of intellectuals headed by poet Said Akl to standardize a Lebanese dialect by adopting the Latin script, as done by Kemal Attaturk in modern Turkey. Ironically,

For a newly founded state such as Lebanon, competing claims of community affiliation remained very strong, not least because it served, through confessionalism, as the mythical foundation of the state. The historian Ussama Makdisi argues pertinently that confessionalism as a political system emerging in late nineteenth-century Mount Lebanon should be read as a highly modern institutional innovation that paved the way for changing political structures.[38] In such arrangements, political claims were not simply social in nature in the sense of obeying a specific hierarchy of affiliation (nation first, religion, class, or tribe second). To the contrary, different community attachments or solidarities gained importance according to political contexts. It is through one's affiliation to a sect, group, etc., and thus by imagining community, that one could aspire to control the state. There was a paradox between the uniting, "nationalist" implications of trying to control, confront, or simply relate to the state while at the same time having to identify to particular sects in order to do so.[39]

The Islamic resurgence that gradually gained popularity from the 1950s witnessed a political momentum with the Iranian revolution that brought Ruhollah Khomeini to power in 1979 as a repertoire of shared symbols, idioms, stories, and ideas to imaginings of community that were suddenly backed by a state. In effect, Islamic articulations of community belonging existed before Khomeini came to power. And if language was an important anchor of nationalist imaginaries, Arabic came to be seen as the language of the Qur'an, and not just a sophisticated literary language that was the anchor of modern secular civilization as developed by nineteenth-century Arab intellectuals,[40] even if Islamic movements also conformed to certain political and cultural contexts that preceded them and from which they learned.

If the argument of this book is that Hizbullah has less of a comprehensive ideology than a particular treatment of the past that produces ideological coherence, then its ideological production resembles what Freeden has called a thin-centered nationalism.[41] This is also in line with Partha Chatterjee's observation that post-colonial political formations were

before becoming a staunch Lebanese nationalist, Said Akl was part of Antun Saadeh's Syrian Socialist Nationalist Party that advocated for a greater geographical Syria, which included Lebanon, parts of modern-day Turkey, Palestine, Jordan, and Cyprus.

[38] Ussama Makdisi, *The Culture of Sectarianism: Community, History, and Violence in Nineteenth-Century Lebanon* (Berkeley: University of California Press, 2000).

[39] This is the experience of the Christian right in the 1970s and early 1980s that culminated in the election of Bashir Gemayel as the president of Lebanon. Hizbullah was later on confronted with similar dilemmas.

[40] These intellectuals were associated with what came to be called the *nahda* (renaissance). See Nadia Bou Ali, "Hall of Mirrors: The Arab Nahda, Nationalism, and the Question of Language," D.Phil. thesis, University of Oxford, 2013.

[41] Michael Freeden, "Nationalism a Distinct Ideology?" *Political Studies* 46 (1998), 748–765.

unable to escape the nation-state paradigm.[42] Freeden is right to point out that "all types of nationalism seek institutional recognition,"[43] and this falls very well in line with Hizbullah politics. In this sense, a thin-centered ideology is not comprehensive in that it does not attempt to answer all the questions.[44] Yet I would slightly disagree with some of the criteria Freeden outlines for this type of ideological construction. Although Hizbullah may prioritize, albeit implicitly, "a particular group," this group is not really "the nation" as the latter's contours are still being negotiated in the case of Lebanon.[45] Moreover, Hizbullah never promoted a "positive valorization" of one's nation.[46] Due to the pan-national character of this resistance project, Palestinian solidarity trumps attempts to fall back to a Lebanese centricity.[47] What is missing here is a more nuanced understanding of the politics of nationalism and religion.

Ideology, Nationalism, and Islam: Between Secular and Religious Time

As mentioned earlier, Anderson argues that the difference between national and premodern "religious" imaginaries of community rest on a specific notion of time. Nationalism, accordingly, involves a horizontal (with no beginning) understanding which goes along with the rise of secular sensitivities, whereas religious notions of time imply that community belonging involves a point of origin such as prophecy or creation and the start of a particular line of conduct that religions aim to uphold. Anderson's argument that nationalism presents a break from previous premodern community imaginings rests on this clear division of notions of time. But with groups such as Hizbullah, and arguably other "Islamists" in the Middle East and beyond, the line between the secular and the religious is blurred as these organizations operate in a nation-state setting while using identification techniques that borrow but are in no way similar to premodern ones. It is possible that nationalism is at the heart of secular sensibilities as argued by Anderson,[48] but this may not mean absence of non-religious imaginaries.

---

[42] See Partha Chatterjee, *The Nation and its Fragments: Colonial and Post-Colonial History* (Princeton: Princeton University Press, 1993). For the Middle East see Massad, *Colonial Effects*, which focuses on the role of Jordanian state institutions and the drafting of state laws in the construction of the national subject.

[43] Freeden, "Nationalism a Distinct Ideology?" 754.

[44] Ibid., 751.

[45] Ibid.

[46] Ibid.

[47] Even if the constituency and larger public of Hizbullah may valorize Lebanese belonging, I am mostly focusing on the cultural production of the party.

[48] Anderson, *Imagined Communities*, 25.

Yet, if "secularism" implies a horizontal sense of time with no beginnings, as argued by Charles Taylor,[49] then we definitely have something else emerging with Political Islam. Does nationalism/secularism represent a rupture from "premodern" understanding of time centered on religious narratives and affinities that were cyclical or vertical and involving an origin or actor that enters the time-continuum, such as God or the beginning of a tradition?[50] What happens to these signifiers in a different socio-economic context such as that prevailing under the modern state and the various economic and technological structures that are associated with it?

In her study on various narratives developed by Hizbullah activists around the Ashura ritual, Lara Deeb argues against this cyclical–linear binary, appealing to a more complex process that did not necessarily involve a "return to the past" but a "progressive" understanding of time where the future might be better.[51] Anderson's "modern-national-empty versus religious-messianic (and, by extension, non-modern) schema" did not leave space to account for what Hizbullah partisans, the group that Deeb interviewed, were elaborating through their practices of piety.[52]

Here I build on Deeb's argument, which reverberates with ongoing discussions on the difference between nationalist and religious imaginaries understood in terms of a difference between secular and nonsecular understandings of time, a conceptual division I wish to transcend. Talal Asad argues that nationalism, especially coupled with the concept of the modern state, "requires the concept of the secular to make sense," as the nation is said to be "in this world" even though sometimes "under God."[53] Later in his text, when discussing the difference between nationalist and religious imaginaries in the Arab world, Asad argues, "it is easy to see that while the 'Arab nation' is inconceivable without its history, the Islamic Umma ['community' in Arabic] presupposes only the Qur'an and the Sunna."[54] While officially or according to prevailing texts this may be a relevant claim, Islamic traditions have deployed a highly complex sense of history (as opposed to relying only on Qur'an and Sunna) in order to legitimize different Islamic sects, schools, or trends of thought. Most importantly for Political Islam, the use of history, of a particular human legacy and its endlessly recounted

---

[49] Charles Taylor, *A Secular Age* (Cambridge, Mass: Harvard University Press, 2007).

[50] In premodern imaginaries religious narrative is also a reflection of rural life with its cyclical nature.

[51] Lara Deeb, "'Emulating and/or Embodying the Ideal': The Gendering of Temporal Frameworks and Islamic Role Models in Shi'i Lebanon," *American Ethnologist* 36:2 (2009): 242–257, 244.

[52] Ibid.

[53] Talal Asad, *Formations of the Secular: Christianity, Islam, Modernity* (Stanford: Stanford University Press, 2003), 193.

[54] Ibid., 197.

stories have fitted the nationalist imagination in different ways. Stories are told that may refer to the life of the prophet or his family in a way reminiscent of nationalist foundational myths. These become of paramount importance in envisioning social causes. In so doing, these groups have very modern technological tools at their disposal to produce political action such as in ritualizing remembrance acts.

Textual Strategies for Writing the Past

In this context, the Qur'an is the main referential text used to devise conceptual tools; it helps in imagining social reality and the past, and contributes to constructing national communities. It is what the anthropologist Brinkley Messick has called the "paradigmatic text," meaning that it represents the spoken words of God, while any other text is "written" and thus has secondary ontological value.[55] This logocentric textuality – or what can be called metaphysical statements – which the philosopher Jacques Derrida finds at the heart of the social sciences and in other contemporary writings,[56] is similarly pervasive here in the use of the Qur'an. Any form of writing that consecrates the importance of this source of reference (the Qur'an) epistemologically contributes to inscribing the "Islamic." Islamic jurisprudence is built on the continual reinterpretation of the Qur'an, but also, to a second degree, the Prophet's sayings (*ḥadīth*), and – especially in the case of Shi'i jurisprudence – the sayings of the heirs of the Prophet, his family, and the Imams.

The main intellectuals who can produce such interpretations are the clerics, the *'ulamā'* (the knowledgeable).[57] The *'ulamā'* have a specific social function, akin to that of academics and others producers of knowledge in the modern age. Most political Islamic movements rest on the legitimizing strategies of clerics who are heavily involved in reassessing the relationship between community, religion, and politics in the modern age. In the case of Hizbullah, the main figures include Mohammad Hussein Fadlallah, Mohammad Mahdi Shamseddine, Ruhollah Khomeini, and Baqr al-Sadr.[58] This does not mean that these are all affiliated or supporters of the

---

[55] This idea is taken from Jacques Derrida, *De la grammatologie* (Paris: Éditions de Minuit, 1967). See Brinkley Messick, *The Calligraphic State: Textual Domination and History in a Muslim Society* (Berkeley and Los Angeles: University of California Press, 1993).

[56] Derrida, *De la grammatologie*.

[57] For early 1980s Hizbullah ideologue Ali Kurani, the *'ulamā'* are the bearers of knowledge, or what he calls the people of knowledge (*ahl al-'ilm*) and the leaders of the Islamic community (*al-umma al-islāmiyya*). See Ali Kurani, *Ṭarīqat ḥizb allāh fīl-'amal al-islāmī* (Beirut: Maktab al-I'lam al-Islāmī, 1986).

[58] On Fadlallah's legacy see Jamal Sankari, *Fadlallah: The Making of a Radical Shi'ite Leader* (Beirut: al-Saqi, 2005). On Baqr al-Sadr see Chibli Mallat, *The Renewal of Islamic Law: Muhammad Baqer as-Sadr, Najar and the Shi'i International* (Cambridge: Cambridge

party. Others, such as Ali Kurani, were part of the general social field from which Hizbullah emerged, and perhaps considered themselves as part of the movement; Kurani wrote one of the earliest systematic and theoretical treatises on the Hizbullah phenomenon, yet was never really part of it and was early on moved to Qum (See Chapter 6).

However, modernity saw the rise of new social (and intellectual) actors, namely modern academic and media institutions. Journalists, university professors, activists, and laymen of all kinds are engaged in this practice of producing knowledge and information. They have challenged the mono-poly of the clerics over intellectual elaboration. Clerics may even lean on them to produce authoritative statements, by for example drawing on "scientific" claims to propose new conceptualizations of social reality. Through a change of style and focus in writing, clerics had to carve out a new space for themselves that would help to regain, preserve, or con-solidate their social influence and position. This process does not differ significantly from what Bourdieu studied when describing the social dis-tinction resulting from academic and other intellectual practices.[59] The Shi'i intellectual sphere, whose activities ranged from classical juris-prudence to political pamphleteering by clerics, has increased its effort at reconceptualizing reality. And as will be seen below, the Shi'i intellectuals engaged with a rewriting of the Islamic past (mostly clerics) have been concerned with varying political realities and contexts throughout time, from before the creation of Lebanon until the present today.

Writing the Islamic and the Politics of Remembrance

Al-Islām wa mantiq al-quwwa (Islam and the Rationale of Force)[60] is a theoretical treatise by Mohammed Hussein Fadlallah that symptomizes this treatment of Qur'anic texts by conceptualizing power through an Islamic imaginary. One of the most vocal and visible figures in the early 1980s (the period of Hizbullah's emergence and rapid establishment as a force for militant activity against Israeli military presence on Lebanese territory), Fadlallah was to become one of the most important Shi'i clerics by the end of the 1990s – what is called a *marja'* in Islamic tradition, literally meaning "a reference" or source of imitation – respected in the Islamic world by Hizbullah's friends and foes alike as a facilitator of

University Press, 2003). On Shamseddine, one can look at Hizbullah party member Husayn Rahhal's *Muhammad Mahdi Shamseddine: dirāsāt fī ru'ah al-islamīyya* (Beirut: Center of Civilization for the Development of Islamic Thought, 2010).
[59] See for example Pierre Bourdieu, *Homo Academicus* (Stanford: Stanford University Press, 1990).
[60] *Quwwa* could also be translated as power, or strength.

religious and national dialogue. This book, written in the early 1970s, exemplifies the kind of hybrid text that follows the classical jurisprudential method of rearticulating Qur'anic statements into handy dicta conducive to social action.[61]

As outlined above, Fadlallah uses modern techniques of referencing and conceptualizing. He defines the term society by borrowing from the conceptual formulations of an Iraqi sociologist.[62] There was originally no word for "society" in Arabic; the word that was introduced some time at the turn of the nineteenth and twentieth centuries is *mujtamā*ʿ, which an Arabic–English dictionary of the time translates as "meeting place." Talal Asad points out that this absence of the modern concept of society signals a particular conception of self, with regards to legal instances, as linked to family or tribal affiliations and not to an abstract concept of a society made of aggregates of individuals.[63] The relations between people and an abstractly imagined society that interacts with a political state is one of the main features of the modern age.

From there, Fadlallah introduces a concept of "social power" that he "Islamicizes," in the sense that he reflects on its meaning through the reading of suras and Prophet's sayings. This mode of writing the Islamic is an instance of what I described above as a "dualism of image and reality": referring to Qur'anic suras, and to any text considered sacred. In so doing, Fadlallah contributes a useful and legitimizing theory of militancy authenticated by textual practices, and actualizes its use.

Fadlallah's argumentative style had great resonance throughout Shiʻi Islamic revolutionary ideological constructions, especially in the early 1980s. This prolific textual production has developed through time and espoused different concerns. The style remains mostly unchanged, but the use of the text invokes different concerns, and consequently adopts different meanings. This transfer quality of the text is of paramount importance. In later writings, as we shall see in Chapter 6, the deputy secretary general of Hizbullah and cleric Naim Qassem would develop his concept of *mujtamā*ʿ *al-muqāwama* (literally, "society of resistance").[64]

A book on the secret of Hizbullah's victory against Israel in the July 2006 war was published by Dar al-Amir (a publisher sympathetic to the party) and written by Arwa Mahmood, a Master's student from the University of Cairo. Naim Qassem wrote a preface for the book, describing it as a scholarly elaboration of the militant practices of Hizbullah as a force

---

[61] For a detailed biography of Mohammad Hussein Fadlallah see Sankari, *Fadlallah*.
[62] See Hassan Saafan, *Ususs ʻilm al ijtimāʻ* (Beirut: Dar al-Nahda al-ʻArabiyya, 1975), quoted in Fadlallah, *al-Islām wa mantiq al-quwwa* (Beirut: Dar al-Malak, n.d.), 114.
[63] See Asad, *Formations of the Secular*, 223.
[64] Naim Qassem, *Mujtamāʻ al-muqāwama* (Beirut: Dar al-Maarif al-Hikmiyya, 2008).

that symbolizes resistance. Mahmood argues that the sine qua non of Hizbullah's battlefield success is the piety of its combatants. The evidence consists of interviews with several clerics in the top echelons of the party such as Naim Qassem, Nabil Qaouk, a member of Hizbullah's Executive Council, and others. In turn, clerics refer to Qur'anic verses in order to illustrate their points and also to provide intellectual references for combatants.[65] Qassem has a detailed section on piety and other socially differentiating markers. I discuss the one on *jihād* in Chapter 6.

This writing process outlined above can be classified as Islamic insofar as it claims inheritance from a specific past, by which I mean a collection of writings or other types of archived inscriptions or traces that can be given meaning.[66] Thus, writing the Islamic is writing difference. It is inscribing in the written the trace of what it is not. These can be thought of as "writing strategies." The different ideological constructions invoked by writers, orators, poets, and others, appropriated as part of the organization of Hizbullah, are never just "out there," but are read by party members, party allies, enemies, and other actors very differently at different points in time.

I propose to think of tradition as a set of writing strategies that are communally accepted so as to have a performative use. Whereas textual strategies are the ideological as such, what matters here is not whether these are "really" preserving or transmitting a particular "tradition" – they may do so in terms of replicating particular religious teachings – but rather the actual efforts deployed to do so and their political consequences or how this process enables strategies of action. These strategies of action that are represented by "a discursive tradition"[67] is where "politics" meets "religion," given that ethics and pious practices are conducive to community-driven or collective action. This also helps shed light on what Islamic signifiers really in terms of actual political practice, and its relation with party and state institutionalization.

Early Writings: *al-'Ahd* as a Template

In line with my argument on ideology above, this book focuses mostly on early textual materials because they provide templates for later texts. *Al-'Ahd* is important because it contained all the various ideological productions of the party since its first appearance in 1984. Official party speeches are reproduced in it, along with Friday sermons, martyr commemorations,

---

[65] Arwa Mahmood, *Kital hizbullāh* (Beirut: Dar al-Amir, 2008).
[66] Here again I partly draw on MacIntyre's conception of tradition and its relation with past. See MacIntyre, *After Virtue*, 204–225.
[67] Ibid., 20.

Hizbullah's operations, and other events related to Hizbullah's political and military actions. Its editorials, columns, and analysis usually reflect the prevailing event of the week, but also contain the various declarations made by Hizbullah officials, and related material.[68]

Al-'Ahd's debut slightly preceded Hizbullah's Open Letter to the Downtrodden, and was published uninterruptedly from then. Going through its pages from the beginning of the 1980s, one can observe how the evolution of the paper was roughly paralleled by developments in Hizbullah and its political environment. In years where Hizbullah faced difficulties, for example during the confrontation with the Syrian regime in the later parts of the 1980s, it was printed on lower-quality paper. The subsequent post-war settlement between Syria and Iran over the fate of the resistance project is reflected in the early 1990s with a new theme adopted by the newspaper. It also reflects the various institutional developments undergone by the party and outlined below. In 2000, after the liberation of the South of Lebanon, *al-'Ahd* was renamed *al-Intiqād*, only to revert to *al-'Ahd* after 2010 as it became available online only.[69]

Al-'Ahd not only tells us about Hizbullah's ideological efforts but, as it became a hub for Shi'i militant intellectuals of different currents expressing ideas at one point or another, especially during the 1980s and 1990s, it sheds light on the sociology of knowledge of various segments of this community and their contribution to the project of resistance. In certain cases it attracted figures who are not aligned with Hizbullah's politics today. For example, the prominent Shi'i scholar Hani Fahs contributed interesting political Islamic theoretical work to *al-'Ahd*. Today he works to dislodge Hizbullah's monopoly over Shi'i political thought through his own think tank, al-Markaz al-Lubnānī lil-Dirāsāt wal-Hiwār wal-Taqrīb.[70] Wajih Qanso and Wajih Kawtharani are other examples of Lebanese University professors who wrote papers on Islamic themes published in *al-'Ahd*. Qanso is currently affiliated to Fahs's think tank and has published a book on alternative ways of reading Shi'i political thought – in this case, not sanctifying some form of *wilāyat al-faqīh* (leadership of the jurist), as espoused by Khomeinist theories and followed by Hizbullah.[71] Kawtharani has published a book criticizing the alleged monopoly

---

[68] The leader of the parliamentary coalition of Hizbullah, Mohammad Raad, acknowledged that in my interview with him (June 2010). As I mention below, Raad is the founder of *al-'Ahd* and was its main contributor, especially in the early years.
[69] www.alahednews.com.lb/.
[70] The Lebanese Center for Studies, Dialogue, and Rapprochement.
[71] Wajih Qanso, *'A'imat ahl al-bayt wal-siyāsat* (Beirut: al-Mada, 2008).

of the Iranian *walī al-faqīh* on Hizbullah as an organization, questioning the national affiliations of the party.[72]

Most of the prominent party members who emerged during the 1990s were at some point columnists or journalists at *al-'Ahd*. Chief among them is Mohammad Raad, who was the director and chief editorialist for the newspaper during the 1980s before becoming the leader of the Hizbullah-affiliated parliamentary coalition.[73] Since 1992, Raad has been part of Hizbullah's Shura Council,[74] the party's main deliberative body, a sign of his seniority in the party's institutional structure. To a great extent one can say that *al-'Ahd* was Raad's project. Other key ideologues of the party such as Ali Fayyad, who later became the director of al-Markaz al-Lubnānī lil-Dirāsāt wal-Hiwār wal-Taqrīb and is now an MP, and Nawaf Moussawi, who is today in charge of Hizbullah's foreign relations committee, all passed through *al-'Ahd* at one point or another. While *Al-'Ahd* did not act, in the full Andersonian sense, or it was poorly read as a national newspaper, it did signal the presence of an intellectual community. It was published periodically, helped structure imaginaries of time and space, reminding its readership of histories of people and struggles, and shaping a collection of opinions that represented Hizbullah as an existing entity.

The Rise of the Ideologues pre/post-1990s and the Institutionalization of Cultural Production

As Hizbullah entered the post-war era in Lebanon, especially after 1992 as it engaged in the first post-war legislative elections, the cultural production of the party underwent a series of changes. Due to the innovations and sophistication of media, and the institutional developments the party was undergoing, intellectuals[75] came to fit into a new economy of knowledge that had an impact on overall ideological production. As institutionalization was equated with specialization, there was a slow dissociation of the various general Islamic cultural practices from the narrower resistance-related activities. This was never really completed, and the boundary between the cultural spheres was in constant negotiation, showing the extent and limits of oversight Hizbullah as an

---

[72] Kawtharani, *Bayna fiqh al-islāh al-Shī'ī wa wilāyat al-faqīh* (Beirut: Dar al-Nahar, 2007).

[73] Mohammad Raad, interview with the author, June 2010.

[74] Aurélie Daher, *Le Hezbollah: mobilisation et pouvoir* (Paris: Presses Universitaires de France, 2014), 4.

[75] I adopt Pierre Bourdieu's general conceptualization of an intellectual or producer of knowledge/information as fitting a particular economy of symbolic capital that in turn produces social status and legitimacy. See Bourdieu, *Homo Academicus*; Pierre Bourdieu and J. B. Thompson, *Language and Symbolic Power* (Cambridge, Mass.: Harvard University Press, 1991).

organization asserts over the cultural production that interpellates its community at large. I explain below some facets of why this is so.

The institutionalization of Hizbullah at the end of the civil war led to a change in the social positioning of Hizbullah-affiliated intellectuals. They came to occupy different organizations, committees, and other media-related divisions allocating writing strategies in the different corners of the growing cultural phenomenon in and around the party. The contrast with earlier *al-'Ahd* writing dynamics cannot be overstated.

One important facet of this is that ideological production gradually moved from being anonymous to involving authors who were named.

This new exposure occurred at a time when Hizbullah decided to run for the legislative elections of 1992. Suddenly many new faces started appearing and spoke on behalf of Hizbullah, arguing about the topics of the day, voicing political positions, criticizing, etc. This also meant that the clerics were no longer alone. *Al-'Ahd*'s columns were crowded with the opinions of the various parliamentary members. Appearing gradually were Mohammad Raad, Ali Hajj Hassan, and others, giving public statements, and being present at all sorts of ceremonies commemorating martyrs and other grand celebrations along with clerical leaders such as Abbas Moussawi (until his death in February 1992), Hassan Nasrallah, Naim Qassem, and of course, Mohammad Hussein Fadlallah. Contributors to *al-'Ahd* from that period also included Sobhi Tufayli, the first secretary general of Hizbullah, through his weekly editorial, Mohammad Fneish, Mohammad Hassan Yaghi, and Sheikh Khodr Tliss, all of them member of the newly founded Political Bureau.[76]

Thus, most of those who had written anonymously in *al-'Ahd* now appeared to have party positions in other institutional areas. It is not a coincidence that the change in party position coincided with media developments. Mohammad Raad became leader of the parliamentary coalition Solidarity with the Resistance and a member of the Hizbullah Shura Council.[77] Ali Fayyad, who briefly wrote the column Rashqat hajar in *al-'Ahd*,went on to lead the newly established research center of Hizbullah (Center for Documentation and Research), which became one of the main media archiving institutions of the party. Mohammad Fneish, a new figure in the early 1990s, became Hizbullah spokesperson as the chief of the newly established Political Bureau, and also as a Shura

---

[76] It is interesting to note that Sobhi Tufayli, who was the first secretary general of Hizbullah, continued writing in *al-'Ahd* after his first "fall-out" with the party in 1992.

[77] Asadollahi, *al-Islāmiyyūn*, 188.

Council member. After 2005, Fneish came to occupy several ministerial positions allocated to Hizbullah.[78]

In this vein, the institutional repositioning and reordering of tasks within Hizbullah's organization was paralleled by another interesting development. The increasing visibility of Hizbullah officials and Hizbullah-affiliated intellectuals triggered what could be called an "individualization" process that impacted on writing strategies and went hand in hand with the growing institutionalization or "corporatization" of the party. Although writing strategies were still being articulated in similar ways, intellectuals operated in a new social context of discursive interaction, and developed different interests and ambitions. They became university professors, journalists, intellectuals, political figures, and institutionalized party members with fixed positions in a gradually more complex institutional setting in which several objectives were combined: defending the resistance project and elaborating new symbolic tools for social differentiation, while at the same time preserving their own specific status in an increasingly sophisticated socio-economic field.

This individualization of ideological production, wherein political figures have different social and institutional functions that impact on their discourse, means that paradoxically these actors conform more to a particular set of discourses.[79] The responsibility placed on political actors is such that it was important to "stick to the template." The visibility of members individualized their ideological practices, yet at the same time made them conform to a standardization process of cultural production. One could reverse this equation and say that it was the standardization of the process of cultural production through this institutional sophistication that permitted, or perceived as safe, this individualization process.

The general point to make here is that Hizbullah did not need to be fully in control of ideological production, even if its institutions constantly screened and oversaw publications and media production. There seems to be not only conformity but also an element of trust prevailing in the way ideology replicates itself in the general social field. I would argue here for a fine-tuning of Althusser's argument that the state is the apex of the institutional structure through which ideology trickles down to social actors.[80] A case like Lebanon shows that in the absence of strong state powers, social actors and

---

[78] For example, Fneish was energy minister from 2005 to 2006, and state minister for agricultural reform in 2009.

[79] This is a phenomenon that is present in most aspects of modern life, such as modern academia, journalism, etc., where growing instutionalization pushes social actors to conform to styles of literary or other economic production in order to gain status.

[80] Louis Althusser, "Ideology and Ideological State Apparatuses," in *Lenin and Philosophy, and Other Essays* (New York: Monthly Review Press, 1971).

semi-state structures create their own ideological conformities by relying on trust and loyalty.[81] This explains why, as we will see soon, several newspapers such as *al-Akhbār* and *al-Safīr* were considered by Hizbullah as a natural conduit for pro-resistance discourse. Another important point here that explains the possibility of conformity is that statements made in media and other fields of the economy of information are less important for their particular content than for their form, which defends the presence of a political party or cause.

As a symptom of this, when Hizbullah members started appearing in public, *al-'Ahd* gradually ceased to be the dominant "voice of Hizbullah."[82] This shift toward a total visibility of those who "express" Hizbullah to the outside world was paralleled by a change in media structures. It also coincided with several other news outlets recognizing the legitimacy of the resistance and participating in the general archiving efforts. At the beginning of the 1990s, although most Hizbullah members with public positions were visible in the media, some level of anonymity still existed. For example, Nawaf Moussawi, who replaced Mohammad Raad as the editor-in-chief of *al-'Ahd*, also did not sign his writings, and thus was not "visible" until he became an MP in 1992.

There are different reasons for the decline of the personalized newspaper; one of them was the takeover of information by audio-visual media, namely the creation of al-Manar TV station in 1989.[83] It was also at this time that Hizbullah founded its Media Unit to organize relations with other media outlets, and al-Nour radio station. Yet to be sure, there was no deliberate decision to sideline *al-'Ahd*. Proof of this is that *al-'Ahd* continued to be quite rich in contributions until after 2000, when it was transformed to *al-Intiqād*. In 2010 *al-Intiqād* was renamed *al-'Ahd* as the newspaper became a solely internet-based news website. According to the head of Unit for Media Relations, Ibrahim Moussawi, *al-'Ahd* was always the favorite name for the news outlet, but when the Lebanese state introduced media regulations in 2000, the name had already been taken by another media body, so, for copyright reasons, Hizbullah had to adopt *al-Intiqād* (The critique). Moussawi explained that once the news outlet became available only on the

---

[81] Of course here trust can be backed by economic and other incentives, but it need not always be so.

[82] For an outside audience, *al-'Ahd* was never the "voice of Hizbullah." The latter mainly appeared through press releases and declarations, statements by its leaders that were re-transcribed, and the various media sympathetic to the cause of the resistance.

[83] For a detailed overview of the history of al-Manar's production see Olfa Lamloum, "L'histoire sociale du Hezbollah à travers ses médias: système de représentation et inscription territoriale," *Politix* 22:3 (2009), 169–187.

internet, where copyright considerations did not apply, it was able to revert to *al-'Ahd*.[84]

When asked why *al-'Ahd* ceased to be an essential media device for the party, Mohammad Raad, the leader of the parliamentary coalition Solidarity with the Resistance, answered that "it did not look good" for the party to have an official media outlet when all other mainstream newspapers in Lebanon were "officially at least" independent – noteworthy here is that this rule does not apply to TV channels, which are all openly affiliated to political parties, a sign of Hizbullah's keenness on working with prevailing social protocols as partly arguing for a clearer assignment of roles, a clear sign of the growing institutionalization of Hizbullah. For Raad, a newspaper should have a range of opinions whereas a political party should only issue press releases and propose occasional articles in newspapers, but should not control a newspaper because the latter would lose credibility as a bearer of a "neutral" point of view.[85]

Also, and more importantly, according to Raad, the fact that other Lebanese newspapers and media devices carried party messages repeatedly across time meant that they more effectively legitimized those points of view. In his opinion, the party stance was liable to be undermined if it was only voiced in an official Hizbullah newspaper. Hizbullah saw it as more appropriate, if not strategic, to allow the rest of the Lebanese press to carry Hizbullah's message. For example, *al-Safir* was one of the most pro-resistance newspapers,[86] especially throughout the 1990s in its contributions to the writing of the history of the resistance in, at times, more effective ways than any single Hizbullah effort.[87] Finally, *al-Akhbar*, established in 2006, finished the job of completely marginalizing the role of *al-'Ahd*. Through the loss of Hizbullah's anonymity, and the engagement of Hizbullah-affiliated intellectuals in the public sphere, Hizbullah actors were individually and collectively able to voice opinions on what Hizbullah "thinks" or what Hizbullah's "ideology" is about, and enable an increasingly complex media and cultural field to disseminate the party's views and positions.

These institutional novelties took place following the first Hizbullah congress held on 5 November 1989. This congress took important

---

[84] Ibrahim Moussawi, interview with the author, July 2010.
[85] Mohammad Raad, interview with the author, June 2010.
[86] As Raad explained, there were no formal links with *al-Safir*, "only the presence of friends within the newspaper sympathetic to the cause."
[87] See, for example, the *al-Safir* publication of a rich collection of newspaper articles and pictures on the resistance divided into several themes: *Hizbullāh: al-muqāwama wal-taḥrīr*, 13 vols. (Beirut: As-Safir Arab Documentation Center, and International Edition 2006).

security decisions along with institutional media reforms such as the election of Sobhi Tufayli as the first secretary general of Hizbullah, for a period of two years. Abbas Moussawi succeeded Tufayli in 1992, but was assassinated by the Israelis on 14 February 1992. As mentioned above, Tufayli and Moussawi are considered to be the founders of Hizbullah at the time that the first Pasdaran troops, the Iranian elite military squads sent by Khomeini, arrived in 1982, shortly after the Israeli invasion.[88] The election of Hassan Nasrallah in 1992 was quickly followed by the party's decision to engage in the Lebanese legislative process, a move often (and inaccurately, as is argued in this book) conceived as a decision to become more "open" or "pragmatic," and more "Lebanese."

In reality, this change in tactics involved more efficient strategies for disseminating Hizbullah's cause of resistance by a much more pro-active policy of navigating an increasingly dense institutional and organizational complex. Whereas the literature on Hizbullah has explained its post-1992 political legacy as undergoing a "Lebanonization" process,[89] I would argue differently: this "opening up" helped in defending and more effectively serving their foundational project: the Islamic Resistance. Through all these legitimizing techniques, and under the leadership of Nasrallah, Hizbullah has succeeded in entrenching its project in the politics of the country and the region without either becoming explicitly Lebanese or ever ceasing to be its own version of "being Lebanese." Most importantly, the various political directions that Hizbullah took obeyed the existential rationale of how to protect the military resistance project.

All throughout the 1990s, Hizbullah's production of knowledge was disseminated among the growing bodies of committees, organizations, and institutions. This specialization of themes tackled in these publications was continued in *Baqiyatullah*, a monthly magazine created at the beginning of the 1990s that developed what was started in *al-'Ahd*'s cultural pages. *Baqiyatullah* consisted of a selection of opinion and analysis texts by Iranian clerics, former contributors to *al-'Ahd*, a plethora of Lebanese clerics and laymen teaching at the Lebanese University or at special religious schools, and newcomers dedicated to the rearticulation of ideas and concepts around Islamic tropes (*jihād*, resistance, martyrdom, and so on) and its various social, political, economic, and spiritual ramifications. What started in the pages of *al-'Ahd*, such as regular testaments of martyrs, found an increasingly developed form throughout the

---

[88] The centrality of these two figures in the foundation of Hizbullah is convincingly argued by Aurélie Daher in *Le Hezbollah*, 76–77.
[89] See here particularly the works of Joseph Alagha and Nizar Hamzeh.

issues of *Baqiyatullah*, which also featured all types of Iranian idioms and aesthetics, such as Persian styles of drawing. Once *Baqiyatullah* was created, *al-ʿAhd* became more focused on political events and analysis.

In cultural terms, *Baqiyatullah* represented a specialization process running throughout the media industry related to Hizbullah as it geared its product toward a specific social niche. What was first produced along-side multiple forms of information in *al-ʿAhd* was now available to a much more specialized public. Indeed, different organizations started working on expressing "the cultural" in multitudes of ways (as seen with Athār al-Shuhadāʾ in Chapter 2). Many other media outlets came to emulate this institutionalization of cultural production, mainly through the television and the internet.

Once groups are institutionalized, the particular "artistic" or "intellectual" directions taken are multiple. Books published by research centers, university publishing houses, etc. were often introduced by sentences of this sort: "The opinions present in this book may not necessarily reflect the opinions of the given institution publishing it."[90] A particularly revealing line is the one on the first pages of a transcript of a collection of speeches made at a conference organized by a Hizbullah-related think tank on the "Ethics of the Resistance":[91] "The opinions that are present in this book represent the opinions of those stating them." In this case, although the aim does not appear to be protecting the overall views of a particular institution, party, or cause, it seems necessary to designate the individuality of voices. This preservation of a viewpoint that may not exist at a particular point in time is facilitated by the dissemination of many publications and enables a perpetual quest for self-definition, for fixing meaning or presence while projecting an image of ideological coherence. As an illustration of the industry, according to data collected by Stefan Rosiny, there are more than fifty Shiʿi publishing houses (mostly labeled "Islamic") that were founded between the end of the 1980s and 1990s, compared to an impressive total of 136 over the course of the twentieth century[92].

Launched in 1991, al-Manar TV station gradually became the center of a flurry of "Islamic" discursive practices through informal agreed-upon rules of discussions. This cultural sphere used slogans familiar to Hizbullah's writing strategies and beyond, some borrowed from Iran,[93] which became more and more elaborate with time: Video clips, soap

---

[90] Articles published in *al-ʿAhd* sometimes still have this type of disclaimer.
[91] *Qiyām al-muqāwama* (Beirut: Dar al-Hadi and Maʿhad al-Maʿāref al-Hikmiyya, 2008).
[92] Stephan Rosiny, *Shia's Publishing in Lebanon: With Special Reference to Islamic and Islamist Publications* (Berlin: Das Arabische Buch, 2000), 22–23.
[93] See Asadollahi, *al-Islāmiyyūn*.

operas, talk-shows and other types of TV programs were steeped in this borrowing of Iranian cultural production (if not sometimes rediffused as is), but also developed a local style over the years. [94]

Yet in this flurry of cultural production, Hizbullah was forced to standardize ideological templates. For example, after July 2006, Ashura and all other annual campaigns that fragment the calendar year (as seen in Chapter 2) were organized by a specific group, the Unit for Media Activities, the aim of which, according to Ibrahim Moussawi, was "to set the unified code for all the campaigns, especially the religious ones." This "unified code" was the standardization of how cultural production should take place. It is that unit that set up and organized the Mleeta museum. It also "provides the official motto and slogans for all occasions, it designs them and carries them out as well."[95] It is not to be confused with the Unit for Media Relations, at the time headed by Moussawi,[96] which serves as a link between Hizbullah and other media bodies in the world.

As al-Manar developed, along with other media devices and artistic initiatives, it facilitated a complexification of the relation between what was dubbed the *hāla islāmīyya* (the Islamic situation, or disposition)[97] and the more narrow or "political" resistance project. The organizational separation between the social agents responsible for cultural production reflects a decentralization of general Islamic articulations developed by multiple segments of social groups and narrower Hizbullah core writing strategies that are more related to issues of the legitimacy of resistance. The industry of artistic creation (video clips, radio shows, documentaries, films, musical compositions, and so on) regarding "Islamic" idioms would take a course of its own, targeting a social niche just like any other artistic practices present in other segments of society (whether in the diverse social setting of Lebanon, or elsewhere).

---

[94] I know of instances where all kind of social actors contribute to al-Manar programs such as martyr-related productions, writers and designers who are not specifically Shiʻi.

[95] Ibrahim Moussawi, interview with the author, July 2010.

[96] At the time of writing, Moussawi is the head of al-Manar TV's news and news programs. He is also the vice president of al-Manar.

[97] See the works of Mona Harb and Lara Deeb for an application of this notion in different cultural practices of the Shiʻi community.

2   Martyrology and Conceptions of Time in Hizbullah's Writing Practices

We remember together the recalling (*zikra*) of the martyred leaders (*al-qāda al shuhadā'*), the leading family (*al-'ā'ila al-qā'ida*) the martyr Sayyed Abbas Moussawi our Secretary General, our leader, our teacher, our beloved (*habībuna*) and our inspiration (*mulhimuna*) and his wife the knowledgeable and striving (*mujāhida*) martyr Um Yaser and his young son Husayn, and his grace the Sheikh of the Islamic Resistance Ragheb Harb and the great striving (*jihādī*) leader Hajj Imad Mughnieh. These are the title of our victory. And we always remember this recalling (*zikra*), for our own sake and that of our children, our grandchildren and our generation, and not for their [the leaders'] sake. We remember them so that the near past, that we lived and that we participated in creating, stays. This near past that is near, that is connected to the present and that is overlooking over the future. So that it stays in our consciousness and awareness (*wa'yuna*) and that of the generations to come.

(Hassan Nasrallah, Week of the Leader of the Resistance, 16/02/2015)

On 30 January 2014 the secretary general of Hizbullah, Hassan Nasrallah, as has become customary, appeared on TV to give a speech praising the latest military operation carried out by his group against an Israeli army vehicle that was moving in the Shebaa farms, territory occupied by Israel since 1967. The operation, carried out against what Nasrallah called "one of the enemies' elite troops," was dubbed the Heroic Martyrs of Quneitra Operation. The name referred to an Israeli ambush a week before in the region of Quneitra, which is situated in the Syrian non-occupied Golan region, and which had killed senior Hizbullah and Iranian military commanders. During his speech, Nasrallah praised a successful operation that according to him "rewrote the language of warfare" between Israel and Hizbullah to the advantage of the latter. The naming of the operation after fighters who had died in combat followed a tradition that stretched back to the earliest moments of the organization in the 1980s. Moreover, this was not just a rhetorical exercise, but involved a rationale for fighting exemplified by the succession of events just mentioned, and characterized the style of the resistance. Remembering martyrs, and more generally a human legacy, is the cornerstone of the cultural production of Hizbullah that not only builds ideological coherence but is also conducive to effective social mobilization and militant action. This chapter seeks to explain the various rituals and techniques developed by Hizbullah to remember its dead, and how this fed into imagining the nation.

In the Lebanese context, there is an ongoing negotiation between the state and Lebanon's various communities over the articulation of a legitimate national narrative, since each has its own understandings of history.[1] In other words, at play here, to draw on Sune Haugbolle, is "Public memory" and "Private memory," or "state-sanctioned memory" and "local memory."[2] However, in the case of Hizbullah, its local, confessional memory has slowly become one of the dominant narratives, especially due to the increasingly important role the party has played in state institutions. While Hizbullah's slogans aimed to redefine the historical markers of the Shi'i community, the party also rewrote imaginaries of the nation. Mainly through the use of the highly polyvalent notions of the resistance project (*mashrū' al-muqāwama*) or resistance community (*mujtamā' al-muqāwama*), the organization succeeded in developing different imaginings of community that it has invited all other Lebanese communities to embrace.

For Shi'i political movements, the Ashura ritual, which recalls the killing of Husayn – the son of Ali and grandson of the Prophet – in the battle of Karbala, could be considered the paradigmatic act of remembrance that feeds into writings of history. As Michael Fischer has argued, Karbala "provides a model for living and a mnemonic for thinking about how to live."[3] The act of transmitting a particular quality of life from one generation to another is what ties the community together, or makes the community possible.

Strikingly, however, none of the detailed narratives of the "Karbala paradigm" developed by Iranian cultural institutions and agents (mostly clerics) and described by Fischer, especially their understandings of history and of Sunni narratives of the Islamic past, are even mentioned in the early issues of *al-'Ahd*.[4] It is not that the battle of Karbala has no symbolic value in the cultural productions of Hizbullah-affiliated intellectuals – far from it. Rather, the latter's understandings of this event, of the history of other events, and of the present follow different strategies

---

[1] For example, see Lucia Volk, *Memorials and Martyrs in Modern Lebanon* (Bloomington: Indiana University Press, 2010); and Sune Haugbolle, "Public and Private Memory of the Lebanese Civil War," *Comparative Studies of South Asia, Africa and the Middle East* 25 (2005): 191–203.

[2] Haugbolle, "Public and Private Memory," 201.

[3] Michael Fischer, *Iran: From Religious Dispute to Revolution* (Cambridge, Mass.: Harvard University Press, 1980), 21.

[4] Ibid., 13–27.

from those deployed in Iran, due in part to their different institutional and political settings. The writings of Hizbullah-related intellectuals are relatively basic, focused as they are on the idea of resistance against Israel and occupation, or related injustice. Similarly, although the *madrasa*[5] (or in the Lebanese case, the *hawza*) was an important site of social mobilization for political Shi'ism, in the run-up to the creation of Hizbullah the development and success of the movement followed a locally contingent path as its social mobilization strategies involved a series of ritualistic practices that, although resonant with Iranian and other such practices, was quite specific to the Lebanese situation and the experience of territorial occupation.[6]

Many works exist on the various aspects of and changes to the ritual practice of Ashura in modern times.[7] For an understanding of how Hizbullah builds ideological coherence, however, it is necessary to turn our gaze away from Ashura and toward the multitude of other commemorative events – mostly for martyrs who died in battle – that came to break up "calendrical time."[8]

Important aspects of ritualistic acts of remembrance include not just discursive rearticulation, but also periodicity. Hizbullah's commemorations of martyrs gradually came to occupy every day of the calendar year. Each martyr or group of martyrs was remembered a first time following the act of martyrdom, then a second time after one week, then again after forty days, and then once more after one year.[9] Eventually acts of remembrance were repeated annually. As Hizbullah's military operations against the Israeli army increased and more casualties were incurred, commemorations quickly began to crowd the calendar space. If on one day Hizbullah commemorated the funeral of a *shahīd*, the next day it would already be commemorating the "week" of another martyr or group of martyrs. Likewise, a few days later the militant group might be

---

[5] Ibid., 27–32.

[6] On the importance of the *hawza* and the clerical intellectual see Abisaab, "The Cleric as Organic Intellectual."

[7] To name but a few, Lara Deeb, "Living Ashura in Lebanon: Mourning Transformed to Sacrifice," *Comparative Studies of South Asia, Africa and the Middle East* 25:1 (2005); Sabrina Mervin, "Les larmes et le sang des chutes: corps et pratiques rituelles lors des célébrations de 'ashûrâ' (Liban, Syrie)," *Revue des mondes musulmans et de la Méditerranée* 113–114 (2006); Elizabeth Picard, "The Lebanese Shi'a and Political Violence in Lebanon," in *The Legitimization of Violence* (London: United Nations Research Institute for Social Development, 1997).

[8] For this expression see Wedeen, *Peripheral Visions*.

[9] In this case, Hizbullah is merely using social rituals of mourning traditionally practiced by most communities (The various Muslim, Christian, and Jewish sects) in the Middle East. In so doing Hizbullah is employing "traditional" or available ritualistic practices for contemporary political concerns.

commemorating the passing of the "fortieth" day since the death of yet another martyr or group of martyrs. The oft-repeated slogan, "every day is Ashura, every day is Karbala," made much sense in this light. The calendar year was gradually filled with commemoration. This investment of time was significantly beneficial to the resistance, as it enabled the elaboration of communal or national imaginaries conducive to political action. With years passing and martyrdom acts and commemorations multiplying, the periodical and very real commemoration of martyrs during these early years slowly paved the way to fix two major dates that are marked on a yearly basis: Shuhadā' wa-Qadat al-Muqāwama (Martyrs and leaders of the resistance), which eventually become Yawm al-Shahīd (Day of the martyr), and Usbū' al-Muqāwama (Resistance Week). I shall explain shortly how these dates are linked to the legacy of the resistance.

The Martyr as Witness in the Text and the Promise as Era

If martyrology produces particular imaginings of community through periodicity and the breakup of the calendar year, martyrs testify to a particular ethical practice that can only be understood because the martyr is never present in one time dimension – whether past, present, or future – but rather exists between dimensions.

In a very early issue of *al-'Ahd*, an anonymous writer laid out his take on the notion of *shahīd* and *shahāda* (martyrdom) by tapping into the root meaning of the verb *shahāda* (to testify) and its various nominal derivations.[10] The author proposed the following revealing definition of the *shahīd* by bringing it back to the literal meaning of the term *shahīd* (witness): "the *shahīd*: one who looks at and understands his situation, and copes with it or acts upon it ... And the *shahīd* in Islamic thought is the believer who looks at his situation and his society and the realities of its scriptures, and acts upon it ... even if this involves dying."[11] This etymological exercise emphasizes the notion that the *shahīd* is a witness to a line of conduct that is determined by his social and political context. He testifies to a cause by experiencing a reality that when encountered only in written form remains abstract. In so doing, he embodies it or gives it "presence."

But how can this experience of the martyr who "looks at and understands his situation" be communicated and transmitted? How can this

---

[10] *al-'Ahd* 14 (28/9/1984), 2.
[11] Ibid.

line of conduct be remembered and rendered traceable? This challenge is shared by all intellectuals or political actors who create understandings, dispositions, and sensibilities framed through the "Islamic" signifier. Indeed, as the Islamic is written down, traced, and differentiated, its "presence," or fixed meaning, can only be established through the coming and going of the martyr, the experience of the past, or more accurately, the experience of the different time dimensions in which the martyr seems to belong.

Interesting parallels can be drawn between the articulation of the martyr – the one who witnesses – in the Lebanese and Iranian cases. In her study on the Iranian culture of martyrdom, Shahla Talebi argues that *shahādat*, or witnessing, can be "imagined as a gift: an exchange of life and death for the sake of life and justice."[12] This Maussian understanding could not be more accurate, for it places acts of martyrdom at the center of communal continuity.[13] If gift exchanges happen over successive generations and involve remembering a human legacy, in what ways do they signal a process of knowledge transmission? Drawing on the discussion of witnessing by Ali Shariati – who was a prominent Iranian sociologist and one of the ideological precursors to the Islamic revolution – Talebi emphasizes that "the *shahīd* continues to live on, not in body but . . . as a thought."[14] But what is it that is "thought" when the *shahīd* is invoked?

In his book on martyrdom in Islamic traditions, David Cook acknowledges that the martyr acts as a witness, but he argues that the martyr "must have belief in one belief system and possess a willingness to defy another belief system."[15] While I agree that the martyr differentiates himself through acts of witnessing, it is overly simplistic to narrow this idea down to belief. If the word used in religious traditions such as Christianity, Judaism, or Islam is "faith," this cannot be equated with the narrower (and more discursive in content) notion of "belief."[16] Rather than a discursive phenomenon, the

---

[12] Shahla Talebi, "An Iranian Martyr's Dilemma: The Finite Subject's Infinite Responsibility," *Comparative Studies of South Asia, Africa and the Middle East* 33:2 (2013): 177–196, 172.
[13] Marcel Mauss, *The Gift: Forms and Function of Exchange in Archaic Societies* (London: Cohen & West, 1966).
[14] Talebi, "An Iranian Martyr's Dilemma," 182.
[15] David Cook, *Martyrdom in Islam* (Cambridge and New York: Cambridge University Press, 2007), 1–2.
[16] See Asad's discussion, which widens the scope of belief from its "discursive" or "symbolic" bias to a practical, dispositional, and emotional dimension: Talal Asad, "Thinking about Religion and Politics," in Robert A. Orsi (ed.), *The Cambridge Companion to Religious Studies* (Cambridge: Cambridge University Press, 2012). I also rely here on Asad's argument that religion as a private set of beliefs held by the individual is the product of a recent socio-political context that Western Europe developed through the notion of the secular: see Asad, *Genealogies of Religion*.

martyr leaves a trace that then can be used by social actors in a myriad of ways. Revealingly, articles and other cultural productions on martyrs published in *al-'Ahd* seldom discuss belief systems or doctrinal positions. Rather, they focus largely on storytelling describing ways of living that transmit a line of conduct espoused by a martyr. Storytelling offers the martyr the possibility "to witness" and creates a space in which ethics can be understood and embodied. Most importantly, stories are efficient substitutes for theoretical articulations of ethics. On the rare occasions when Hizbullah-affiliated intellectuals have tried to explain their doctrinal positions in *al-'Ahd*, they have tended to stop short of a full explanation, and instead revert to the power of the witness as a self-explanatory trace. In brief, to the question "Who are you?" a Hizbullah intellectual or official would answer, "This is what *we did*," this is the Resistance Project.

Jacques Derrida has elaborated the link between witnessing and the transmission of ethics through his notions of specter and debt. Derrida argues that one can learn ethics only from "the other" and "death"[17] because this transmission of knowledge occurs through time, involving as it does a constant "hanging" of the specter – in our case, the martyr – in time. The specter is able to transmit ethical lines of conduct insofar as he exists between timeframes. Because he haunts the present without really being present, the specter initiates a "politics of memory, of heritage and generations."[18] For Derrida, however, the specter's ability to produce feelings of responsibility toward the other is what builds the possibility of a present, or, to draw on Anderson, a feeling of simultaneity. The very possibility of ethics and a notion of justice depend on acts of remembering, which are also the basis for ideological coherence and continuity.

The martyr witnesses because he "exists" between timeframes, and in so doing produces imaginaries of community conducive to political action. Hizbullah-related intellectuals emphasize the concept of "the promise" as the act that ties together different time dimensions, linking people to martyrs and martyrs to God or the Islamic tradition. The martyr promises or swears (*'ala al-'ahd*) to fulfill an oath. Different social actors, whether militants or the community at large, promise to honor that martyr's line of conduct, which becomes a tradition of practice.[19] The conduct is then reinterpreted and reenacted via repetitive promises across time and generations. The notion of *al-'ahd* (the promise) appears several times in the Qur'an. It is no coincidence that on the front page of each

---

[17] Jacques Derrida, *Spectres de Marx: l'état de la dette, le travail du deuil et la nouvelle internationale* (Paris: Galilée, 1993), 14.
[18] Ibid., 15.
[19] MacIntyre, *After Virtue*, 211.

issue of *al-'Ahd*, next to a picture of Khomeini, a Qur'anic sura states: *innā al-'ahda kāna mus'ūlan* (the promise was responsible).

Al-'ahd is the commitment to a line of conduct that has been preserved by a human legacy though the act of witnessing. Key to understanding the Islamic resistance's fight against Israeli occupation is its attempt to control time dimensions. The ideological translation of the act of resistance is a promise that enables ethical traceable lines of conduct in time, and that is reiterated in text form. For this reason, the discursive component of textual presence is less important than the various other phenomena (such as ethical practices) it deploys. Witnessing plays a necessary role in bridging the epistemological gap left by intellectual transmission.

The First Texts in *al-'Ahd* Commemorating Martyrs

One of *al-'Ahd*'s first texts on martyrs who died conducting operations against Israel paraphrases a famous statement made by Imam al-Sajjad, an important Shi'i figure of the first-century hijra.[20] The text in *al-'Ahd* reads: "The two happy martyrs, Ahmad Khalifeh and Nasser Mansour, two stars (*kawkabayn*) joining the convoy of martyrs (*qāfilat al-shuhadā'*), convinced that killing/death (*al-qatl*) is a habit to them, and their dignity (*karāma*) from God is a testimony (*shahāda*), striving for liberty for the Islamic *umma*, through participating in the destruction of the Zionist tyrant (*jabrūt*)." Imam al-Sajjad's original statement, a famous *ḥadīth* of the Prophet's family collection of *ḥadīth*s, was directed at Ibn Ziyad (the Umayyad governor of Basra toward the end of the seventh century): "Do you threaten me with death, O son of Ziad? Death is a habit to us, our dignity deriving from God is a testimony of that." Noteworthy here is that the dignity to which Ali, son of Husayn, testifies is a line of conduct, an ethical disposition, and not merely a discursive belief in a cause. This sentence is constantly repeated in Hizbullah secretary general Hassan Nasrallah's speeches, and is often used by martyred fighters in their testaments.

Articles on fighters from the Islamic resistance who died in combat against the Israeli army are known as *sirat al-muqawama, zākirat al-shuhadā'*,

---

[20] *al-'Ahd* (18/8/1984). Ali, son of Husayn, son of Ali bin Abi Talib, is considered to be the third Imam in Twelver Shi'ism. He had different titles, such as Imam al-Sajjad and Zayn al-'Abidīn (the ornament of the pious), as it is said that he was very devout and prayed constantly. In the Shi'i tradition all the Imams died from either poisoning or in battle, starting with Husayn's death in the battle of Karbala and including Zayn al-'Abidīn, until the last Imam, who is believed to have disappeared into occultation, but will return at some time in the future.

meaning literally "the legacy of the resistance, the memory of the martyrs." The Arabic word *sīrat* includes the sense of a line of conduct, or an ethical act. The stories consist mostly of interviews with the families of martyrs.[21]

The second article published in *al-'Ahd* on martyrs, which was embedded in a new section on martyr biographies and remembering, was on the fighter Rida al-Sha'ir. Nicknamed the "martyr of Western Bekaa," al-Sha'ir testified to the conditions under which fighters were trained and prepared to confront the enemy.[22] The article's subtitle read: "Hamzet al-Bekaa, he took mountains as a home. His wife: he used to eat wild plants during days of confrontations." The article itself consisted mainly of the testimony of Umm Muhammad, his wife, who apparently raised his children "according to a conscious Islamic education" and played an important organizational role in the resistance. She also conveys the community's difficult experiences confronting the occupying army through highlighting the resistance of al-Sha'ir and the rest of the family. This family testimony and others like it in *al-'Ahd* are geared toward highlighting the resistance as a project of being-in-action. Beliefs are seldom discussed, and when they are invoked it is only as nominal slogans.

Published several months after the article on al-Sha'ir, the martyr biography of Ahmad Taleb, who was also from Western Bekaa (most of the early fighters were from this region, which falls outside areas once occupied by Israel), sheds light on the act of witnessing. The subtitle reads: "The day of his martyrdom he saw himself sleeping above the arms of Imam Husayn. His wife: before he left he said 'be patient, as I am certain of my martyrdom [here read as "testimony"].'"[23] The article details Taleb's courage through acts of the lived experiences of Hizbullah fighters. We read that he fought the cold of winter as his group prepared for battle; he insisted on leading the group into battle as he screamed "O Husayn"; he found death as he threw a grenade into an outpost of the Lebanese proxy army of Israel, causing heavy damage and casualties;[24] and, echoing the notion of haunting, "with all this, Ahmad Taleb did not leave [this world], but his *ghost* is still chasing after the

---

[21] In an interview the leader of the Hizbullah parliamentary coalition, and former editor-in-chief of *al-'Ahd* in its formative years, Mohammad Raad, described to me the painstaking process that *al-'Ahd* journalists had to go through in order to get information from families of martyrs in regions that were either occupied by Israel or highly sensitive at the security level. Mohammad Raad, Lebanese MP, interview with the author, June 2010.

[22] *al-'Ahd* (20/9/1986).

[23] *al-'Ahd* (13/12/1986).

[24] This army is known as the South Lebanon Army (SLA), led by General Antoine Lahd.

collaborators in Lusy, and Sarira, and on the Dalafeh bridge, forbidding them from returning a second time (emphasis added)."[25]

Types and Times of Mourning the Martyr: Markers of the History of Resistance

Hizbullah identifies several types of martyrs, classified according to the way they died. There are those who died in combat, those who died during military clashes, and those who purposefully took their lives in order to cause damage to Israeli military property or take the lives of Israeli military personnel. Martyrs in the latter category are called *istishhādiyyūn*, a word deriving from the root verb *shahāda*, which in the age of the nation-state came to mean "died for this or that cause." Whereas the concept of the *shahīd* goes back to Ali bin Abi Talib's death, and in Islamic jurisprudence meant "died while fighting in the cause of God," the concept of *istishhādī* as used in the modern period is a complete innovation. Classically, it meant "requiring someone to give evidence as in a court of law"[26] – thus again we see the connotation of testifying as action.

As suicide attacks had no jurisprudential precedence in Islamic legal theory, Hizbullah-affiliated intellectuals created fresh referral strategies in order to propose new readings of different social realities. For example, the deputy secretary general of Hizbullah, Naim Qassem, has attempted to link one Qur'anic sura to a general rationale for *istishhādī* operations.[27] This sura states:

Indeed God has purchased from the believers their lives and their possessions, that they expend it in obedience to Him – for example by striving in His way – so that theirs will be [the reward of] Paradise: they shall fight in the way of God and they shall kill and be killed;[28] that is a promise which is binding upon Him in the Torah and the Gospel and the Qur'an; and who fulfills his covenant (*'ahd*) better than God? That is, no one is better in fulfilling it.[29]

---

[25] *al-'Ahd* (13/12/1986). Lusy, Sarira, and the Dalafeh bridge are regions in the South of Lebanon.

[26] For a discussion of this point see Talal Asad, *On Suicide Bombing* (Columbia: Columbia University Press, 2007), 52.

[27] Mustafa Amin, *al-Muqāwama fī lubnān: 1948–2000* (Beirut: Dar al-Hadi, 2003), 458.

[28] This sentence is independent and constitutes an explication of the (above-mentioned) "purchase"; a variant reading has the passive verb come first [sc. *fa-yuqtalūnawa yaqtulūn*, "they shall be killed and shall kill"], meaning that some of them are killed, while those who remain fight on.

[29] Sūrat al-Tawba, verse 3, translation available at http://altafsir.com/ViewTranslations.asp?Display=yes&SoraNo=9&Ayah=0&toAyah=0&Language=2&LanguageID=2&TranslationBook=3.

Qassem uses this verse to emphasize that the act of testifying (*shahāda*) is dependent upon the notion of a contract or covenant (*'ahd*), here between God (through the tradition of the written texts) and the believer. The believer is the social actor who becomes committed to a line of conduct that only materializes over a period of time. The promise that binds the person to the group or community is also the base of its continuity. Messianic time, or time that involves a promise that a line of conduct will be respected in the future, gains significance through writings about the one who testifies.

In Lebanon, Hizbullah was not the first group to organize what have been called "suicide attacks." The first *istishhādī* operation on Lebanese soil was carried out by the Iraqi al-Da'wa Party in mid-December 1981 and targeted the Iraqi embassy in Beirut. Other political actors such as Amal, the Syrian Socialist Nationalist Party (SSNP), and the Communist Party (i.e. not just "religious" groups) have conducted highly successful suicide operations that, similar to those by Hizbullah, were used to claim political legitimacy, likely because of their earlier presence and thus older social ties in the Lebanese South.[30] These militant practices may have created a climate of competition, or at least put new emphasis on the importance of claiming and articulating a human legacy in order to assert difference from other groups. Hizbullah, for example, has claimed to be the first militant organization to plan and execute a suicide attack directed solely against Israeli military targets.[31]

Yet this strategy of legitimization also involved delineating an ethical practice peculiar to each group. In *al-'Ahd*, the first article to do this, written in 1985 by Mohammad Raad in his column Tahht al-majhar (Under the magnifying glass), reflected on a flurry of *istishhādī* operations and argued for reconsidering them.[32] Though not condemning the operations, Raad called for renewed focus on their overall purpose and effectiveness in inflicting military losses, reminding his readers that this practice is not simply a "sacrifice" but also a witnessing of fighting for the cause with impeccable ethics as a way of doing, i.e. on this case as inflicting losses to the Israeli occupier and thus serving the cause of resistance. In this sense also, a fighter should be a *mujāhid*, someone who strives towards excellence or perfection of being-in-action.

The first *istishhādī* to be claimed and remembered by Hizbullah was Ahmad Qasir. On 11 November 1982 the seventeen-year-old Qasir drove

---

[30] Starting from the withdrawal of Israeli forces from the coastal city of Saida as well as other southern areas and their settling south of the Litani river, Hizbullah started claiming martyrdom operations more systematically.

[31] *al-'Ahd* 72 (8/11/1985).

[32] *al-'Ahd* 58 (3/8/1985), 2.

a white Mercedes packed with explosives into Israeli military headquarters in Tyre. The blast killed 141 soldiers. Qasir's identity was only revealed two-and-a-half years after the operation.[33] In order to account for this delay, official Hizbullah statements later invoked security: Qasir had asked the party to respect the safety of his family, who lived in Israeli-occupied territories. Hizbullah only began claiming *istishhādī* martyrs much later, after 1988, simply because between 1985 and 1988 it carried out no suicide operations. By 1988 media devices such as *al-'Ahd* and related cultural efforts had been developed by a slowly growing organization, making claims more of a successful media event.[34]

In the official narrative of Hizbullah, Qasir "opens the era of the *istishhādīyyīn*" (*fātiḥ 'ahd al-istishhādīyyīn*). Notice that "era" is another translation of the word *'ahd*. Hizbullah *istishhādī* operations and any other form of *shahāda* "open" the proper history of the Islamic resistance, the resistance as a project, differentiating it, through this event, from other forms of militant action. Another such event was the assassination of Sheikh Raghib Harb, one of the precursors to resistance against the Israeli army. On 16 February 1984 Lebanese collaborators with Israel shot and killed Harb with a Kalashnikov. As the story goes, he was returning home after praying the *'ishā'* prayer when assailants attacked him in his home village of Jebsheet.[35] Harb was first mentioned in *al-'Ahd* in its very first issue of 28 June 1984, several months after his death. The newspaper reported that the Islamic Republic of Iran had just issued a stamp in his name.[36] As with Qasir, Harb's militant legacy occurred at a time when Hizbullah had not yet begun to openly claim resistance efforts against Israel since it was still in its formative stages.

Regardless of the organizational relationship between Raghib Harb and the emerging organization of Hizbullah, Harb became the "sheikh of the *shuhadā*'," and the anniversary of his death is commemorated every year through a series of gatherings which open the door for a profusion of articles in *al-'Ahd* about the Islamic resistance. The newspaper first marked this event in 1985 by publishing several pages on Harb's life

---

[33] In *al-'Ahd* 48 (24/5/1985). The following week, in issue 49 (1/6/1985), *al-'Ahd* published an interview with Qasir's family.

[34] The irony here is that looking through the data of the time Hizbullah carried out significantly fewer suicide operations than other organizations on the ground such as Amal, the SSNP, Baath, the Communist Party, etc.

[35] There are two versions of the story. One is that Harb reached his house and that the killers found him there, knocked at his door, and as he opened it, killed him instantly. The other claims that Harb was intercepted in the street by the killers driving a Chevrolet car while he was going to visit friends. The presence of varying versions would later boost the creativity of storytelling on Harb's martyrdom.

[36] *al-'Ahd* 1 (28/6/1984), 1.

and work, and a selection of his speeches.[37] The front page of the issue read: *Dalīl al-qāfila* (the guide of the convoy).[38] The biography of Harb[39] described his confrontational stance toward Israel and mentioned his imprisonment by Israeli forces on 18 March 1983. The next four pages reported on commemorations and film screenings organized in Beirut and in Western Bekaa, where several speakers addressed the crowds and key political figures read aloud a list of quotations on his martyrdom (*shahāda*) and poetry by anonymous writers, as well as displayed several pictures of the sheikh with other *ʿulamāʾ* of his village, his mother, and the rest of his family. These visual traces in *al-ʿAhd* attested to particular ways in which the cause should be represented: women wear the black chador, Raghib's mother is draped with his *ʿabāya* (clerical gown), and Raghib is photographed with his *maṣbaḥa* (rosary). This format of pictures, symbols, and texts put together on the occasion of a remembering is referential in the sense that it serves as a template for a myriad of acts of remembering reproduced annually, which gradually became more complex as years passed.

Most importantly, Hizbullah proclaimed its political existence, its presence, through the haunting by Harb's ghost. In an "Open Letter to the Downtrodden" published on 16 February 1985 – two days after Harb's martyr commemoration – Hizbullah made its first official appearance in media channels and other political communities. The letter presented the party's worldview and several political objectives, including liberating occupied land and bringing down the Lebanese government, which at the time was presided over by Amin Gemayel, who was believed to be giving in to Israeli and American demands. First communicated through a press conference given by Sayyid Ibrahim al-Amin, the formal spokesman of the organization, the Open Letter was published in full in *al-ʿAhd* along with details on the press conference and Harb's commemoration.[40]

Gradually, Hizbullah linked the resistance's military operations and main exploits to other important dates in the party's history, connecting future operations with the anniversaries of past martyrs. This reinforced the idea that all operations were carried out *ʿala al-ʿahd* (keeping the promise). On 26 February 1986, two years after the death of Raghib Harb, *al-ʿAhd* reported on an operation dubbed "the gift of the Islamic Resistance to the soul of the shaykh of the *shuhadāʾ*, Ragheb Harb." Carried out by Hizbullah fighters, this operation resulted in the capturing

---

[37] *al-ʿAhd* 34 (16/2/1985).
[38] *Dalīl* is most accurately translated as "the one who points to directions" (signs).
[39] Ibid., 5.
[40] *al-ʿAhd* 35 (23/2/1985). I discuss this letter in a forthcoming article on Hizbullah's representation of party, community, and state.

of two Israeli prisoners. The front page of the issue depicted an image of these prisoners lying unconscious on beds in a room on whose walls hung pictures of Harb, Musa al-Sadr, Khomeini, and the dome of the al-Aqsa Mosque in Jerusalem (which later became commonly used during Jerusalem Day commemorations).[41] The image's caption reads: "The two Israeli prisoners before the condemning of one of them." The editorial explains why this offering was being made to Harb. On the second page were pictures of objects belonging to the Israeli military prisoners, such as a Jewish kippah, personal identification papers, and jackets.[42]

Operations accumulated and dedications systematically followed. In one issue, an Islamic resistance operation made the front page with its "gift to the shaykh of the *shuhadā'* [referring to Raghib Harb] at the anniversary of his fourth [annual] remembering."[43] The resistance captured two main positions (Saidun and Rimat) of the Israeli proxy army in Lebanon. The front page displayed images of seized weapons bearing the logo of the Phalange Party.[44] One such image contained a picture of Raghib Harb and Khomeini hanging on the wall behind the collected bounty of weapons. Below the image, an article described the operation, comparing it to the previous operation offered in the memory of Harb (described above). Also included was an interview with Harb's family that revealed new stories and anecdotes about his life. Every new act of remembering became an occasion to present more information on or knowledge of the martyr.

In *al-'Ahd*'s 17 October 1989 issue, the front page depicted an immense crowd gathered for what the headline called "The Day of the Shahīd: The Day of Commitment to the *istishhādiyyīn*."[45] On the occasion of the annual remembrance of Ahmad Qasir's martyrdom, Hizbullah organized the first joint commemoration as a single tribute to all of the *shuhadā'* who died fighting Israel. The picture on the front page

---

[41] Musa al-Sadr is another important figure for Hizbullah as the first to found a political movement, Amal, which represents the Shi'i community in Lebanon. Many Hizbullah members came from a branch of Amal called Amal al-Islāmī, which thought that the main leadership of Amal in the beginning of the 1980s had deviated from the political objectives of al-Sadr such as the fight against Israel. Jerusalem Day is a commemoration instituted by Khomeini that annually remembers the occupation of the al-Aqsa Mosque, a sacred site of Islam.

[42] *al-'Ahd* 36 (26/2/1985).

[43] *al-'Ahd* 191 (20/2/1988).

[44] The president of the Lebanese Republic at this period was Amin Gemayel, the brother of the assassinated president Bashir Gemayel, who had led the Lebanese Forces, an offshoot of the Phalangist Party. For this reason, Hizbullah, which is antagonistic to this party, labeled the Gemayel presidency as Phalangist, which is a slight oversimplification, as Gemayel had his differences with what were gradually becoming various Phalangist factions.

[45] *al-'Ahd* 282 (17/10/1989).

showed Islamic resistance soldiers in impeccable uniforms, brandishing their weapons. Inside the issue, details of the festivities were displayed. One picture showed the podium at which Hizbullah leaders assembled and the first secretary general, Sobhi Tufayli, appeared to be giving a speech. Behind him were posters of the main *istishhādīyyīn*, Ahmad Qasir, Ali Saffieddine, and Assad Berro. One such poster portrayed a drawing of a rose most probably symbolizing the anonymous *istishhādī* dubbed "Abu Zaynab." And as the parades were taking place in Dahyeh, Abbas Moussawi was in the south giving a speech, demonstrating this crowding not just of time but space. One learns from these early commemorations that the various divisions of military units in Hizbullah took the names of specific *shuhadā'*. As pictured in the issue, present at the parade were the Martyr Mohammad Bajiji group, the Hassan Saaluk group, the Abu Ali Shahla group the Faraj Balluk unit, the al-Ḥur al-'Āmilī group, the Leader Ahmad Qasir group, and so on. Also demonstrating were hermetically veiled people in black representing *istishhādī* groups and carrying explosive devices.

Several months later, on the sixth anniversary of Raghib Harb's assassination, *al-'Ahd* featured a new commemoration: Usbū' al-Muqāwama al-Islāmīyya (Islamic Resistance Week).[46] What had once been the "Week of the Martyr" was now an annual commemoration. This particular issue of *al-'Ahd* included an unprecedented ten-page section on the history of the Islamic resistance, its various achievements, and the human legacy that gives it meaning through action. In the issue immediately prior, *al-'Ahd* had reported on yet another commemoration, the triumph of the "Islamic Revolution era" (the word *'ahd* here again means "era") in Iran.[47] Its front page read: "As their leader Ruhollah Khomeini has just passed away, the resistance fighters are commemorating through qualitative operations (*'amaliyyāt naw'iyya*) the opening of the era."[48] The intense periodicity of commemorations shows the high frequency with which people are "interpellated"[49] to be part of the common cause, showing the link between acts of remembrance and political practice.

In February 1992, while returning from the eighth commemoration of Harb's death in Jebsheet, the then secretary general of Hizbullah, Sayyid Abbas Moussawi, was killed by an Israeli helicopter missile strike on his car, along with his wife, son, and driver. Suddenly, Raghib Harb's day of

[46] *al-'Ahd* 295 (16/2/1990).
[47] *al-'Ahd* 294 (9/2/1990).
[48] Ibid., 1.
[49] I am using here Althusser's notion: see Louis Althusser, "Ideology and Ideological State Apparatuses," in *Lenin and Philosophy, and Other Essays* (New York: Monthly Review Press, 1971).

memory gained greater substance, as Moussawi was added to the commemoration. Just as Harb had been dubbed the "sheikh of the *shuhadā'*,"
Moussawi was now the "sayyid of the *shuhadā'*."[50] *Al-'Ahd* commemorated the martyrdom of Harb and Moussawi together every year during
Usbū' al-Muqāwama, with articles increasingly growing in size and cover-
ing different topics.

Sixteen years later, the third-highest-ranking Hizbullah member, Imad
Mughniyya, was assassinated around the same time of year, on 12
February 2008, in Damascus, adding another prominent martyred leader
to the "Islamic Resistance Week" (which was subsequently titled Zikra al-
Shuhadā' al-Qada [Remembering the martyred leaders]). In a radio
interview in 2013 given on the occasion of Islamic Resistance Week,
Hizbullah parliamentary member Nawaf Moussawi was asked if he had
an explanation for why Israelis always seem to choose that particular
period to kill resistance leaders. Moussawi half-seriously speculated that
Israel must have found it to be a strategically opportune moment to attack
since Hizbullah's leaders always mobilize to specific areas at that time for
commemorations that the organization views as extremely important.
Ironically, the making of these commemorations was at the heart of
Hizbullah's ideological coherence, demonstrating the extent to which
all facets of the "lived" experience of the resistance against Israel was
the direct reservoir of ideological coherence.

The Day of the Shahīd and the Remembering of the Martyred Leaders
mark the beginning of the Era of the Resistance (*'ahd al-muqāwama*)
labeled as Islamic in Lebanon, through the legacy of Raghib Harb and
Ahmad Qasir, as well as other martyrs who came to testify to the same
political cause. Hizbullah, through the recalling of its particular human
legacy, differentiates between its own particular project of resistance and
a wider "Islamic Resistance" that has been taking place since the death of
the Prophet, depending on the specific writings of histories with which
Hizbullah-affiliated intellectuals engaged. These commemorations are
not stable in content and fixed in time; they constantly incorporate new
manifestations depending on the different types of testimonies or
martyrdoms within specific timeframes.

All of these early ideological formulations find resonance in the
advertising banner for a commemoration that took place on 11
November 2009. The banner, which was plastered on most billboards
of Beirut's southern suburbs and the road to the South, depicted a

---

[50] Sayyid is a term given to people whose family lineage can be allegedly traced to that of the
Prophet Muhammad. When they are religious figures, they wear black turbans (as
opposed to white for ordinary sheikhs such as Harb).

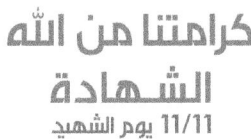

Figure 1 A billboard poster for Martyrs' Day commemoration that took place on 11 November 2009. It depicts the picture of the first martyr, Ahmad Qasir, with his face made up of the faces of many martyrs. The caption, referring to a statement made by Imam al-Sajjad, reads: "Our dignity deriving from God is a testimony."

previously unreleased portrait of Ahmad Qasir made up of hundreds of faces of martyrs (Figure 2). This type of portrait was not without precedent. As early as 1992, following the annual Ashura commemoration, *al-'Ahd* had published a very similar caricature of a silhouetted face wearing the black turban of the sayyid, which was composed of a myriad of other faces representing the martyrs as legacies of the resistance (Figure 1).[51]

---

[51] *al-'Ahd* (11/7/1992).

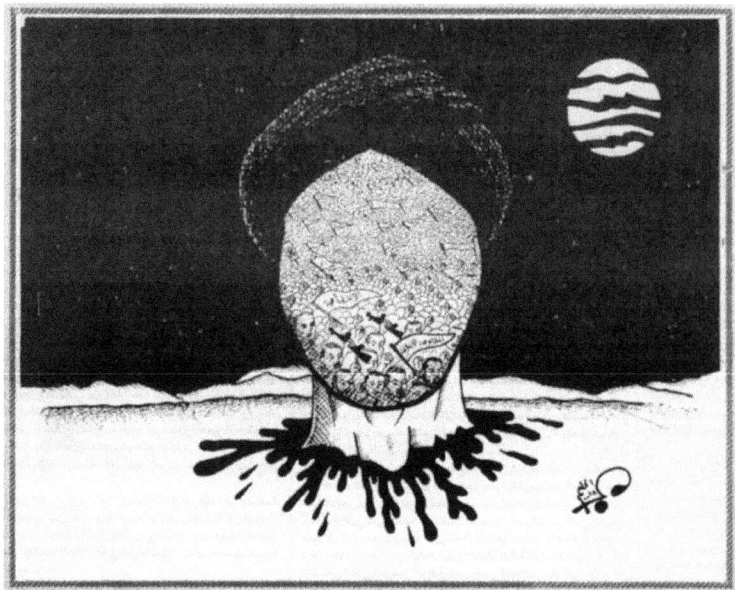

Figure 2 A drawing of the head of an imam/sheikh with a black turban and the head severed from its body (drawn from *al-'Ahd*, 11 July 1992)

An Interlude: "Calendrical Times"

One way of imagining time and history is through different bindings of texts. Calendars, for example, can outline a breakup of events, sayings, thoughts, prayers, and so on, in a chronological, ordered sequence. Hizbullah's Islamic Resistance Support Association (Hay'at Da'm al-Muqāwama al-Islāmīyya) issues annual calendars with famous quotes and events end-noted on each date. These calendars have the Gregorian and the Islamic dates juxtaposed to each other, referring alternatively to commemorations marked in either nomenclature.[52]

---

[52] Examples of dates commemorated are Ashura (10 Muḥarram), Jerusalem Day (last day of Ramaḍān), Liberation Day (25 May), Yom al-Ghadīr (18 Zhī al-Qa'da), the anniversary of the Iranian Islamic revolution (11 February), the birth of the Mahdi (15 Sha'bān), and so on. Note that one of the only Islamic dates instituted in the modern era is Jerusalem Day; the rest of the contemporary commemorations use the Gregorian calendar.

On the reverse side of the first page of the 2008 calendar is the following Qur'anic verse:

And We made the night and the day two signs. Then We effaced the sign of the night and made the sign of the day sight-giving; that you may seek bounty from your Lord, and that you may know the number of years and the reckoning, and everything We have detailed very distinctly.[53]

This verse is followed by a text that elaborates the importance of the calendar as a repository of wise sayings spread throughout its pages, and thus across time, so to speak. On the front of the following page under the date 2 January, a saying of Imam Ali reads, *al-shukr turjumān al-niyya wa-lisān al-taw'iya* (thankfulness is the translation of expression and the language of awareness). The back of this page mentions two military operations that took place on 2 January 1987 against the SLA, which resulted in the killing of several soldiers, the destruction of three vehicles, and the confiscation of weapons. On the third day, "the main operations that took place in the year 1995" are listed on the back of the page: four such attacks and their results.[54] On the front of this page is written a saying of the Prophet: "Exchange salutes so that rancor leaves your heart" (*tasāfahu yazhab al-ghal min qulūbikum*). Sometimes sayings include references to political positions. The page for 25 August 2009, for example, is marked with a quote by Musa al-Sadr: "Islamic and Christian coexistence is a treasure to hold on to." In addition to religiously marked references, the calendar also quotes anonymous poetry, sayings, and proverbs, titled "the poet" and "Arabic sayings and proverbs."[55]

At the beginning of this chapter I considered the interplay between ethical reflections and historical markers that allow for the narration of a political cause through the coming and going of the martyr, or through injunctions of the human legacy. Calendars synthesize this process not only through their references to general rules of conduct and proverbs but also through their intensive condensation of overlapping timeframes, from what one might call prophetic historiography (e.g. the birth and death of religious figures, such as the Prophet and his family, or important battles), to the lives, deeds, and sayings of Shi'i-related *shuhadā'*, and contemporary world political issues (such as the beginning and end of

---

[53] Sūrat al-Isrā', verse 12. Translation available at http://altafsir.com/ViewTranslations.asp? Display=yes&SoraNo=17&Ayah=0&toAyah=0&Language=2&LanguageID=2& TranslationBook=3.

[54] This categorization of operations according to days, months, and years was first published in *al-'Ahd* starting from the early 1990s. See as early as *al-'Ahd* 333 (16/11/1990), 21; 502 (20/1/1994); and 504 (11/2/1994).

[55] These calendars also contain English and other "Western" proverbs on some of its dates, as well as random scientific and technological "information."

World War I and II) including the expulsion of the Palestinians and the establishment of the state of Israel in 1948. What is important in this representation of time is that every era comes to be associated with a cause. It is in this sense that time is neither strictly linear nor cyclical. Calendars mark anniversaries of events involving resistance, from anti-colonial battles, to independence days, from the Lebanese national pact to the first Israeli invasion of Lebanon in 1978.[56] Yet each era has its own promise, its 'ahd.

Judicious overlap can take place between the use of the Islamic and Gregorian calendars. Given that the Islamic calendar is cyclical, Ashura is constantly rotating from one week or month to the next, occurring "earlier" every year. In 2009, for example, the Day of the Shahīd coincided with the middle of the week of Ashura commemorations. In 2005 and 2006 the commemorations of the martyrdom of Harb and Moussawi fell on roughly the same week as Ashura. The different themes articulated in these commemorations thus overlapped, keeping time saturated with recallings day after day. For example, in February 2006 Nasrallah's speech commemorating the martyrdom of Harb and Moussawi focused on the pious characteristics of these individuals, for during the week of Ashur Nasrallah typically spoke about Islamic virtues and linked them to fighting oppression and injustice. A Nasrallah quotation from that time stands out as further evidence of my argument. Remembering Harb and Moussawi, he stated that "the past becomes present with what and who is in it, so that we face the future" (yaḥḍur al-māḍi bi mā fīhī wa-man fīhī ila al-ḥāḍir li-nuwājih al-mustaqbal).[57]

The great detail used by Hizbullah to describe past military operations and their commemorations is sometimes coupled with a description of phases of combat or strategic techniques, always in the background. For example, 19 January 2008 falls on 10 Muḥarram 1429 in the Islamic calendar and commemorates Ashura. On the reverse side of the page for this date is a small text recalling the start of the use of Katyusha rockets against Israeli targets in 1995 as well as the rationale for this military technique: "a reaction to Zionists' targeting of civilian positions in the South and an attempt to foster a deterrence force." These calendars also detail the various prisoner swaps that took place between Hizbullah and Israel. For example, 29 January is the "day of the liberation of Lebanese

---

[56] Ironically falling on 14 March, the day massive demonstrations took place in downtown Beirut against the Syrian political presence in Lebanon and after which the political coalition against Hizbullah took its name. One reads on this calendar that it was on 14 March that Hizbullah's non-Shi'i division of fighters, al-Sarāya al-Lubnānīyya, was formed.

[57] Hassan Nasrallah, speech, 16/02/2006.

and Palestinian prisoners," following the release of Sheikh Obeid, who had been imprisoned by the Israelis.

Athār al-Shuhadā᾽ (Relics of the Martyrs) and the Question of Trace

Aside from the military infrastructure of Hizbullah, the Mu᾽assasat al-Shahīd (Martyr's Association) was one of the first organizations to emerge through Iranian logistical aid. *Al-'Ahd* first mentioned this institution in a very early 1984 issue. According to this article, the Martyr's Association was founded just after the Israeli invasion of 1982, describing it as "one of the most important Islamic institutions that participates in reducing the weight of problems and social issues incurred by Muslims in the different Lebanese regions as a result of the constant belligerent assault by the Lebanese regime, the Crusaders, and the Israeli enemy."[58] Founded with the significant support of its eponymous twin organization in the Islamic Republic of Iran, the association takes care of the families of those martyred or injured while "defending Muslims on battle fronts."[59] In practice, the association is dedicated to providing all kinds of facilities and services to the families of Hizbullah fighters who died in combat against Israeli military forces.

On the 2008 annual anniversary of the Day of the Shahīd, *al-'Ahd* pointed out that the association "intends to offer total care to the family of resistance martyrs in these different realms: social, cultural, consultative, psychological, educative, living standards, accommodation, and health, in order to build a believing [pious] family that is independent and striving so as to protect the road followed by those who sacrificed themselves, those who dedicated their lives to build the nation, its borders and sovereignty."[60]

A special branch of the association, Athār al-Shuhadā᾽ (Relics of the Martyrs), has been set up to collect objects, mostly textual and acoustic, either belonging to or produced by martyrs, or collected and created by the friends and relatives of a martyr. The collection is extensive, and includes letters, testaments, diaries, articles, studies, stories, memories, translations, plays (some written and others in video format), rosaries, books, clothes, and so on. As explained by one of the association's employees, martyrs' activities – as captured and represented by

---

[58] *al-'Ahd* (30/12/1984).
[59] Ibid.
[60] *al-'Ahd* (11/10/2008).

these objects – were not only military in nature but also encompassed sports, social practices, and artistic creations.[61]

Hizbullah as an organization collects information on each of its fighters independently of Athār al-Shuhadā'. Accordingly, conflicts may occur between the two, and in some cases Hizbullah is forced to seize sensitive military- or security-related information. Athār al-Shuhadā' therefore focuses solely on "cultural" aspects of the martyr's life. After the death of a combatant, researchers try to gather as much information as possible by approaching the martyr's family and close friends, figures from his village, and when possible his military companions.

Although only recently instituted as a sort of formal database collecting agency, Athār al-Shuhadā' continues a process started by al-'Ahd's journalists, as outlined above. But this process, first elaborated in the mid-1980s, has been scrupulously enlarged to include collecting all types of objects. Whereas al-'Ahd did standard journalistic accounts based on one-time interviews with families, Athār al-Shuhadā' collects actual relics and other objects, which it stores in digital form searchable by subject and type. The testimonies of martyrs or their family members that were fitted into one newspaper article in al-'Ahd now stand on their own as archived material, and the collected artistic creations, short stories, novels, poems, and so on come to form a rapidly enlarging reservoir of information.

The presence and use of traces makes the transmission of knowledge-as-ethics possible. An employee at Athār al-Shuhadā' told me that there are two types of sources about "being a martyr" or "living as a martyr": primary and secondary. Whereas the direct testimonies of martyrs, whether spoken words, writings, or relics, are considered a primary source, the testimonies of others about martyrs or any textual or nontextual object related to the martyr are secondary sources. In his study of textual traditions in Yemen, Brinkley Messick argues that the Islamic tradition has always preferred the spoken over the written, with the Qur'an acting as the paradigmatic text because it is the spoken word of God, and any other textual work, including interpretation or commentary, secondary and considered as "text."[62] Here, although martyr testaments are written, ontologically they have the importance of the "oral": they are primary sources – the sayings of the martyr himself along with his own artistic creations (stories, poetry, etc). In other words, there is a sacred element to martyr testaments and any other "artifact" or "trace" that the martyr leaves behind. Likewise, although the Qur'an circulates as a written medium, the book is the expression of the spoken

---

[61] Athār al-Shuhadā' employee (anonymous), interview with the author, July 2009.
[62] Messick, The Calligraphic State.

word of God, his sayings, passed on through the Prophet. In contrast, testimonies about sayings, life episodes, and social practices of the Prophet and his close companions, although orally transmitted, have the same importance as the "written."

But following Derrida, there is no fundamental ontological difference between the written and the spoken. On the contrary, oral expression is a form of writing, subject to a process of endless interpretation.[63] Social actors use traces to create hierarchies of meanings in order to establish continuity across time-as-era and imaginaries of community. In the case of Hizbullah-affiliated intellectuals, therefore, they develop hierarchies of knowledge about the martyr in order to create the martyr's presence. The martyr then testifies unrelentingly, through all of these relics, all of these traces (the Arabic word *athār* literally means "trace"), and in so doing he produces knowledge. He contributes to the construction of Hizbullah's ideological coherence not just as a political organization or as an abstract cultural sphere of idioms and symbols, but as a "physical" trace bearing a meaning that can be used and reused by individuals and groups in infinite ways.[64] It is in this sense that Hizbullah's cultural backbone is the legacy of the martyrs. And to this effect, it is Hizbullah-affiliated intellectuals' main ideological anchor to recall the martyrs and their testimonies.

The presence of martyrs enables representations of land, history, and people, and invites members of the "interpellated community" to write to or about the martyrs, resulting in the whole community interacting with the specter. Letters dedicated to martyrs are the most common form of text, and they are constantly published in *al-'Ahd* and then catalogued in the database of Athār al-Shuhadā᾽. Important time junctures, such as the *istishhādī* operation of Ahmad Qasir, attract many more letters from a wider public, and even invite different types of literary experiments.

In 2001, Dar al-Amir, a publishing house close to Hizbullah, released a romanticized biography of Hadi Nasrallah, the son of Hassan Nasrallah, whose *shahāda* in an operation against the Israelis in September 1997 caused a great deal of agitation within the Lebanese political community. Written by Nisrine Idris, the biography was entitled *'Urss Aylūl* (the September Wedding), referring to the month in which the martyrdom of Hadi Nasrallah took place. Mohammad Hussein Bazzi, the editor of Dar al-Amir, an author of several books on the resistance, and a main contributor to the new cultural production around Hizbullah, the Project of the Resistance, and other "Islamic" discursive articulations, wrote the

---

[63] Derrida, *De la grammatologie*.
[64] In this vein, I am highly indebted to Lisa Wedeen's conceptualization of culture as meaning-making practice that illustrates the practical and material implication of this notion. See Wedeen, "Conceptualizing Culture."

preface in which he recalled martyrs by deriving forms of conduct from Husayn, the paradigmatic martyr in Shi'i historiography. For Bazzi, what is remarkable is not just that Hadi was the son of the secretary general of Hizbullah, or that his family had direct links to the Prophet (which makes Nasrallah a sayyid), Ali, and Ali's son Husayn, but that "he was Husayn" (*kāna al-Husayn*)[65] in that he faced and addressed the same ethical questions that Husayn did when confronting enemies. In order to capture this ethical presence, he had to *be* him or to be haunted by him. He, along with all the other martyrs, was Husayn, the paradigmatic martyr, haunting people's unfolding present through their actions.

---

[65] Nisrine Idriss, *'Urss aylūl* (Beirut: Dar al-Hadi, 2001), 3.

اننا لا نريد أن نحقق مشروعا للمسلمين، وانما نبني مشروعا اسلاميا. وهذا هو الفرق بين مشروع
المسيحيين، ومشروع المسلمين وبين أن يكون الموضوع مشروع مشروع مسيحيا في مواجهة مشروع اسلامي
(السيد ابراهيم الأمين، العهد، 21 ذو القعدة1404، ص6)

We do not want to realize a Muslim project, but we want to build an Islamic
project. And this is the difference between the Christian project [in Lebanon]
and the Muslim project, or having the subject being a Christian project in the
face of an Islamic project.   (Sayyid Ibrahim al-Amin, *al-'Ahd* 18/08/1984, 6)

ان على أتباع المسيح ان يثبتوا لكل الآخرين انهم فعلا ملتزمون بتعاليم المسيح.. لا أن ينادوا بالمحبة فاذا
بهذه المحبة تقف عند حدود آخر مسيحي منتسب بالهوية فقط للمسيح.

(*al-'Ahd* 27 11/1/1984, 2)

The followers of Christ ought to really prove to others that they are
committed to the teachings of Christ. They cannot just call for love when
this love only involves the other Christian who subscribes by identity
only to Christ.   (*al-'Ahd* 27 11/1/1984, 2)

From the early 1980s, Hizbullah-affiliated intellectuals drew the political
"other" into a largely consistent narrative. It was against a background of the
civil war and its harsh divisive reality that Hizbullah was first formed. Stories
came together based on an assessment of actions that took place on specific
recorded dates and at junctures of past political events.

Writing the history of the other enables a process of political appraisal, and
through this reading of history stems a general "substance" that explains the
moral intentions of actions. Sometimes this substance is given the label
'aqīda siyāsīyya, a word that translates as "doctrine," and, in this political
context, as ideology. However, this translation misses the ethical components of the concept.[1] Just as Hizbullah says it has an *'aqīda* that sets it apart
from other political formations in Lebanon, Christian politics obeyed

---

[1] In the word *'aqīda*, there is the element of certainty that the beliefs that are espoused are
unquestioned. This is probably why it was commonly translated as "doctrine," but also as
ideology in the political sense. Yet the way it is used by Hizbullah seems to imply an ethical
component, in the sense that these doctrines, especially in the realm of politics, lead to
particular actions that are either harmful or beneficial to human beings; or that cultivate
specific virtues.

a particular "rationale" of work. And for Hizbullah, Political Maronitism, which refers to the domination of the Lebanese political system by a Christian elite since the inception of the modern state, has its ʿaqīda.[2] In so doing, from the early 1980s, Hizbullah-affiliated intellectuals drew the political "other" into largely consistent narratives.

This reappraisal of the political other – whether labeled as an enemy, an ally, or as just another political entity present in the environment of Hizbullah – involved rewriting prevailing accounts of history that have already been elaborated by the other. In this case, it involves addressing the different Maronite constructions of the nation, the Palestinian call for resistance, the earlier legacy of "secular" political opposition to the regime, and representations of the enemy, namely Israel, a topic discussed in Chapter 4. This process of historical appraisal feeds into conceptions of the nation, or at least this imagined sense of belonging to a community. By delineating a particular writing strategy, the Christian emerges as a compatriot, albeit one who has followed unacceptable political paths.

Early Hizbullah representations of Christians shed light on a highly mis-understood subject – the relationship between the party and the Christian Lebanese – and its various political formations. The literature is split between theorizing a shift in Hizbullah's representations of the Christians from an attitude of radical confrontation, to one where they are considered as fellow nationals, or, supposing that this initial confrontation is still there, only masked by media propaganda, awaiting the establishment of an Islamic state where Christians would become second-class citizens, or *ahl al-dhimma*. The issue in both of these theories is a deep misunderstanding of Hizbullah's representation of what it is to be Lebanese, from the 1980s up to the present day. As explained in Chapter 1, this has mostly to do with a misunderstanding, first, of the performative dimension of ideological material deployed over time, and second, of the general cultural background that witnessed Hizbullah's emergence.

In fact, nowhere in the issues of *al-ʿAhd*, or in the speeches, official press releases, or even interviews of the party, was the label *ahl al-dhimma* ever used. Alagha points to the use of this expression in the books of a certain Muhammad Zʿayter, who is a relative unknown in the intellectual circles of the party. Despite the fact that Alagha calls Zʿayter

---

[2] For example, see Khodr Tliss' column on Political Maronitism in *al-ʿAhd* (15/05/1992), 8, when he was a member of Hizbullah's Politburo. He was killed in 1998 during armed confrontations between Sobhi Tufayli's opposition group and the Lebanese army. The first SG of Hizbullah, later split with the party over the issue of participating in the legislative elections of 1992. Although he continued writing in *Al Ahd*, along with Khodr Tliss (who although close to Tufayli, ran for legislative elections). Tufayli gradually radicalized his stance towards the Lebanese state, which culminated in the confrontations of 1998.

a "Hizbullah intellectual,"[3] the latter's writings are nowhere to be found in publications related to the party, and he was never close to them in any way, according to sources from within Hizbullah. Even if we suppose that he was connected to the party in a secretive way and that the party later tried to distance itself from him and his radical discourse, one would still expect to find leads in the hundreds of issues of *al-'Ahd* throughout the 1980s and 1990s. In reality, the language and writing style of Z'ayter[4] stands in contrast to Hizbullah-affiliated intellectuals' writing strategies, especially as described throughout this book. Z'ayter's texts appearing sometime in 1987 are markedly different from the writings of *al-'Ahd*, the Open Letter, speeches, interviews, and all other ideological production that appeared from 1984 onwards.On the contrary, most of Hizbullah's concerns are in line with those of the constituency and intellectual circles it emanates from: to find a political formula to live with the rest of the Lebanese. This formula was not well thought out at first and remains blurry in these publications, if not ending up resorting to accepting confessionalism and consociational democracy as the least worst solution (provided that the military resistance remained). How can we then explain the relentless lessons in patriotism, and in Christian ethics, and the subsequent Muslim–Christian institutional efforts deployed in the post-war period? What Hizbullah has engaged in since its inception is a redefinition of what it is to be Lebanese, stranded by the experience of occupation, the marginalization of the state, and alienation from a portion of the population.

Writing one's own history and addressing that of the other brings the hegemonic and the ideological into play,[5] involving two writing exercises. First, addressing dominant political narratives of the Lebanese nation, the hegemonic so to speak, is to write about Political Maronitism, to be forced to confront it; and second, the ideological, to propose a different representation of it so as to change it. Representations of Maronites, and of Christians more generally, have changed following the end of the wars between 1975 and1990 and following the rapprochements of the next two decades. Yet this does not signal a "shift in ideology," a "Lebanonization," or "modera-tion" of Hizbullah. Rather, it shows that the initial writing strategy of

---

[3] Alagha, *Hizbullah's Identity Construction*, 36–38.

[4] Z'ayter has two books that have passed down to us, both seemingly published around the same period in the late 1980s, but dates remain uncertain. See Muhammad Z'ayter, *Nazra 'ala tarh al jumhūriyya al islāmiyya fī lubnān* and *al-Mashrū' al-mārūnī, fī lubnān: juzūruhu wa tatawwurātuhu* (no publication details available, but published in 1987–8). If anything, Z'ayter could have been a remnant of earlier Islamic formations from which Hizbullah diverged at its inception (see Chapter 6).

[5] As explained in Chapter 1. See Comaroff and Comaroff, *Of Revelation and Revolution*, introduction.

delineating a tradition played an important role as relations with the political other gradually changed according to context.

In this chapter I argue that Hizbullah-affiliated intellectuals' representations of the political "other" involve a type of writing strategy: placing that other into a "tradition of history" so as to judge its actions and propose political lessons. Hizbullah's intellectuals proposed new ways to understand the culture of the other based on effective ways to operationalize confessional imaginaries. In both cases, for Hizbullah voicing political demands and building relations with the other, it came down to judging whether an ally or enemy belongs to a shared tradition. Inscribing the other into a tradition made him worthy of being part of a particular political community that included Hizbullah by literally inscribing him "in time" (the Christians, for example), or else by ejecting him out of it (for example, the Israeli or Zionist).

The Background

Political Maronitism as a political regime was especially relevant in the pre-1975 war era and was characterized by the control Maronite Christians had over the institutions related to the state. Political parties and formations opposed to this system argued that it produced asymmetric forms of power, giving the bulk of political prerogative to the Christians, which eventually led to the beginning of the hostilities in 1975. Mostly comprising leftists, pan-Arabists, or Arab nationalists of all sorts as well as ad hoc Sunni political formations, these groups criticized the monopolization by Christian groups over the apparatus of the state and the domination over the majority of institutional positions. The confessional political system allocated to each sect's specific administrative quotas allowed the Maronites to keep most of the privileges given their hold on executive power, represented by the position of president of the Republic, the head of the army, and other key institutional posts.

Political Maronitism owed its genesis and consolidation to a more generalized political system of confessional institutional sharing and allocations that was developed in the second half of the nineteenth century following the popular revolts of the 1860s. The confessional sectarian system of political representation came about as a result of Western meddling and local political ambitions against the backdrop of a gradually weakening Ottoman grasp over those regions.[6] It was on the basis of these modern political developments that the modern state of

---

[6] For an interesting analysis of the birth of confessionalism as a modern political and social practice in the aftermath of the 1860s see Makdisi, *The Culture of Sectarianism.*

Lebanon was founded by linking the mountainous region to the coastal area. Most rules were unwritten, and it is mere convention that political representation and administrative positions are set as they are. However, the end of the civil war era saw a rewriting of prerogatives during the Taif meetings of 1989 that culminated in the agreement that set the stage for what was dubbed "the post-war and reconstruction era."

This agreement did not change the actual administrative positions, the president still being a Maronite, the prime minister a Sunni, the speaker of Parliament a Shi'i, and so on, but it has rewritten the prerogatives of each, most importantly putting the president and the prime minister on the same level, the result being that they could veto each other's actions, leading to constant paralysis of executive in the country. In order to save a custom that had "made things work" ever since some form of semi-independent political structure existed in Mount Lebanon, the new situation of the 1990s just tried to give each party more of its dues. The actual "technocratic" use of the position of prime minister or any other was not as important as group representation. In a sense, the state's importance as a powerful institution that mobilizes resources, plans and changes the management of territory, population, and history has always been weak in the face of the various parochial groups' interests.

Groups' perceived security had to operate under the guise of an overarching state which in turn was fragmented in order to be put to political use. But in turn, these groups could not derive legitimacy unless they had their own specific imaginary of a nation-state in which other groups are accounted for. In the process, each political formation created its own understanding of the community, whether parochial or national, as it came to make a claim over the state. Initially, the first to engage in this exercise were Maronite intellectuals: seeking to construct narratives positing the specificity of the nation, they wrote the major historical events that came to represent the timeless nation of Lebanon where Christians played a formative and pioneering role.[7]

When Hizbullah emerged at the beginning of the 1980s, the different warring factions in Lebanon had undermined the state's ability to be the sole monopolizer of the means of coercion. Small divided militia-controlled geographical areas[8] had emerged all throughout the country. Until the Taif Agreement, which paved the way for a new political formula, the Lebanese war era could be partly read as attempts made by

---

[7] See the discussion of Maronite writing of history below and Ahmad Beydoun, *Identité confessionnelle et temps social chez les historiens libanais contemporains* (Beirut: Librairie Orient, 1984).

[8] These were occasionally called cantons, alluding to the Swiss and Belgian political systems.

remnants of the old political system to reassert their pre-war positions. This was embodied in the regime of Amin Gemayel, who became president after his brother Bashir was assassinated in September 1982, a few days after the latter's election. Even though Bashir and Amin (and, for that matter, other Christian political figures) had different approaches to politics, from the perspective of groups such as Hizbullah, they were similar in that they sought to regain Christian prerogatives over the state. In this sense, the breakdown of the state was a reality that began in the mid-1970s,[9] yet most Christian political elites hoped for a return of Political Maronitism as the foundational regime for the national pact.

The Christian Other: An Old and Turbulent Compatriot

Predictably, for a media outlet that posited itself in opposition to the political regime in place, early issues of al-'Ahd discussed Political Maronitism extensively, informing its readers with minute and endless details about Christian politics in Lebanon, especially before the end of the war in 1990. Across the pages of al-'Ahd, early writings criticized the actions labeled as Political Maronitism by virtue of understanding it as an ethical line of conduct. In order to do so, just as it was done in order to recall the martyrs of the resistance's legacy, Hizbullah-affiliated intellectuals engaged in a particular writing of the past, but in this case the history of the other.

An analytical article[10] in the second issue of al-'Ahd compared two different plans for compromise[11] proposed by the party that then held the presidency, the Phalangist Party, a Christian group that was one of the main protagonists in the unfolding of the civil war in 1975 against Palestinian armed groups and different Muslim and leftist political coalitions in Lebanon. Al-'Ahd described "the first plan," jointly drafted by the Phalangists and another Christian group, al-Ahrār, as differing from earlier plans that were proposed by Christian political elites, in that it "proposes a real balance between powers in terms of central ruling." But it was criticized for not really addressing the question of Israeli occupation and the proper ways to deal with it. In the view of the article's author(s), any plan that did not take into consideration the occupation issue was a dead end, especially if it came from parties suspected of having collaborated with Israel all along. Indeed, in the same al-'Ahd article, what the author described as the older plan called for building Lebanon according

---

[9] Farid el-Khazen, *The Breakdown of the State in Lebanon (1967–1976)* (Cambridge, Mass: Harvard University Press, 2000).
[10] al-'Ahd 2 (4/7/1984), 2.
[11] *Tasswiyya* is the Arabic word used.

to "a Maronite orientation (naz 'a), of crusader origins, western oriented, and Israeli in its ambitions." Given past Christian political practices, this plan (and perhaps any plan) could only be a diversion, a cover legitimizing Israeli occupation. Any solution that did not address this latter issue appeared to deliberately sidestep the supposed purpose of national reconciliation or compromise. The underlying question of this analysis would be, why trust the Maronites knowing what they have been doing until now? What sort of knowledge was assumed in the formulation of these questions by the al-'Ahd author(s) in this second issue of the paper? Moreover, what were the social practices involved in the different attempts at writing the other? Answering these questions, and thus understanding the actions of the Maronites, or Christian politics in general, led to a historical delving into events that shaped the space of Lebanese politics, constantly drawing lessons for current political action.

In the early 1980s, in certain mountainous areas, Christian villages were sacked and vandalized, driving their inhabitants to take refuge in other more Christian dominated areas. In 1984, Phalangists and other Christian groups were asking for the return of these displaced families. An early al-'Ahd front-page editorial titled "The massacre, the language," describing Christian politics, is quite revealing of the extent to which writings could be understood as actions.[12] The editorial started with this enigmatic statement: "At certain levels of consciousness (wa 'i) everything becomes a language and every action can be transformed into a discursive expression." In other words, a language is not only a method of thinking, but a direct expression of a way of living, a direct translation of actions on the ground. According to the editorial, "expressions" acquire a specific pervasive power of their own, especially when they are issued by "a civil group or an organized political party." The text then gives examples: "Since the April 15 1975 massacre of the Ain el Remmaneh that was the key to the Lebanese war, and along with el Dankura and Karantina, Tal El Zaatar, Black Sunday, Ehden, and Safra [sites of other massacres in the 1970s], the 'civilized' texts written on the operations of these allies of Israel has not changed, right until today with the Sabra and Chatila massacres" (emphasis added).

The editorial was followed by a detailed description of the massacres of Sabra and Chatila (16–18 September 1982) and linked language to method:

[12] al-'Ahd 12 (15/9/1984), 1.

The massacre of Sabra and Chatila is the method (*nahj*) used by all fascists since the beginning of history, and it is the only language these racists know of and they learned some of its lessons in the battles of the mountains [where massacres against Christians were perpetrated by Druze militias] but they still need to learn more.

The editorial concluded: "We know the line of oppression very well from Satan, to Pharaoh, to Hitler and to all the devils, petty and great, not the least Pierre [Gemayel] who went to hell two weeks ago." Gemayel was the leader of the Phalangist Party, the main armed Christian militia group on the Lebanese arena since the outbreak of hostilities.

These texts, among so many others, signaled an attempt to capture the culture of the other through making sense of his actions, through grasping his *nahj*, a word that we can roughly translate as method, approach or process. Extracting meanings seems necessary in order to issue some form of a judgment or ethical standpoint. In so doing, the culture of the other can be traced back, through a study of events. When brought together by these writers, they come to form, in the case of Christian politics, Political Maronitism in all its different facets, each dependent on the context of the particular text concerned.

In the same *al-'Ahd* issue, in an editorial entitled "The language that we understand,"[13] *al-'Ahd* criticized the recent militia-driven armed confrontations taking place in Trablus, a city in the north of Lebanon, and distanced itself from these practices. It claimed, instead, to abide by a single, "alternative language," one that declares that Israel is the sole enemy, one language that creates dialogue between the different parties that speak this language and are ready to fight Israel and their allies the Phalangists.

In this case, Hizbullah's *nahj* (or *'aqīda*, for that matter) is the struggle against the oppressive political actor, such as Political Maronitism, imperialism, or Zionism. This is also why Political Maronitism and Zionism do not differ at all "ideologically, in rationale, and through their practices" as claimed in a long analytical article that was serialized in three consecutive issues of *al-'Ahd*, sketching the historical relations between certain Christian political elites and the Zionist state.[14] Through this "archival rather than analytical" text, the author(s) sought to map out the formation of a political consciousness of that particular other through various events, starting from the birth of the Maronite Christian sect until the present, the formation of a specific political consciousness of that other.

---

[13] *al-'Ahd* 9 (25/8/1984), 1.
[14] *al-'Ahd* 12 (15/9/1984), 10.

In that quest to understand and capture the other national, Hizbullah-affiliated intellectuals, like many previous historians, delved into Maronite historiography. Where did the Maronites come from? When did they settle in Mount Lebanon? What were their general attitudes to the environment they were part of? What "identification" markers did they articulate: did they think of themselves as Arabic, Byzantine, Islamic, and so on? Early twentieth-century historians, who were predominantly Christians, have dealt at great length with these questions, profoundly shaping the different currents of writing history in modern-day Lebanon.[15]

The serialized article cited above jumps between principal historical episodes as reported by the main historians, from the first migration waves of Maronites to 1860, when the first interconfessional massacre is reported. The latter date is commonly read as the moment of birth of modern-day Lebanon through the creation of the confessional allocation of political prerogatives under the patronage of French and British embassies as well as Ottoman administrative reforms (*tanzimat*).[16]

The State through Perceptions of Community: Perception of the Other as Citizen

The historian Ahmad Beydoun argues that, depending on their sectarian affiliations, Lebanese historians developed particular narratives of past events.[17] For example, Fakhr al-Din's legacy as a political figure of the seventeenth century has been the crux of a struggle to capture relations between the different confessions making up Lebanon. A politically and economically ambitious *amīr*,[18] Fakhr al-Din had succeeded in extending his influence to territories that would comprise most of modern state Lebanon. He maintained relations with several antagonistic powers such as the Vatican, certain Italian states that were crucial to his trade interests, and the Ottoman Empire, which was the formal source of his official legitimacy, and on whose behalf he levied taxes.Earlier writings of modern Lebanese history have portrayed Fakhr al-Din as an important pillar in the founding of the modern state of Lebanon. As Beydoun argues quite persuasively, Lebanese historians produced versions of Fakhr al-Din's story in

---

[15] For a detailed analysis of the main debates see Beydoun, *Identité confessionnelle*.

[16] The *tanzimat* initiated a short-lived process of change brought to an end by the demise of the Ottoman Empire. The *tanzimat* aimed at centralizing the Ottoman Empire by emulating some of the administrative apparatus of Western powers.

[17] Beydoun, *Identité confessionnelle*.

[18] *Amīr* could roughly translate as prince, a title given to feudal families during the Ottoman Empire, responsible for collecting taxes.

order to articulate certain claims to authenticity in light of political power relations in present-day Lebanon. For some nationalist historians (mostly Christians), Fakhr al-Din was said to have "united" Lebanon for the first time since "prehistoric" times as he came to control a territory roughly the size of present-day Lebanon. Fakhr al-Din therefore epitomized the state as a generic concept, the entity he ruled over the genuine ancestor of the modern state of Lebanon.[19]

Moreover, in a political system built on a particular perception of and interaction with different confessional communities all expressing different political visions, the actual question of the confession of Fakhr al-Din oriented historical ideological constructions in different directions and gave one a national "'preeminence" over the other. The Maronite version is predictable: Fakhr al-Din converted to Maronitism, at least in spirit as he "unites with a libanism of Maronite origin who ends up espousing the Catholic faith."[20] Beydoun quite caustically describes the eccentric dimension of this debate about the true nature of Fakhr al-Din's confession.[21] Without going into the different manipulations of historical narratives, suffice to say that any claim about a "correct" version of events most of the time involved a symbolic battle pitting one sect over another.

An early al-'Ahd article argued that Christian militias were driving Muslims out of Jubayl and Kiserwan, two mostly Christian regions to the north of Beirut, even as negotiations were underway for the return of Christians to certain mountain regions, from which they had been expelled as a result of the war between Druze and Christian militias in 1983–1984. The article complained that this was going unreported by the mainstream press.[22] The interesting point here is that this article did not just denounce the claim of double standards in dealing with refugee questions, it decided to address very seriously a contemporary Christian argument of that time, namely that Muslims were "an alien body in Christian areas." The article sought to counter this claim by demonstrating the presence of Muslim populations in Jubayl and Kiserwan since time immemorial. A subtitle in the article read, "Islamic presence in Jubayl and Kiserwan is not a sudden and foreign one," and another read, "its origins dates back to 636 AD since Muslims opened the area."[23] (Opening and conquest (*fāth*), which is an

---

[19] Ibid., 440.
[20] Ibid., 550.
[21] Ibid., 545–547.
[22] al-'Ahd 6 (3/8/1984), 5–6.
[23] "Opened" here is my translation of the term "*fātah*," referring to the first Islamic conversions since the Prophetic revelations. The root verb *fātaha* means to open and is commonly used in this sense.

"Islamic" signifier, has a reactionary meaning, in the sense that it is used in reaction to actions perpetrated by the political/social other.)

The author of this article quoted freely from *Lubnān al-ta'ifī*, a book by the renowned Palestinian historian Anis al-Sayegh, to explain the slow disappearance from Jubayl and Kiserwan of "Islamic and civilized presence" following Fakhr al-Din's decision to remove Muslim villages ("uproot" is the term used) from Kiserwan in 1622. We then read that the Maan and the Chehab families of *amīr*s followed al-Din's political line until 1860, when a major intersectarian crisis took place, leading to a new political arrangement on confessional lines. It was al-Din, in reality, who instigated divisions between Sunnis and Shi'is, and fought the Muslims in every corner of his territory, with the blessing of foreign powers such as the Vatican and France. Meanwhile, he tried to play by Ottoman rules, appearing to respect Islamic legal norms in order to be able to pursue his ambition for dominion even further. In sum, in this account Fakhr al-Din became the precursor of Political Maronitism. Sayegh's book revolved around tracing down confessionalism as a socio-political tradition since the time of the Phoenicians. Whereas Sayegh argued that Christians were to a certain extent persecuted by Muslim political regimes at various points in time,[24] and that the relations between Maronites and Muslims were much more complex than generally assumed,[25] the author of the *al-'Ahd* article shifted the focus of concern. Among other things, this illustrates the debt that these Hizbullah-related writers owe to earlier leftist writers and intellectuals. This version of understanding Fakhr al-Din's legacy presents interesting discursive topics using Islamic tropes.

Many of these texts found in *al-'Ahd* move from older pan-Arab nationalist (or related) historical writings to later writings that may be called "Islamic," by the simple expedient of replacing the word "Arab" with "Islamic." But in these rearticulations of narratives from "Arabic" to "Islamic," variations and differences do exist, even if they are subtle. Two main arguments direct these newer writings of history, and make texts particularly "Islamic." First, that it was Muslims who were persecuted rather than Christians; and second, that Fakhr al-Din simply epitomized Political Maronitism. In so doing, Hizbullah-related writers wholeheartedly embraced either Christian versions of history or their strategies of writing it. In the article cited above, for example, one reads that Christians consistently followed the same policy, both before and

---

[24] Anis Sayegh, *Lubnān al-ta'ifī* (Beirut: Dar al-Sira al-Fikri, 1955), for example 59–77.

[25] Especially since the Maronites and the Byzantines clashed around the seventh century A.D.: ibid., 66–67, but here the debate is endless, as Maronites were at times alleged to have allied with the Crusaders against "Muslims forces," as Sayegh would claim (74). Beydoun describes the general political undertones of this debate well in his book.

after Fakhr al-Din, of marginalizing Muslim forces in the region through alliances with outside forces, espousal of the confessional system that would give them the upper hand politically, and so on. Whether Fakhr al-Din was a Christian convert (or a Maronite at heart) was no longer the main question. The historical polemic that shapes the contours of modern Lebanese history has ceded the discursive space to Fakhr al-Din being an agent (or ancestor) of Political Maronitism.

The Islamic emphasis notwithstanding, this mode of writing history accepts the Christian (or Maronite) discourse as official, takes it seriously, and builds on it, offering yet another example of the hegemonic shaping the contours of the ideological. This moreover accords with the general portrayal of Shi'i intellectuals' writings of Lebanese history. Beydoun draws a detailed genealogy of the main texts written by Shi'i historians, and focuses on Ali al-Zayn in the case of Fakhr al-Din. According to Beydoun, al-Zayn "would probably search for precedents to his frustration,"[26] that would justify his ambiguous relation with the state[27] and in turn provide for the momentum to criticize the prevailing system in order to seek change. Then, to come back to the al-'Ahd article mentioned above,[28] the writer posited a striking analogy between the practices of Fakhr al-Din and the more recent ones of the Phalangists in the 1970s (and their successors, the Lebanese Forces). But instead of the Vatican or other powers, it was the military presence of Israel that fostered divisive politics such as those perpetrated against the Muslims of Jubayl and Kiserwan in the 1980s. In connecting the two epochs lies a consistent politics of Muslim marginalization, especially since the founding of the modern Lebanese state under the French mandate. Seemingly, all the Christian political groups that emerged in Jubayl and Kiserwan in one way or another engaged in hostile practices toward Muslims, but the Phalangists seem to exemplify its most extreme form. Thus, in a section on "the implication of the 1975 events," the article develops the idea that "the Phalangist party has conspired against the Muslims in this region [Kiserwan and Jubayl] executing at their expense the politics of Fakhr al-Din . . . in order to create a Christian Canton under the shade of the Israeli flag."[29]

The article then listed measures taken by the Phalangist Party to marginalize the Muslim population, for example prohibiting them from

---

[26] Ibid., 551.
[27] Representations of the state as a sanctifying entity will be dealt with at length in Chapter 4. This chapter focuses on the subject in so far as it involves representations of the other.
[28] al-'Ahd 6 (3/8/1984), 5–6.
[29] Ibid., 6.

exercising their most basic legal rights, such as getting married or inheriting. The Muslim population was also forbidden to perform the call to prayer, its mosques were destroyed, and other holy sites or figures that bore any Islamic imprint were subjected to hostile practices. Finally, they were ousted from some villages, such as Laqlouq. The conclusion of this long historical exposé was to condemn the politics of returning Christian refugees to the Shouf (another part of Lebanon) when the return of Muslims (or mostly Shi'i) refugees from Jubayl and Kiserwan was not even on the table.

Much later on, a book titled *al-Muslimīn al-Shī'a fī Jubayl wal-Kisirwān*, published by Dar al-Hadi in 2007, expanded this original idea, which, its author, Ali Jaber Haydar Ahmad argued, had been overlooked by Lebanese historians.[30] That this book, despite being very elaborate in content and in the extent of its archival work, should share this concern with the subject is not especially remarkable. The sense of urgency in the above-mentioned *al-'Ahd* article had almost disappeared, and the tone was instead "more scholarly." The book acknowledged that many problems are not always defined by the binary categorization of a Muslim–Christian conflict, and portrays the Lebanese conflict as more complex, involving intra-Muslim clashes, changing alliances among Christians, and so on. And yet the book stuck to the goal of legitimizing the presence of Muslims, and specifically Shi'i, when discussing Jubayl and Kiserwan, in the particular context of imagining community presence in Lebanon.

al-'Ahd itself returned to the issue in a later edition,[31] publishing the full proceedings of a talk given by Lebanese University professor Wajih Kawtharani about "the Lebanese entity, its formation and the position of its social forces." In this case, the analysis of Political Maronitism was much more detailed, unfolding slowly throughout the period stretching from the nineteenth century until today. The conceptual framework was also much more elaborate: a Maronite *'asabiyya*, or "group feeling"[32] is thought to have undergone several stages, from the Maani emirate (of Fakhr al-Din) and the dominance of influential families to the creation of the modern state of Lebanon. In the process, Kawtharani is reported to have detailed the various socio-economic forms of monopoly

---

[30] Ali Jaber Haydar Ahmad, *al-Muslimīn al-Shī'a fī Jubayl wal-Kisirwān* (Beirut: Dar al-Hadi, 2007).

[31] *al-'Ahd* (20/4/1985), 9–11.

[32] *'Asabiyya* has a pejorative connotation in Arabic, especially in this context, meaning someone who is too radical about belonging to a group; the word comes from *'asab*, which means "nerve," and could characterize the feeling of excitement deriving from being part of a collective or community.

and exploitation practiced by the Maronite elite with the help of French political actors, merchants, and traders.

It is worth pointing out that Wajih Kawtharani later became one of the most vehement critics of Hizbullah. Yet these discursive elaborations could still be considered as strategic to Hizbullah's overall machinery of archiving. To a certain extent al-'Ahd's journalists and other intellectuals picked up on all types of discourse that fed into questioning the prevailing power system, and especially when leftist, "critical," or even Islamic discursive material was available. This encompassed anything that could be said about Political Maronitism or the rewriting of history in general, especially when it took the form of a scholarly conference given at the Center for the Lebanese Union of Muslim Students, from where main cadres of Hizbullah, such as Mohammad Raad, originated.[33] Noteworthy also is the difference between the performative dimension of this material from intellectuals outside the more formal organizational structure of Hizbullah and the one of self-proclaimed ideologues who have no intellectual influence on the party such as Muhammad Z'ayter, as shown by its media and other literary productions.

Reading the Other and Lessons in Patriotism

As previously argued, al-'Ahd and later publications related to Hizbullah contain writings based on a relentless reading of texts the other writes or produces. This ranges from local media, especially Christian ones, to American and Israeli think tanks and research centers. Reading the other involves not just a quest to place this other politically, but also to justify the particular line followed by Hizbullah or the Islamic resistance as a new alternative. Through this relentless tit for tat with other commentaries and texts, one of the ways Hizbullah-affiliated intellectuals are engaged in a particular representation of the nation is by judging what it is to be a patriot.

In some cases, sarcastic editorials such as the regular Tahht al-majhar, whose author was at the time anonymous, periodically assessed political events and the various media's analyses of them. Tahht al-majhar was a witty, politically sharp, and highly analytical piece of writing that was consistently published on the second page of al-'Ahd. The leader of Hizbullah's parliamentary bloc, Wafa' lil-Muqāwama, Mohammad Raad, revealed to me in an interview that as the editor-in-chief of al-'Ahd

---

[33] See Chapter 1 for a discussion of the cultural precursors of Hizbullah. In the case of al-Ittihād al-Lubnānī lil-Talaba al-Muslimīn, as one of the precursors to Hizbullah, see Daher, Le Hezbollah, 52–54.

during most of the 1980s[34] he was not only writing these columns but most of the other opinion and analysis pieces. In one such early column Raad explained the peculiarity of the Islamic project, or Hizbullah, or the Islamic movement, by comparing it to other movements or socio-political manifestations such as the left, or the right, the secular, the colonial, etc.

Depending on the context, these comparisons illustrate specific differ-ences by locality. In another editorial on "the specificity of Lebanon and the Islamic project" (*khusūsiyāt lubnān wal-mashrū' al islāmī*),[35] the author presented the Islamic revolution (of Khomeini or Iran) as a successful alternative to the two regional poles prevailing at the time: the United States (as a Western power) and the Soviet Union (as an Eastern power). He said that the Islamic revolution threatened both these powers and their projects. In the last two paragraphs the author comes to the other subject of his title, alluding to Maronite (or general Christian isolationist) narratives without relinquishing the notion that Lebanon has some form of specificity: that Lebanon's specificity is very clearly recognized by the Islamic revolution in Iran does not mean that Muslims should not be committed (*fī hāl min al-iltizām*) to the central command of the Islamic project (*al-mashrū' al islāmī*) in the world. If that is not the case, the specificity argument would have as an objective to isolate Muslims from its legitimate and unique leadership represented by the Islamic revolution and its leaders, which is exactly what the USA and Israel are working on in order to isolate the *umma* from its mother revolution (*thawratiha al-um*).

One underlying concern in this passage is the absence of a "positive" elaboration of what specificity would mean, which shows that the writer is mostly focused on blocking the isolationist (Christian) argument. Revealingly, Raad found the idea of the specificity of Lebanon unaccep-table only if it had to be built on an isolationist argument symbolized by the "cantonization" of political groups practiced during the 1980s. In later articles, all throughout the 1980s, most arguments of national specificity went through the condemnation of the prevailing power or narrative that has dominated the way the Lebanese state has been ima-gined (i.e. by Christian elites). During this period, then, Hizbullah-affiliated intellectuals' notions of patriotism betrayed this reactive focus and cynical outlook. The Islamic signifier helped in diffusing the possibility of clearly defining what they offered as an alternative to what seemed to be a fraudulent Christian patriotism.

---

[34] Mohammad Raad interview with the author, June 2010.
[35] *al-'Ahd* 53 (29/6/1985), 2.

Two years after the above-mentioned article, a front-page editorial entitled "The Guardians of the Revolution[36] who defend ... Lebanon" summed up the controversy around "the role of Iran" in the representation of both Hizbullah and Christian political actors.[37] "It did not cross one's mind that Amin Gemayel[38] would be so insolent as to ask the Iranian Revolutionary Guards to leave Lebanon while equating them with the Zionist occupiers!" These lines prefaced a very inflammatory text, most probably written by Raad, arguing for the necessity of having the Revolutionary Guards helping the Islamic resistance in its fight against the Zionist occupation. Raad reminded the reader of the state of disarray prevailing in 1982 once the Israelis were well advanced into Lebanese territories, how in the midst of this occupation "the butcher and collaborator Bashir Gemayel got elected," and how Ariel Sharon was assisting a Phalangist military presence in Baabda. The editorial also recounted all the murderous practices of the Phalangists in order to conclude that it is not they who can judge whether the Revolutionary Guards are fit to stay or leave. If it was not for them, the article carried on, "Lebanon would just be another Israeli settlement just like occupied upper Galilee." And the article concluded: "We used to say: the land is to whom built it, and now, listen to us saying: The land is to whom liberates it, and as we are those who are working on liberating, we will proceed in the way we like."[39] This passage seems to emphasize that if any form of national specificity should be brought to light it can only come from a radical change in the prevailing political paradigm. Only Iranian support can help render that change concrete. Indeed, what is revealing is that at no point in this type of writing (also mirroring political speeches given by Hizbullah's "officials" of the time[40]) was there a frontal attack on the very idea of Lebanon and the elaboration of a transnational Islamic imaginary sense of belonging to a territory or to history. To the contrary, Hizbullah-affiliated intellectuals seemed to be pitted in a relentless dialectical struggle with the other in order to justify their political stances.

---

[36] The Revolutionary Guards are an Iranian military institution that helped Hizbullah in its formative years.

[37] al-'Ahd 171 (4/10/1987), 1.

[38] Amin Gemayel was the president of Lebanon at the time and was the author of the ill-fated 17 May Agreement.

[39] Ibid.

[40] These speeches are retranscribed in the pages of al-'Ahd, all throughout the 1980s, including those of Ibrahim al-Amin, Abbas Moussawi, Sobhi Tufayli, Hassan Nasrallah, Hussein Moussawi, and others.

In another Tahht al-majhar column,[41] Raad reacted to a piece written by the editor-in-chief of *al-Nahār*, Jubran Tueni. Raad did not mince his words:

In his American and Zionist *Nahar*,[42] Jubran Tueni comes to us with his political analysis that he gets through the Gemayel family preaching of Sawt Lubnan el Hor (voice of free Lebanon) radio, a new mantra[43] that adds to the musical pieces, filled with hatred and nuisance as if they were the voices of owls and the croaking of sick frogs in the dirty swamps.[44]

Tueni seemed to have accused Hizbullah of actually being the ally of Israel based on the notion that the party did not want to take the chance for a diplomatic and peaceful solution with Israel. Raad proceeded to show the absurdity of such a statement and that the real allies of Israel according to "historical evidence" were the Christian right. Through this incisive critique of the other's discourse, Raad concluded with this Qur'anic verse: "Fain would they put out the light of God with their mouths, but God will perfect His light however much the disbelievers are averse."[45] A vehement critic of Hizbullah, Tueni became the target of other columns, and *al-Nahār* seems to have been one of the most attentively read newspapers by Hizbullah-related writers. A couple of months later[46] Raad's tone was even harsher, clearly showing the impulsive anger provoked by statements made in this paper. Tueni was again accused of being dishonest: "We know that you are immature for journalism, and that you are a distracted[47] teenager ... but words are a security ... and security a responsibility ... and thus animals were forbidden to speak."

What could Tueni have written to receive such treatment? On 16 February 1985 the Israeli army withdrew from parts of South Lebanon, retrenching south of the Litani river. In Saida, celebrations marked the victory of the Islamic resistance according to the front page of issue 35 of *al-'Ahd*.[48] The main editorial praised the liberation of the city as a prelude to the liberation of Jerusalem, advising prudence and persever-ance. Another editorial by Tueni, apparently criticizing the display of posters featuring Khomeini and Islamic slogans must have caught the eye of the

---

[41] *al-'Ahd* 21 (18/11/1984), 2.

[42] Here Raad plays on the word *nahār* referring to its Arabic meaning, day, and the name of Jubran Tueini's newspaper, *al-Nahār*.

[43] The actual word used is *muwwāl*, which is an Arabic repetitive style of music improvised at the beginning of a song. It is part of an expression that one is trying to impose another repetitive or boring idea.

[44] There is a rhyme missed in the original Arabic sentence.

[45] Ayat al-Saf (Surat al Tawba), verse 8, translation available at http://islam awakened.com/quran/61/8/.

[46] *al-'Ahd* 36 (2/3/1985), 2.

[47] *Tāyish* and *ahwaj* are the terms used.

[48] *al-'Ahd* 35 (24/2/1985), 1.

writer of Tahht al-Majhar, who responded that Hizbullah's allegiance to Khomeini was open and honest.[49] He added that "For the oppressed have chosen him as a leader ... and he is not the president of our republic but is our prince (*amīr*) and the prince of the Muslims (*amīr al-muslimīn*) in all the parts[50] of the world. As for your president, Israel imposed him to the detriment of everyone and we of course do not accept him."[51]

The article continued by alluding to the cheerful demeanor Christian political forces exhibited when the Israelis first reached Beirut in 1982. "In the past you were happy with the occupation of Saida, because you chose the [political regime of the] mandate over it and today you are sad because Saida freed itself from the occupation on which you were betting so do not claim to be a *saydāwī*[52] O Jubran and do not think you can win the hearts of its people." This flaunting of patriotic standards, of sticking to the "right" cause, reappears endlessly in *al-'Ahd* in reaction to the writing of others, especially when the Christians put forward some authentic claims to Lebanese nationalism and accuse Islamic movements of jeopardizing this ideal.

In this Tahht al-Majhar column, which called for Amin Gemayel to be put on trial, along with his party and his "Forces" (referring to the Lebanese Forces),[53] Hizbullah showed a clear understanding of the divisive and conflicting nature of Christian politics, although it grouped them all under one banner that claimed some form of political, if not cultural, superiority over the rest. The column explained: "And it is not permissible that the face of the presidency that shows its collaboration with the enemy, and its crimes, be substituted with another face, the one of patriotism (or nationalism, *watanīyya*), and consensualism (*hiyādiyya*). It is the same regime bringing Amin Gemayel to power that brought his brother Bashir before him. Bringing down this regime requires the bringing down of all of its symbols and its torturers (*jallādīn*)." The column continued, "This uprooting process should happen from its origins. Everything should be uprooted, so that there may not be another Zionist that can burgeon [the Arabic word used here is *yanbut*]."

---

[49] An argument that has been voiced until today. See more about affinities with Iran in Chapter 5.

[50] *Bekaa* is the word used for "parts," and is also the name of the region where the Islamic resistance began.

[51] *al-'Ahd* 36 (2/3/1985), 2.

[52] *Saydāwī* is Arabic for "from Saida."

[53] It is noteworthy that the Lebanese Forces were not under the command of Amin Gemayel, so the *al-'Ahd* writer is grouping together what are in reality different political groups, probably because, conceptually, they are all different faces of Political Maronitism.

These statements may to some extent have captured representations of the official regime. It is through this medium that Hizbullah
officials and intellectuals may have later understood the conflict that
pitted the Lebanese Forces against the head of the Lebanese army,
General Michel Aoun, who had been appointed prime minister by
Amin Gemayel. Christian politics was understood as being plagued
by divisions, backstabbing, and other immoral activities, and therefore should be rejected all together. Before Taif and its ensuing
redistribution of political prerogatives, any type of Christian political
action was read under the paradigm of Political Maronitism.
Accordingly, for Hizbullah-affiliated intellectuals, Michel Aoun's
political initiatives of fighting the Syrians and then trying to
dismantle the Lebanese Forces were but a remnant of Political
Maronitism in its death throes.

On 16 February 1985, Sayyid Ibrahim al-Amin read the Open Letter to
the Downtrodden, on the occasion of the commemoration of Raghib Harb's
martyrdom. Reprinted in al-'Ahd,[54] the letter represented a synthesis of the
ideas discussed and developed in the preceding editorials.[55] In fact, most of
the articles covered in the first year of al-'Ahd's publication are different
textual manifestations of the arguments summed up in clear and concise
ways in the letter. The Open Letter demanded that (a) occupation or foreign
forces leave Lebanon; (b) the Phalangist Party be brought to justice to be
tried for the crimes "against Christians and Muslims"; and (c) "our people"
be allowed to decide freely on the regime they want for the country. Whereas
the full extent of the letter will be discussed in Chapter 5, it had a special
section addressed to the Christians of Lebanon that concerns us here.
The Letter is addressed "to the downtrodden," and definitely seemed to
include Christians along with Muslims. Again here the same themes elaborated previously in above-cited articles of al-'Ahd are developed. The Letter
strove to distinguish "Christ's teachings" from the practices of parties such
as the Phalangists.

The Letter differentiated between an "authentic" Christian tradition
and that exemplified by Political Maronitism. In effect, the Letter,
steeped in Qur'anic quotations, called upon the Christian population to
take their future into their own hands and free themselves from the grip of
the elites representing Political Maronitism. Let's look at the difference
between Christianity as a religious tradition, Political Maronitism as
a political movement, and the possibility of a common nationalism.
Hizbullah-affiliated intellectuals often reiterated the idea that Islamists

---

[54] al-'Ahd 35 (24/2/1985), 5.
[55] It would not be surprising if Raad had participated in the drafting of the letter.

were in fact coming to the rescue of the Christians. For example, a front-page editorial entitled "Intifāda am ja'ja'a," which appeared a week after the reading of the Open Letter, went as far as arguing that Islamists had actually saved Christians in Lebanon from the Zionist/Phalangist threat.[56] The Christian other is seen as part of an imagined community that comes to be shaped around the geographical and historical boundaries of the Lebanese nation because it belongs to a tradition or a line of conduct. The representation of Christians developed in the 1980s sheds light on the later arguments of citizenship that were elaborated in the Memorandum of Understanding between the main Christian political force in Lebanon, the Free Patriotic Movement (Michel Aoun's political formation), and Hizbullah in 2006.[57] The Christian–Hizbullah rapprochement that took place more than a decade later was the result of a gradual build-up of diplomatic efforts that took place in the post-civil war period between a pro-Syrian Christian elite that was now in power and protected Hizbullah's resistance project (the presidential mandate of General Émile Lahoud was a case in point). But it took another decade, more precisely after the assassination of former prime minister Rafic Hariri, the Syrian withdrawal, and the return of Michel Aoun from exile, for the rapprochement to consolidate into an official agreement. Hizbullah-affiliated intellectuals recognized that Aoun was a patriot after all, a "good Christian." Previously Aoun had been the most vehement critic of Hizbullah because of the latter's alliance with Syria.

From my various discussions with party members, I gathered that Hizbullah's perception of the Tayyar movement was framed by their understanding of Christian politics' relations with Political Maronitism. As mentioned before, Hizbullah's animosity toward Christian politics during the civil war was not only because there was no Christian group that questioned the Political Maronitist regime, but also because most groups clung to it until the Taif Agreement and the subsequent forced exile of Aoun to Paris. This representation of Aoun's movement in the post-war period prevailed until the return of the latter from Paris in 2005. Aoun's political confrontation first with Syria and then with the Lebanese Forces was read through that lens. Once Political Maronitism was defeated after the end of the civil war, and once most Maronite elites were marginalized, the door was opened for a possible rapprochement. Revealingly, Hassan Nasrallah constantly claims in his speeches that the

---

[56] *al-'Ahd* 39 (23/3/1985), 1.
[57] Paper of Common Understanding between Hezbollah and the Free Patriotic Movement (6/2/2006), available at http://static.tayyar.org/Content/uploads/PdfLibrary/150528041 932259~fpm_hezbollah2.pdf.

particular political environment of the Lebanese war period made it impossible for such contacts and representations of the other to develop.

The Memorandum of Understanding signed between Hizbullah and the Tayyar on 6 February 2006 focused on articulating notions of nation and citizenship. Logically then, there was no direct mention of any Islamic state, demonstrating that for Hizbullah this was never a coherent political argument. In an interview,[58] Ziad Debs, a Tayyar member who was present during the talks, explained that the discussions between the two parties quickly moved beyond Christian anxiety over a possible Islamic state as it came to be understood as a proposal that has different performative senses in different political environments. Debs kept on insisting that the memorable insight of these talks was that as soon as "the ice was broken," Hizbullah and Tayyar members realized that "they have much more in common that at first thought. Both were staunch patriots."[59] Among other points, the paper emphasizes consensual democracy as the best system for Lebanon because it expresses "the essence of the pact of shared coexistence."[60] *Ta ʿāyush* (coexistence), and *muwātana* (citizenship) are two terms that would recur in Sayyid Nasrallah's speeches and interviews, as exemplified by a historic TV talk-show hosted by Jean Aziz[61] that he and Michel Aoun gave on OTV in 2008, exactly two years after the signing of the Memorandum[62]. Differently stated, once confessionalism as a political system, stripped of its Political Maronitist variants, and as projecting a specific national imaginary, could be rearranged, or could propose redistributive measures more conducive to coexistence, it became a viable system and invited the different parties to accept each other. But the style of representation of the other was still the same. All these elaborations of an authentic Christian tradition that were voiced in reaction to a violent period find an interesting echo in a post-war setting that aimed at bridging gaps. It was always the case that "Lebanese" was defined according to sect, even if outside politics. This also shows that on the question of relating to the political other, Hizbullah has not only been "part of the system" but has also contributed to how the system functions, rearticulating national community belonging.

To be sure, this task was difficult to achieve. During most of the 1990s Hizbullah was still wary of most political parties, even after receiving

---

[58] Ziad Debs, senior Tayyar Party member, interview with the author, June 2009.
[59] Ibid.
[60] Paper of Common Understanding, 1.
[61] Columnist at *al-Akhbār* newspaper and the host of a TV talk-show at Tayyar-affiliated OTV.
[62] TV Interview by Jean Aziz, OTV (6/2/2008).

guarantees from the Syrian and Lebanese security systems that the work of the resistance would be left unhindered. Hizbullah's rhetoric toward the Christians gradually changed after the Taif Agreement, given the new power balance in place. Legitimacy was given to the actions of the resistance under the aegis of the state, especially during the regime of President Émile Lahoud, an army general who worked on rebuilding the Lebanese army, divided by the 1975–1990 war. Lahoud allowed the Islamic resistance to operate unhindered by institutional security concerns. The ruling elites and the Lebanese communities at large thus gradually accepted the resistance as a legitimate political project.

Recapturing the Christian Tradition

Indeed, although this description seems to allude to a typical case of national reconciliation where different political groups find compromises in a secular public sphere, in truth, representations of the other, which developed over time, tended to blur the boundaries between the political and the religious, as we have seen in Hizbullah's treatment of time and of martyrology (Chapter 2). The critique of Christian politics led Hizbullah-affiliated writers and political speakers to propose a specific recapturing of the Christian tradition. This process fed into an imaginary sense of national belonging based on "corrected" confessional traditions untainted by the marks of unethical practices. This reaction to the "other" translates into numerous advisories on how to recapture history, and thus how to form a viable political community amongst the many confessional traditions in place, even as these traditions were all part of an overarching one, the Islamic. This crossover between history read through an Islamic lens and the contemporary being-in-the-now understanding of citizenship would not exist without a certain amount of tension, as will be seen below.

To illustrate, the commemoration of the birth of one of the most important prophets in Islamic tradition, Jesus, was remembered annually in the same manner as other ritualistic commemorations outlined in Chapter 2. Hizbullah-affiliated intellectuals articulated a classical Islamic point that the teachings of Jesus were the same for both traditions. In so doing, by redirecting Christians toward a more appropriate respect for "Christian Jesus" traditions there is a sort of acknowledgment that Christians have a tradition of their own, worthy of respect if applied "correctly." This is most probably an effect of the perception of the "Lebanese community" as made up of different confessions and their political actions.

In an article that reacted to Lebanese Forces (LF) lashing out against "Islamists," a statement by the latter catches the attention of the al-'Ahd reader: "The spirit of forgiveness, love and modesty that is taught by the birth of Christ, should not make us forget the necessity of being conscious of and obstruct the extremist attack that is invading the Islamic milieus."[63]

Another article among many of the genre argued that Phalangists' or LF practices were a replica of French Crusading adventures of the eleventh and twelfth centuries in today's Lebanon, Syria, and Palestine. The article argued that these "neo-Crusaders" were living proof of the violations of most of Christ's teachings. Indeed: "It is deplorable that we find the Phalangist use Christianity as a cover for their actions."[64] On the same page, Raad's column[65] started in a sentential way: "We search for an honest and authentic belonging to Issa the son of Mariam [Jesus son of Mary] in all those who claim to belong to him by name." And the text continued: "In all honesty we say that we search for the honest pious Christians that truly follow the texts originating from the Christ and that are ready to discuss the history written by the enemies of Jesus Christ the prophet of God." The texts are present; the lesson becomes how to abide by an authentic line of conduct:

Christ's followers have to prove to all the others that they really are committed to the teachings of Christ ... They should not call for love of the other if that love does not go beyond the Christian other who is Christian only by name, while the catacombs of monasteries and churches are being opened to stock Israeli and American weapons in order to kill Muslims, slaughter their children and demolish their houses.

Likewise, in a column commemorating the birth of Jesus one year later, in Tahht al-majhar,[66] Raad recalled the *jihād* of *sayyid al-massīh* (the Striving of Christ) as a catalyst for making resistance fighters stronger and more united. More importantly, it was an occasion to feel the "historical depth and the feeling of a link with the movement of the prophets." This initial approach to representations of Christians would mark later thoughts about Muslims (especially Shi'i or Hizbullah-related) tainted by this shock at Phalangists and other "extreme" Christians. This would prompt the question: Do Christians conform to their own tradition, or were they still being led astray, as shown through their civil war behaviour? Moreover, drawing lessons for righteous lines of conduct goes back to a "proper" reading of the Christian paradigmatic texts: the Old and New Testaments.

[63] *al-'Ahd* 27 (11/1/1984), 2.
[64] *al-'Ahd* 39 (23/3/1985), 1.
[65] Ibid.
[66] *al-'Ahd* 131 (27/12/1986), 2.

An example is an *al-'Ahd* article[67] published in the mid-1990s, commenting on the Vatican's recognition of the state of Israel through the drawing of lessons from the Christian holy books. The main themes of the analysis revolved around the argument that through reading the story of the prophet Jesus one could conclude that Jews perceived Christians as enemies. This article argued that, by recognizing Israel, the pope accepted the violation of Palestine as the land of the prophet who was persecuted by Jews.

One way to draw lessons or "set the record straight" was to invite priests and other Christian-related writers to contribute to *al-'Ahd*. Very early on, Hizbullah organized conferences, where priests and clerics from all confessions discussed the "culture of resistance" or of *jihād*, coexistence, citizenship etc. Later on, books published by Dar al-Hadi or al-Markaz al-Islāmī lil-Dirāsāt al-Fikriyya[68] would group the talks given at these conferences[69]. Specially themed conferences on Muslim and Christian coexistence have abounded all since the early 1990s. Similarly, at commemorations, as mentioned in Chapter 2, confessional presence not only signals solidarity but legitimacy too.

The "post-Taif" period saw more contributors enter this discursive sphere of *al-'Ahd*. This goes hand in hand with the increase in interaction between Hizbullah and the different political players in Lebanon, culminating with the party's decision to participate in the first parliamentary elections after the war, in 1992. An article dating one year after the first post-war legislative elections illustrates these issues: A column[70] featured a quote from Bulos Khury, a prominent Orthodox patriarch, who stated that, instead of allying with Israel, the Christians should opt for a union with Muslims as the solution for fighting colonialism and imperialism. Khury continued that this would free the Middle East from its aggressors. Clerics of different confessions and intellectuals writing about Christian issues found a suitable space in *al-'Ahd*'s cultural pages in order to air their ideas about the place and state of religions in contemporary societies.

One big absence from these dialogue sessions was the left, or the "secular" constituency. The confessional system is the only one that conforms to the official concept of an inclusive Lebanon, and secular groups are therefore excluded. In effect, this is one aspect of the later

---

[67] *al-'Ahd* (15/9/1994), 20.
[68] Literally translated as: The Islamic Center for Intellectual Studies.
[69] See for example the transcription of the conference organized by Ma'had al-Ma'ārif al-Hikmiyya in 2003: *al-Islām wal-masīhiyya: buhūth fī nizām al-qiyām al-mu'āsira* (Beirut: Dar al-Hadi, 2003).
[70] *al-'Ahd* (16/10/1993), 6.

concepts of citizenship (*muwātana*) that Hizbullah and the Free Patriotic Movement would elaborate. It exemplifies coexistence in a "secular" sphere, but is a peculiar understanding of the secular made up of the different groups that are politically recognized. If anything, sects (Christians, Muslims, Druzes, and so on) in this case are political and social groups who share this imagined entity called Lebanon. The religious is ultimately a sense of belonging to a territory/history, infused with rituals and practices of public piety.[71]. It is in this sense that Hizbullah ends up taking the Lebanese national paradigm seriously, as it has always been a product of it.

---

[71] See for example Saba Mahmood, *Politics of Piety: The Islamic Revival and the Feminist Subject* (Princeton: Princeton University Press, 2005).

4   The Debt to the Left and the Enemy: The Politics of Resistance

قوة المقاومة هي في استحضار مجريات الأحداث في تنشيط الذاكرة بشكل دائم، وهذه معركة أساسية.
(حسن نصر الله – 2009)   !العدو دائماً يراهن على الوقت حتى ننسى ... وما حننسى والسما زرقة

The strength of the resistance is in mentally actualizing the unfolding of events (*istihdār majrayāt al-ahdāth*) in order to strengthen memory, and this is a fundamental battle. The enemy is always betting on the passing of time so that we forget ... And we won't forget, as long as the sky is blue!
(Hassan Nasrallah, 2009)

Given that Hizbullah emerged as a military organization dedicated to the fight against the Israeli occupation of the South, its representation of other political formations on the ground can be read through the lens of the different militant activities. As we have seen with representations of the Christian other, Hizbullah early on engaged in an appraisal of the effectiveness of the various leftist, pro-Palestinian, or secular organizations' fight against Israel. And, as argued in this book, it was through a particular treatment of time and of the past that Hizbullah created political difference. In this case, the resistance as a legacy of action was reclaimed and understood in a time continuum that proposed new understandings of community where the "Islamic" was imagined in different ways. This helped not just to differentiate between the activities of other organizations fighting Israel and those of the Islamic resistance but also to form an understanding of the enemy, the Israeli army and state and its dominant ideology: Zionism.

Whereas the Christian other was imagined as part of a Lebanese community that has different religious traditions, secular organizations were harder to fit in. Hizbullah intellectuals never developed a theoretical framework that differentiates between Islamic and secular politics in the early issues of *al-'Ahd*, but there was a definite appraisal or critique of acts of resistance from which we can derive a particular representation of the political other and of representations of community. Key to this critique was how these organizations were understood as having failed to develop a consciousness of history.

As a social movement arising from a contentious situation, Hizbullah's various slogans resonate with leftist paradigms in general. Thinking of politics through concepts such as the oppressed and the oppressors, social justice, and so on, framed representations of the other. While commentators have noticed this fact, few have analyzed the difference between leftist and Islamist notions,[1] especially in the ways it produced ideological coherence. If I may simplify for the sake of the argument, Hizbullah, along with other Islamic movements, presents itself as a counterweight to the left's dismissive attitude to the importance of history. Hizbullah's conceptions of time in bringing ideological coherence to the oppressor/ oppressed understanding of socio-political structures is reminiscent of the warning issued by Walter Benjamin when examining the properties of historical materialism.[2] Just like any political party, organization, or state, the Arab left and other secular organizations in the Middle East faced the issue of ritualizing the past, and the significant absence of such practices amongst Lebanese leftist formations contrasts clearly with the example of Italian communists, who used Christian rituals to construct communist imaginaries, as depicted by anthropologist David Kertzer.[3] Although it is outside the scope of this book to engage in a study of uses of the past and representations of history for leftist and other pro-Arab intellectuals – practices that are as diverse as the existence of these movements – suffice to say that for some of the major currents there was a negative view of what the past can teach in terms of shaping the quality of political action. This was part of a broader understanding of modernity that is mostly Western centered.[4] The politics of remembrance, even though indebted to leftist ideological frameworks,[5] breaks with this treatment of history by understanding resistance through a positive, progressive consciousness of history. It constantly draws lessons from past events, and the just-lived[6] as well as the more distant past, producing different time dimensions:

---

[1] Saad-Ghorayeb analyzes the difference as a moving away from class-based accounts of oppressor/oppressed to an "Islamization of class analysis whose defining elements, poverty exploitation and poverty, become Islamic virtues." See Saad-Ghorayeb. *Hizbullah: Politics and Religion*, 17.

[2] Walter Benjamin, "Theses on the Philosophy of History," in *Illuminations* (New York: Schocken Books, 2007 [1968]).

[3] D. I. Kertzer. *Comrades and Christians: Religion and Political Struggle in Communist Italy* (Prospect Heights, Ill.: Wareland Press, 1980).

[4] See for example, Samer Frangie, "Theorizing from the Periphery: The Intellectual Project of Mahdi Amil," *International Journal of Middle East Studies* 44 (2012): 465–482.

[5] For a detailed historical overview of Lebanese Shi'i mobilization from leftist to Islamic movements see Rula Abisaab and Malek Abisaab. *The Shi'ites of Lebanon: Modernism, Communism, and Hizbullah's Islamists* (Syracuse: Syracuse University Press, 2014).

[6] Lara Deeb, "Exhibiting the 'Just-Lived Past': Hizbullah's Nationalist Narratives in Transnational Political Context," *Comparative Studies in History and Society* 5:2 (2008): 369–399.

a general religious one, and one more particular to the "Islamic Resistance" in Lebanon.

Hizbullah intellectuals, and before them Shi'i clerics who addressed this question, have argued that leftist notions were already present in Islamic traditions long before Marxist articulations of social reality, and that one did not need to espouse Marxist ideas in order to make sense of political issues related to power and social justice.[7] Yet if anything, it is possible that Hizbullah's main debt to leftist organizations stemmed from its organizational framework or the politicization of its ideas.[8]

Producing Difference

The year 1982 was a turning point, not only because it witnessed the Israeli army enter and occupy practically half of the country,[9] but also because it dramatically changed the balance of power and caused most players to reassess their political objectives, constraints, and opportunities.[10] For example, the invasion placed the Shi'i organization Amal, which had positioned itself as the foremost political representative of the sect, in an awkward position. Amal was split between engaging with the new regime, accepting the fact of occupation and going through the state to deal with the question, adopting a more militant confrontational approach to the Israeli presence, or simply keeping all these alternatives open. This ambiguous stance led to the secession of an "Islamic Amal" (Amal al-Islāmī) from among its ranks, of which the future secretary general of Hizbullah, Hassan Nasrallah (along with senior party members such as Hussein Moussawi), was part.

The separation of Islamic Amal from Amal and the subsequent founding of Hizbullah brought to the foreground a political ambivalence as it was a clear indication that Hizbullah built its political difference on the issue of armed resistance against the Israeli military presence. In this sense, whereas Hizbullah and Amal are both confessionally *denominated*, meaning that they both have a Shi'i make-up and address a Shi'i constituency, Amal also has a confessional *political*

---

[7] See in this case the works of Mohammad Baqr al-Sadr, especially his *Falsafatuna* and his *Iqtisaduna*. Mohammad Hussein Fadlallah's numerous speeches often articulate these ideas.

[8] As'ad Abukhalil, "Ideology and Practice of Hizballah in Lebanon: Islamization of Leninist Organizational Principles," *Middle East Studies* 27:3 (1991).

[9] The Israelis had previously invaded part of the South in 1978 and then partially withdrew, keeping the contested territory of the Shebaa farms. But this military incursion displaced large numbers of people, triggering initial resistance efforts.

[10] For a detailed background of the political and security situation at the eve of the formation of Hizbullah, see Daher, *Le Hezbollah*, 67–75.

program, unlike the then emerging Hizbullah, whose objective was the fight against Israel. Whereas Amal was more likely to accept state-brokered agreements if they involved political gain for the sect, those who later formed Hizbullah chose not to engage with the existing political system because they perceived it as inherently corrupt and oppressive (see Chapter 3 and representations of Political Maronitism). In effect, Hizbullah quickly claimed, from the first issues of *al-ʿAhd*, that it carried on the "real" message of Musa al-Sadr, the founder of Amal, whose aim was not to form a political party with a confessional agenda like other Lebanese political parties, but to create a social movement. Hizbullah appropriated al-Sadr to its cause, commemorating the anniversary of his disappearance in Libya in 1978 every year.[11] Hizbullah claimed that Amal had lost al-Sadr's original political objective, which was to fight Israel and state marginalization.

In effect, the unfolding of hostilities between the various Lebanese and foreign protagonists left these already marginalized areas further distanced from the state, as different types of social and political groups gained influence, most of them involved in one way or another in the fight against Israel. The most influential and best armed were Palestinian organizations, which had conducted resistance operations since the 1960s, consequently controlling many of the remote border regions of Lebanon. Intermittent clashes erupted in the latter half of the 1970s between inhabitants of those regions and an increasingly aggressive Palestinian resistance movement. When Israel invaded Lebanon in 1982, it highlighted the weaknesses and ambivalent stance of organizations such as Amal, which strove to assert its political control in the South, toward Palestinian organizations. This precipitated the schism within the ranks of Amal: by dealing a heavy blow to the Palestinian resistance in the south, Israel inadvertently set the stage for the emergence of other organizations that would struggle to address longstanding security concerns of the southern region of Lebanon and its mainly Shiʿi inhabitants. Most of Hizbullah's future members came from the organizational base of Amal or were involved in one way or another with more flexible Amal-related political structures.[12] These security settings informed the general

---

[11] The fate of al-Sadr is still unclear, but most stories relate that Libya's president at the time, Muammar Gaddhafi, killed him, either after a heated theological argument or at the request of Yasser Arafat, the leader of Fatah, the armed wing of the PLO then in Lebanon.

[12] For example, in his autobiography Nasrallah describes the transfer of some elements of Amal's formations into the more ordered organization of Hizbullah. See Nasrallah, "al-Sayyed Hassan Nasrallah: al-sīra al-zatiyya," *al-Mustaqbal al-Arabi* 331 (September 2006): 113–118.

understanding from which Hizbullah emerged as a composite of Muslim (Shi'i) organizations[13] and former disgruntled Amal members.

In May 1985 – among other similar events that pitted different militant actors in Lebanon against each other – fighting erupted between Amal and the main Sunni militia group, al-Murābiṭūn, an ally of the Palestinian Liberation Organization (PLO), with which the Christian Phalangists had clashed in 1975, sparking the beginning of the Lebanese war. These clashes quickly spread into the Palestinian camps, stopping and resuming over the following years until 1988. These intermittent but no less deadly clashes were known as the "War of the Camps." *Al-'Ahd*, Hizbullah's main media outlet, and its political leaders constantly stressed the fact that the Party of God was not involved in the fighting, and condemned it virulently. It was around these events that Hizbullah started discussing differences between its militant activities and those of the PLO and other leftist coalitions.

An early Tahht al-majhar column illustrated some of these differentiating strategies. In it, Raad took a quote from Musa al-Sadr – "the honor of Jerusalem is in being liberated by believers"[14] – and interpreted in specific ways. The liberation of Jerusalem, which had been called for by al-Sadr but also religiously ritualized by Khomeini,[15] was used in order for Hizbullah to voice certain complaints about the fate of the Palestinian resistance's efforts over time. In this article, Raad used al-Sadr's claim to "give a lesson" to Yasser Arafat's PLO and his allies of the Lebanese National Resistance. The crux of his argument was as follows: If the Palestinian resistance weakened over the years, distancing itself from its original objective and becoming implicated in the Lebanese wars, this is because of its lack of foresight that only "believers" can liberate Jerusalem.

"Believing" is a state of being-in-an-act that differentiates between various forms of resistance, an act involving an ethical line of conduct. The Tahht al-Majhar editorial took al-Sadr's appellation of "believer" and linked it to another concept Hizbullah came to use: *taklīf shar 'ī* (lit., legal obligation), a legal command or line of conduct to follow issued by a senior cleric (in this case the *walī al-faqīh* and the institutional structure

---

[13] Mohammad Raad lists four of them: the Iraqi-inspired Da'wa Party; the Lebanese Union of Muslim Students (al-Ittihād al-Lubnānī lil-Talaba al-Muslimīn); Amal; and Sheikh Raghib Harb's militant initiatives in the south. Mohammad Raad, interview with the author, June 2010.

[14] *al-'Ahd* 46 (17/5/1985), 2.

[15] Jerusalem Day is celebrated at the end of Ramaḍān and commemorates solidarity with the Palestinians and recalls the occupation of Jerusalem by Israel.

that he projects),[16] from which a "believer" cannot deviate. The believer follows a line of conduct that is "marked down" – written, so to speak (although not specifically on paper). The *taklīf shar'ī* argument reso-nated for years in the way Hizbullah differentiated its combatants from those of other parties and groups and, inevitably, how others would categorize the Hizbullah combatant as a different "type." Thus, all these arguments promoted some form of "Islamicity" of the resistance explaining why Hizbullah did not take part in events such as the War of Camps. For Hizbullah, the appropriate line of conduct (read as Islamic) was resistance against the Israelis. It is important to note here that the first time the notion of *taklīf shar'ī* was invoked in the cultural outlets of Hizbullah was in the context of differentiating its members' line of conduct from another.

A subsequent Tahht al-majhar editorial took the argument even further. Titled "Huna tabda' al-qussa"[17] (Here begins the story), the column looked critically at the label of "Lebanese National" given to the leftist and other pro-Palestinian resistance in light of attacks against the "Islamicity" etiquette that colored Hizbullah's militant activities. For Raad, the "national" label existed to "cut the road in front of the Islamic resistance" and to give the possibility for leftist and moderate rightist powers to participate in the creation of a "new democratic, unique, and unified" Lebanon. And therefore, in order to impose ready-made solu-tions on everyone under the strength of the "national" sword, and spon-sored by the "heroes" of the "Lebanese National Resistance."

As was seen in the preceding chapter with discussions of patriotic claims and Christian politics, "being a nationalist" is mostly a slogan thrown at Hizbullah-affiliated intellectuals as a political solution that would endanger the activities of liberating territory. In this case, the signifiers "nationalism" and "Islam" are pitted against each other inso-far as they involve following a straight ethical line of conduct. In this editorial, nationalism is associated with "isolation from the Islamic region," which was the function of "the colonialist Sykes–Picot Agreement." Moreover,

> it seems evident that Islam (*al-islām*) is not like Nationalism (*al-watanīyya*) . . . Islam in its totality and its broad look is limited by clear notions and precise legal rulings that cannot be played with or duped. As for nationalism, it is an elastic concept to

---

[16] This legal command is issued in its most general form by the *walī al-faqīh*, Khomeini or his successor. But in fact it represents a general mode of conduct internalizing a hierarchical discipline in the organization of Hizbullah. Here I am looking at one implication of its symbolic importance at the practical level for making arguments and claiming legacies.

[17] *al-'Ahd* 49 (1/6/1985), 2.

the extent that Antoine Lahd[18] can be a nationalist ... and nationalism is "right" to the extent of making the Phalangist butchers innocent, and requesting co-existence with the Zionist neighbor, which actually means protecting their borders from "destructive" operations, for "the national interest" or "national security."

The question that can be posed here is why feel compelled, as in the case of the Christian counterpart, to make reactive arguments about nationalist stands toward parties that were traditionally the most influential political antecedent to Hizbullah? These earlier political formations and Hizbullah were in practice fighting for very similar causes. Both were against the political regime in place, which they believed had led to the prevailing warlike status quo. Both were against Israeli occupation, and both tried to fight it. Both also were "pro-Palestinian" in the sense of claiming that an appropriate confrontational stance against Israel is the right way to meet the territorial and population demands of Palestinian refugees in Lebanon and Palestinians in Palestine.

Noteworthy, however, is that throughout al-'Ahd's early period there were very few articles that mentioned themes directly addressing leftist conceptual or philosophical questions. On the few occasions on which they did appear, it was to discuss a very specific difference in lines of conduct in light of a political event, or to make a political accusation at some behavior. Yet, in the post-Taif period a gradual rapprochement took place, that gradually led to formal alliances between Hizbullah and other confessional actors. This was mainly sponsored by the Pax Syriana imperative, but also because Hizbullah had then emerged as the uncontested challenger to Israeli occupation. Moreover, as Taif increasingly crystallized the confessional nature of Lebanese politics, those groups that were outside the confessional equation increasingly lost their popular support, especially their traditional base that had mostly come from Shi'i areas and was subject to Syrian good will. It is in this regard that Hizbullah slowly emerged, at least partly, as a confessional player.

The Palestinian Resistance: Historical Militant and Intellectual Precedents

In order to understand the ambivalent yet symbiotic relations between Hizbullah and the Palestinians,[19] one needs to delve into the historical

---

[18] General Antoine Lahd was the head of the South Lebanese Army, an Israeli proxy that Hizbullah fought against during the period of Israeli occupation (1982–2000).

[19] Laleh Khalili attempts to provide a description of the relation but, as it is focused on recent events, fails to account for its historical antecedents, which explain a much deeper "cultural" relation. See Laleh Khalili, "'Standing with my Brother': Hizbullah,

context that led to various forms of political mobilization in the regions that were denominated as Shi'i, and how this process was deeply connected to the Palestinian resistance movement and practices. When the first Palestinian refugees started arriving in Lebanon in 1948, Lebanon had been properly independent for three years, with a southern region that found itself effectively isolated from the rest of the political entity. As an illustration, roads and electricity were not provided in the South of Lebanon before the mid-1950s. As observed by Jihane Sfeir, representations of territory would drastically change: a Lebanese southerner would probably find himself closer to villages from Galilee than to cities such as Beirut or regions to the north, before the creation of the country.[20] The 1950s saw two events taking place: the influx of massive numbers of people coming from the Galilee; and the imperative to affiliate to a new political entity called Lebanon with its center in Beirut. In fact, for social and economic reasons, the creation of such power hubs irremediably pushed populations to move toward that new center, Beirut, especially following what Palestinians and Arabs have called the *nakba*, signifying the enormous number of Palestinians forced into exile in 1948.

Sfeir proposes that the perceptions of Palestinians switched from being the friendly neighbor, to the "embarrassing guest", to "the enemy from inside" once the war started in 1975.[21] Yet Palestinians served as a catalyst for militant action against the prevailing regime controlling the newly established Lebanese state. Ideological constructions oscillated between outright rejection of the state in favor of pan-Arab alternatives and accepting the state in order to change it from the inside. In a sense, the Palestinian "cause" was used at will in order to reinforce many reworked nationalist imaginaries. The earlier leftist, or other "secular" lines differed greatly from later Hizbullah elaborations, emerging from concerns shared with Amal.

In reality, many future members of Hizbullah either lived side by side with Palestinian militants and refugees or participated in one way or another in common battles against Israelis or the various Christian forces.[22] It was also the norm that some of those displaced from the South came to live in Palestinian camps.[23] During the 1960s and

Palestinians, and the Limits of Solidarity," *Comparative Studies in Society and History* 49:2 (2007).

[20] J. Sfeir, *L'Exil palestinien au Liban: le temps des origines (1947–1952)* (Paris: Karthala, 2008), 62.

[21] Ibid.

[22] Noteworthy here is Imad Mughniyya's involvement with Fatah before joining the ranks of what became Hizbullah.

[23] When the Tal al-Za'tar siege and subsequent massacre took place in 1976, Christian militias assembled all the men in the camps and took them away. Some of them were

1970s, rural migration brought many families from the South to find work in the city, settling in the outskirts of Beirut. Palestinian camps formed after the expulsion of Palestinian families from territories occupied by Israel during the 1948 and 1967 wars were located in adjacent areas to which the Shi'i expelled from the South came to reside. In parallel to this, this period saw the establishment of power centers in Lebanon around Beirut, throwing regions such as Jabal Amil and the Bekaa out of the economically active "market" sphere. In many ways, Palestinian and Shi'i populations had similar social concerns.[24]

Nevertheless, when Hizbullah-affiliated intellectuals started writing, it was specifically in reaction to the operation of militant activities. Hizbullah was after all the resistance project, and its strategies of social mobilization were geared to this effect. The first editorials mentioned demonstrated that it was a "culture" of resistance that Hizbullah's writers were after. This was evident in the speeches of Hizbullah's officials for years to come. The Palestinian resistance, along with its leftist and other militant Lebanese allies, inspired, if not involved, future Hizbullah cadres. A typical example is Imad Mughniyya, who started training with Fatah. Indeed, Hizbullah's members (especially those involved in military activities) all participated in resistance activities sponsored by Palestinian organizations, and continued in the same vein working for a more effective organization that carried the same initial objective of resistance. As argued by Augustus Richard Norton, movements and shifts of affiliation between these very fluid political formations were the norm.[25]

The other implication of this argument is that there was no clear differentiation between representations of the Palestinians and those of leftist or other groups labeled secular because both are understood in terms of their militant activities. When Tareq Atwi (known as al-Ḥur al-'Āmilī in memory of the seventeenth-century Iranian scholar), blew himself up in 1988, the editorial in al-'Ahd the following week praised the operation as a testimony (shahāda), offered to the "Islamic Intifada in Palestine, as if through this offering, he is opposing, blaming, and correcting" the trajectory of Palestinian resistance efforts against the Israelis.[26]

Lebanese and Palestinian, according to a Lebanese witness whose father was taken, never to return.

[24] This argument has been made countless times in the literature on the subject. Saad-Ghorayeb differentiates between "socio-economic" or "communal" factors of politicization and more "religious" forms of activism in general. See Amal Saad-Ghorayeb, "Factors Conducive to the Politicization of the Lebanese Shi'a and the Emergence of Hizbu'llah," *Journal of Islamic Studies* 14:3 (2003).

[25] A. R. Norton, *Amal and the Shi'a: Struggle for the Soul of Lebanon* (Austin: University of Texas Press, 1987).

[26] al-'Ahd (29/10/1988), 1.

The editorial was referring to Atwi's testament, which was published in the same issue, and focused on a critique of previous resistance activities that was considered to have lost its cause in the internecine local Lebanese turf fights. "The martyr Atwi reminds everyone and is not a witness for the language of letters and words that get lost in the air or is forgotten in the binding of books but [is a witness] of the language of blood and soul that is eternal[ly remembered], he reminds everyone of the true enemy."

During this early period as the War of the Camps unfolded, most editorials on these events heavily criticized the Palestinian organization. Arguments revolved around these narratives read as lines of conduct: Yasser Arafat, the leader of the PLO's armed wing, Fatah, had turned his weapons away from serving resistance activity and into internecine Lebanese violence. He also started negotiating with the enemy as soon as he left Lebanon following the Israeli invasion of 1982. A front-page editorial from 2 November 1986 – a year-and-a-half after the war of the camps started – entitled "In all honesty we say" summed up Hizbullah's critique of Fatah's line of conduct:

Arafat failed in the test of resisting against the Israeli enemy during the 1982 invasion, but this was only a further proof to his first downfall (*suqūtihī*) that happened the day the PLO entered the internal war in Lebanon that led him to a stage of weakness and fragility and made him agree to a ceasefire with the Israeli enemy before the invasion[27].

Representations of Palestinians were shown through this ethical lens. As an illustration, a 1991 analysis of Mahmoud Darwish's latest poetry by Hasan Ashur showed the defeatist mood that characterized the Palestinian culture of compromise, with the enemy exemplified by the engagement in the Madrid talks. [28] Although Darwish had been hailed not just by the Arabic public but an international cultural audience as being the poet of resistance, or at least the poet who represents the Palestinian condition in the face of occupation, for Ashur, the style of Darwish's writing, the words he uses, the expressions he favors, all illustrate a state of surrender. To prove his point, Ashur contrasted this style of writing with an earlier "rebellious" style of Darwish in a 1964 poem "to the reader" from his collection of poetry *Awrāq al-zaytūn* (olive leaves), and a series of writings dated 1975 and onwards, to show how the tone of his poetry gradually changed with the changing condition of earlier Palestinian resistance efforts. This semiotic analysis enabled the author

---

[27] *al-'Ahd* (2/11/1986), 1.
[28] Referring to the Madrid peace conference of 1991 in which Mahmoud Darwish participated.

to capture a specific Palestinian "culture." The focus on Darwish's poetry was not a rare instance, but became a regular feature in later issues of *al-'Ahd*, given that Darwish was arguably the most important Palestinian poet in Arabic but also because he actually took part in engagement with Israelis from the early 1990s, if not earlier.

Another way culturally to capture the Palestinian was through representing his territory as "Islamic." This was done countless times in *al-'Ahd* and in political speeches, including through the celebration of Jerusalem Day each year at the end of Ramaḍān. Palestine is an Islamic land, meaning that it contains holy sites for all Muslims in the world which must be protected. An article on mosques in Gaza, "Ghazza um al-masājed" (Gaza the mother of mosques), approaches the problem of the Islamicity of territory through a detailed description of each mosque in Gaza, its history, and Israeli actions carried out. A Khomeini quotation informs the intellectual initiative: "Turn your Mosques into trenches." First there is the al-Aqsa Mosque, which was burnt in 1969, the Mosque of Bir al-Sabe' turned into a museum, the al-Jesser and al-Souk Mosques into a photo exhibition center, and so on. One learns that Gaza is the city that is most rich in mosques in all of Palestine, and this is followed by a long list of Gazan mosques affected by Israeli offensives.

What remains to be said is that at no point did Hizbullah write about Palestinians and their history in Lebanon, or its common history with the Palestinians, as it did when dealing with Maronite historiography. This seems logical because Palestinian history in Lebanon is a subaltern one. There is no Palestinian history to write except one that takes place in Palestine. Palestine then is part of an imagined Islamic reconfiguration of territory that should be won through resistance. The only stories to tell about Palestine involve Palestinians returning to their homes in its various villages, towns, and regions. These are constantly displayed in songs, video clips, and talk shows on al-Manar TV starting from the 1990s onwards.

The Left, the Palestinian Cause, and How the Left Squandered Efforts at Recapturing History

It is through leftist and other so-called secular Arabic political formations that the Palestinian question, and thus by extension general Arabic questions, would be posed through militant practices. In effect, the South was the most fertile terrain for organizing resistance operations against Israel. Each somewhat radical or anti-regime political party had a space in a specific area. The oldest party to have a presence was the Lebanese Communist Party, probably coinciding with the establishment of the state of Lebanon. The LCP was in Nabatiyeh, Marjeyoun, Bint Jbeil, and some port cities – that is, most of the major Shiʻi towns, and some Orthodox villages. Later on, in the late 1950s, the Arab Nationalist Movement and the Baath were mostly present in Saida and Sur.[29]

Starting from the mid-1960s, and probably until the first Israeli invasion in 1976,[30] the LCP and Organized Communist Action (OCA) would train local inhabitants of the South to conduct military operations against Israeli targets, across frontiers and later on in occupied Lebanese territories. According to Petran, as early as 1968 the LCP and OCA "worked with the village inhabitants to organize People's Guards for self-defense."[31] Petran sums up some themes that parties designated as secular tried to work for:

In Lebanon, an imperative for such a movement must be to replace traditional particularist ties (family, kinship, tribal, religious, etc.) that are incompatible with democracy by a national and social class identification that permits development of a secular, democratic political system. Although Lebanese National Movement parties had yet to liberate themselves completely from such traditional bonds, the movement itself, in bringing together Muslims and Christians of practically all sects around political principles, constituted a significant advance.[32]

As much as parties such as Hizbullah were indebted to leftist or what were labeled "progressive" organizations, it is such points that the party would react to, as this disagreement may not have been intentional or voiced in writing. On the contrary, one of Hizbullah's underlying claims was that Muslims and Christians could come together through strengthening the traditions that leftists were so keen to destroy, or at least looked down upon.

Another important issue that left these earlier political formations in a dead-end was their understanding of national questions, in the sense of proposing viable ideological national constructions and actually being able to implement them: the problem was not the political vision as such but the gap between this and practices on the ground. A conference speech[33] by Kamal Jumblatt, leader of the Progressive Socialist Party (PSP), truly exemplifies the extent of these contradictions. In this long conference, Jumblatt argued that both pan-Arab discourse and a Maronite confessional understanding of the nation should be dropped in favor of a nationalist and socially just program. This sense of national justice is based on the notion of evolution, a cryptic concept that was

[29] Tabitha Petran, *The Struggle over Lebanon* (New York: Monthly Review Press, 1987), 72.
[30] Anonymous former communist fighter, interview with the author, summer 2007.
[31] Petran, *The Struggle over Lebanon*, 144.
[32] Ibid., 125.
[33] See Kamal Jumblatt, "Le Liban et le monde Arabe (30/3/1949)," in *Les conférences du Cénacle* (Beirut: Cénacle Libanais, 1949).

never fully explained by Jumblatt, but clearly alluded to getting out of the "backward ways of the past."

For the left then, the creation of some form of "socially evolved," progressive, or "developed" community was the only justification behind the idea of Lebanon as a nation. A first consequence of this is that these leftist notions of social development in the context of increasing social destructuring and marginalization of the population were read or lived merely as socially distinctive strategies and as triggering group differences. And second, by omitting to articulate a solid understanding of history, or at least a unified national construction that permits a respect for memory, the left ended up losing a social connection with its "public." It was not just that the left was elitist,[34] but, first, it could not keep the type of ongoing interaction/archiving mechanisms employed by Hizbullah, and second, it could not build strong, power-enabled politics as its efforts, especially on the ground, were scattered.

Indeed, Hizbullah's biggest critique of the left and other groups was directed against the label of "nationalist" used by the loose coalition (and also by Christian groups). Several al-'Ahd editorials confronted this issue, whether on the front page or in Tahht al-majhar. In so doing, Hizbullah-related intellectuals called into question leftists' understanding of the past and changed the projection of the imagined community, by changing the actors concerned, i.e. accepting confessions or sects as the natural pro-longation of the past, of tradition. Although Hizbullah heavily criticized the asymmetric political system that confessionalism had produced, it used confessionalism as a repository of social consciousness, when other leftist formations completely rejected it on the basis of "progressiveness." This led Hizbullah to turn an aspect of confessional consciousness into a highly effective asset for political action.

In the same line of critiquing the left and other watanīyyīn,[35] one Tahht al-majhar column commented on a charter signed between the different resistance-related groups,[36] the Charter of the National Union Front. Raad here started to criticize the label "nationalist" given to the charter,

---

[34] In any case, to make that claim extensive research should be carried out in order to account for organizational and mobilization practices on the ground during the 1950s and 1960s. But one thing is sure: the discourse of the elite in the capital was quite removed from the practices of militants on the ground in the South.

[35] Watanīyyīn is usually translated "nationalists"; but I wanted to avoid the peculiarly European dimension of this term pertaining to more rigid notions of imaginary senses of belonging. The whole point in these texts is that these words (watanī, qawmī, etc.) may refer to very different types of imagined communities that are endlessly overlapping (Arabic, Islamic, Lebanese, etc).

[36] al-'Ahd 72 (24 Safar 1406), 2. According to the editorial, this front brought together "Amal, PSP, and various leftist groups."

arguing that "Islamist" incorporates "nationalist," whereas the contrary is not the case. Moreover, Islamists' relation to Arabism includes a peculiar definition of the human condition that is probably larger than that of "Arabists." In this contemporary age, only allegiance to the *umma* (as opposed to atomization of forces) can help in the fight against the occupier. Here the *umma* is represented by the Islamic Republic of Iran, which wholeheartedly supports militant efforts. And here is another interesting articulation of "the national": "the success of total national independence is dependent on Lebanon's belonging to the political map that is governed by Islam in the world, and the Islamic State [of Iran] is the only one in our region that is an independent state in reality, culturally and politically." In effect, the desire here is one of independence, and the model is Iran, because it stands with the cause, and all other attempts at creating forms of "independence" failed. If at the time independence could not be foreseen in real terms to encompass the colonial borders of Lebanon, it was imagined and only materialized in the post-war era.

But this editorial most importantly aimed to criticize these groups in terms of resistance efforts. All these labels should be given according to how one fared in the fight against Israel. And accordingly: "those who fought the resistance are the Islamists, the central pillar of the resistance are the Islamists." Moreover, using "nationalist" labels unfortunately closely resembles Christian appellations and other complacent if not allied parties with Israel and the USA. Lastly, standing with the *umma* in effect makes sure that one distances oneself from such affiliations.

The onset of the clashes between various Lebanese and Palestinian groups in 1975 exacerbated that situation and pushed the left (just as in the case of the Christians) to reveal the paradox in its thinking on national security questions. Judging from the charter of the leftist groupings, the Lebanese National Movement (LNM), which includes the PSP and the OCA, show a sense of disarray and of political apathy. For example, a document dated 1975 (14 August), entitled "Democratic Reform of the Political System in Lebanon," contained a clause pertaining to the "reorganization of the Army" which proposed that "the Army's sole function will be to defend Lebanon's frontiers and national independence and to shoulder the national obligation towards the Palestinian Cause and Arab causes."[37] Another point stated, under the heading of fundamental rights and freedom, that: "enacting a modern naturalization law would guarantee the acquisition of Lebanese citizenship by those who qualify for

---

[37] "Documents   of   Lebanese   National   Movements   (1975–1981)"   (leaflet, 18 August 1975), 20.

it, irrespective of racial, sectarian or political considerations."[38] In 1977 another document reiterated this claim with more detail. One point that discussed the strengthening of Lebanese and Palestinian relations stipulated the "recognition of the Palestinian Resistance's right to operate on the Lebanese arena and non-interference with the Palestinian presence in Lebanon, so that the Palestinian Resistance may be enacted to do its part in defending Lebanon against the Zionist enemy, and to provide the appropriate setting for the strengthening and improvement of Lebano-Palestinian relations."[39]

And still, in its "Plan for a Solution to the Lebanese Crisis," presented on 14 March 1980, the LNM did not depart from its earlier political visions for the country. In this document the LNM reaffirmed "Lebanon's Arabness[40] and national independence" through "the consecration of Lebanon's engagements towards the Palestinian cause, the respect due to the Palestinian Resistance's right to the struggle for the recuperation of their land, and the strengthening of the Lebanese-Palestinian relations based on the signed agreements between the Lebanese State and PLO."[41]

In 1982, when the bulk of Palestinian armed personnel and assets were neutralized and forced into exile by the Israeli invasion, the new situation presented the then slowly emerging Hizbullah with an opportunity to change the rules of the game. Everything that the Palestinians, the left, and its related heterogeneous formations controlled fell under Israeli military control. This last development reveals a security paradox, the main point of contention which Hizbullah, through its actions, would end up resolving by taking the Palestinian question "into its own hands." The result was that contradictory utterances during the era of Palestinian militancy ended up being rearticulated by Hizbullah's intellectuals in a different way.

This is probably why al-'Ahd contained very few mentions of leftist movements or discussions of what could be loosely labeled "Arabic questions." It seemed logical that one would find dialectical debates articulating concepts of "Islamic" versus "secular" alternatives, or ideological debates around leftism, liberalism, or Arabness. But instead, nothing was mentioned. The only time the left was mentioned was either when some of its representatives were present at commemorations and rallies, or when a successful operation conducted by one of these groups created a wave of admiration.

---

[38] Ibid.
[39] Ibid., 46–47.
[40] Translated from French: Arabité.
[41] Ibid., 160.

A case in point is that *al-'Ahd* never mentioned the proliferating number of suicide attacks and other military operations in which other groups from the LNM and beyond had been involved since the period of Ahmad Qasir's operation. The only time this happened was on 9 November 1988, when the communist Suha Bishara fired three bullets at the leader of the SLA, Antoine Lahd; he survived after being transported to an Israeli hospital in Haifa, while Bishara was caught and imprisoned. The editorial of the issue following this operation[42] showed great admiration for the courage of Bishara and praised her and the Communist Party's efforts. The editorial took this event as an occasion to stress that what counted were successful resistance efforts against Israelis, regardless of the party carrying them out. More importantly, the editorial did not just show the deep impression triggered by the fact that Lahd was almost killed, it also noted the passing of an era in which other parties had been real competitors for the party. At this time, Hizbullah began to assume a leadership role in resistance efforts against Israel; it seemed to supersede other parties, and it was Hizbullah operations that were achieving significant military advances.[43] In a sense, this was a signal that the Islamic (military) resistance was fully formed and entrenched in the political environment.

From Critique to Strategic Alliance

Because of this common cause of resistance against Israel, the left and other "Arabist" or pro-Palestinian parties would grow to become supportive if not direct political allies of Hizbullah. The 1990s saw the consolidation of these alliances. After the liberation of the South in 2000 – and, more importantly, after the assassination of the prime minister, Rafic Hariri, and the Syrian withdrawal – the alliances had to demonstrate their solidity. The left was divided over the Hizbullah question, reflecting larger ideological transformations taking place in the movement such as the fall of the Soviet Union, and the global transformation affecting social and communist parties that moved closer to liberal ideological frameworks.[44]

---

[42] *al-'Ahd* 229 (12/11/1988), 1.

[43] A list of those operations can be found in volume 2 of the collection of articles *Hizbullah: al-muqāwama wal-taḥrīr*, published by the Arab Documentation Center of *al-Safīr*, pp. 107–133. The largest number of suicide operations were carried out in 1985; this includes all political parties participating in the fight against Israel.

[44] The Lebanese left also had its local context, involving a declining militant leverage, the rise of a Sunni crony capitalist class centered around Rafic Hariri, and its age-old animosity toward "Islamists" of all kind who seemed to have won popularity and partly produced an ideological shift in their direction.

Later on, when asked, Hizbullah officials gave interesting opinions about the left. In an interview with Fida Itani for *al-Akhbār*, Naim Qassem addressed those who had branded Hizbullah's 2010 political manifesto as borrowing from leftist ideals, especially in its discussion of the international situation and Hizbullah's stand toward US policies in the world.[45] Qassem argued in the same vein as al-Sadr and Fadlallah that concepts of "oppressors and oppressed, poor and rich" had always existed "in Islam," before these "ways of describing the world" were elaborated by the left. In effect, the Open Letter of 1984 used exactly the same form to describe how Hizbullah perceived the various political situations in the world, and the Islamic one in particular. Qassem added that although "our vision of resistance differs from the one of the Leftist or the Nationalist, we still agree on its necessity, but rather than discuss the sex of angels, we agree on the principles of boycotting," referring to Hizbullah's opposition to what was perceived as imperialist policies by the West. It may seem fair to say that one of the reasons why "the sex of angels" was not discussed was because there was nothing to discuss on that matter, given that Hizbullah issued ideological statements only when needed. Differences in the "concept of resistance" could only arise if writing strategies were deployed to that effect. So there is no clear difference between the "left" and the "Islamic" in that regard unless it is necessary to articulate such a difference.

The position of Hizbullah toward the left is one of strategic alliance, with the aim of fighting or resisting Israel in any possible way. And that has been, as was said earlier, the main point over which Hizbullah's intellectuals may have critiqued the left – or, more specifically, Palestinian resistance. The prevalence of leftist and other "pro-Arab" formations such as the Baath, the SSNP, and the Communist Party has tended to link anti-Zionism, material marginalization, usurpation of power in Lebanon by a single community, etc. into a general discourse of social contention. Rarely if ever did Hizbullah need actually to differentiate between parties as different as Communists, the SSNP, Baath, and so on. It is as if things could be classified in terms of who is with the resistance and who is not, who has worked efficiently in terms of resistance efforts and who has not.

Representations of the Zionist Enemy

On 13 September 2009, Hassan Nasrallah gave a televised speech on the occasion of the Jerusalem Day commemoration. Touching upon recurrent themes, Nasrallah engaged in a very specific discussion of claims made over the past. After arguing that Jerusalem was a holy site for both

---

[45] *al-Akhbār* (18/12/09): see www.al-akhbar.com/ar/node/169129.

Muslim and Christians, he asked the question: "Aren't there any holy sites for Jews in Jerusalem?" And he immediately answered: "There is a debate because due to their actions throughout centuries not much has remained of the sites of the sons of Israel."

Switching back and forth between "Jewish" and "Zionist," Nasrallah went further in this effort to claim history. It is worth quoting this passage at length:

The Zionists have no right in this land. We are ready to discuss this topic on religious, historic, rational and legal bases depending on holy books including the Old Testament which is widespread and recognized now among the Jews of this time ... The Holy Qur'an tackles repetitively the stories of the children of Israel and the prophets of the children of Israel. Such concepts were mentioned in previous books especially in Torah and the other books God revealed to the prophets of the children of Israel. We recognize based on the Qu'ran and our Islamic teachings that God Almighty promised Abraham (pbuh) to give his descendants the holy Land. We do not deny that. That is present in our Qu'ranic text. Back also to the Qu'ran, the Old Testament, the sayings of the prophets of the children of Israel and the historic events, God Almighty promised the descendants of Abraham the Holy Land; but the descendants of Abraham are not only the Jews and the Zionists as a political or religious trend or as a tribe and race. A great section of Arabs are among the descendants of Abraham (pbuh). The descendants of Abraham are from Ishmael and Isaac. But in the Torah, the Bible, the Psalms and the Qu'ran, God promised the descendants of Abraham the Holy land. Which descendants? They are the good, the believers, the chaste and the pious among them. They are the followers of Abraham the father and the prophet and the followers of religion of Abraham (pbuh). As for the descendants of Abraham who are criminals and killers who slaughtered prophets, spread corruption on earth and perpetrated horrible deeds and great sins, they were not promised in the first place, so one cannot say the promise was withdrawn. In the Old Testament and in history books after Moses (pbuh) crossed with the children of Israel towards Palestine and the Holy Land, the children of Israel worshiped the bull and the idols and disobeyed God and harmed His prophet and conspired against him and his brother Aaron. God ordered them to go astray in the desert of that land for forty years. So they are not promised. When the disobedient and their descendants who denied the blessings of God were terminated – after forty years – the children of the prophet of God Joshua entered the Holy Land. They were the religious, pious and devout descendants of the children of Israel from the descendants of Abraham. Still when they resorted again to corruption and killing the prophets, God Almighty controlled over them who killed them, destroyed them and dispersed them. Now they are digging under the al-Aqsa Mosque in search of a temple which was destroyed three thousand years ago due to their crimes and corruption. Neither in the Torah, nor in the Bible, nor in the Psalms, nor in the Qu'ran nor in any divine book is there but one principle: The land is God's. He bequeaths it to whoever He wants among his good servants. This land is the promise of God to the good among his servants.[46]

---

[46] Jerusalem Day speech, 13/9/2009, translation from Mideastwire, available at https://mideastwire.com/page/index.php (emphasis added).

Among other things, this very rich passage illustrates two points relevant to our argument. First, it shows that Hizbullah takes seriously Zionist historical arguments and justifications, unlike previous resistance groups against Israel, which just dismissed these claims as ideological fabrications. In this speech, Nasrallah used the same textual references used by the Zionists in order to discredit their claims. Second, as for its Christian counterpart, Jewish traditions have been "dirtied" by contemporary political formations with narrowly defined state projects. Only "righteous" people can claim land and, although Jews, Christians, and Muslims are all under the same God, *some* Jews have been led astray, they have put their traditions in danger, and in this sense risk disappearing from history. The corruption of the Jews in antiquity resembles Zionist actions today. But in contrast to what was done for the Christians, Hizbullah-affiliated intellectuals in general and Nasrallah in particular do not engage in a reinvention of the Jewish tradition(s), especially not those related to Arabs or other Jews from the Middle East. It is on the basis of this type of reasoning that Zionist political action cannot make historical claims (and thus should be rooted out from the time continuum).

Here again it is the "believer" or "pious" signifiers that help mark out righteous political conduct. Nothing can be promised for those who did not fulfill these ethical requirements. It is in this sense that politicized Jews have no tradition, no history written for them. Mirroring this conception of time-as-ethics discussed in Chapter 2, the Jewish promise ('ahd) to God was broken. Because the Jews failed to respect it, they cannot write the past.

From the earliest issue of al-'Ahd, Israel appeared as the occupier: it attacked resistance efforts in all possible ways, especially Islamic ones, such as the targeting of 'ulamā'. Articles described military offensives, political decisions and their repercussions, and contain warnings that the occupation would soon be crushed. Starting from the third issue, there was an analysis of Israeli local politics based on a reading of a *Washington Post* article analyzing the stakes of the next legislative elections.[47] On the third page of that issue, another article described in detail, through testimonies, how Israeli intelligence services erected check points and harassed people for endless hours. That report had a long introduction outlining Israeli objectives, described as to "empty the South [of Lebanon] from its inhabitants so that it reduces the potential for militant operations against them."[48]

[47] al-'Ahd 3 (11/7/1984), 1.
[48] Ibid., 3.

Israel as the occupier and the enemy is traceable through military practices. Not one single issue of *al-'Ahd* passed without describing in increasing detail Israeli "occupation" tactics. These descriptions were gradually linked to more "background" material on who "is" the Israeli enemy. This construction of knowledge about the enemy takes very specific directions, in the way information is used. It seems evident that knowledge of Israelis does not follow the same inscription process as that for Palestinians, or Christian and other Lebanese.

Much has been said on Hizbullah's purported anti-Semitism, a term so grounded in European cultural and political history that it is almost nonsensical in this context. However, as is clear in the above, Hizbullah does have a representation of Jews, even if it is inextricably linked to Zionism. An early Tahht al-majhar editorial has a very interesting elaboration of some related questions. Reacting to the nomenclature of "extremist" versus "moderate," and using it to his own conceptual benefit, the writer states:

There are no Jews that are not extremists because there are no Jews who do not legitimize the violation of Palestine ... Jewish emigration to Israel demonstrates that fact, and worldwide Jewish support for Israel is a proof of that, as is the absence of any Jewish organization opposed to the Zionist entity.[49]

These notions elaborated by the Tahht al-majhar column are part of the common narratives prevailing in Lebanon across sects and groups. For someone living in the Middle East in the 1980s, those outside the Arab world never criticized Israel's actions. It was later, during the second half of the 1990s, that Hizbullah started discovering all sorts of opposition groups to the "Zionist project," some of them including Jews from around the Western world. This immediately inspired Hizbullah media institutions to invite Jewish intellectuals, academics, and journalists who were virulent critics of Israel to meet with party members when the opportunity arose. Prominent Jewish intellectuals and journalists sympathetic to the cause, such as Noam Chomsky, Norman Finkelstein, or Seymour Hersh, were all granted easy access to interview Hassan Nasrallah, and were given useful information that served various causes.

Meanwhile, Hizbullah continued observing the enemy, as it had done since the early 1980s. This move from knowledge built on military "lived" practices and physical traces to more normative and analytical understanding of the Israeli, the Zionist, the Jew, and so on, can be illustrated by a column that started in *al-'Ahd* toward the end of 1987. Its title was "Know your enemy" (*A'rif 'aduwak*), and it regularly discussed

---

[49] *al-'Ahd* (5/1/1985), 2.

organizations or themes related to Israeli politics. The first column was on Tsahal (the Israeli army),[50] and gave a top-down, detailed description of its organizational structure. We learn about the number of soldiers in the various divisions of the army, the "organized and auxiliary branches," the types of weapons used, the air force, navy, and infantry, the territorial ordering of military divisions and how they are managed, the number of officers and their role, and so on. The article catalogues in great detail every single weapon, tactic, and organizational aspect of Tsahal.

The second article in this series was on Aman,[51] the Israeli intelligence services, and is similar in style to the one on Tsahal. The third article was on the Jewish Agency,[52] and traced the historical transformation of that organization from a British mandate-sponsored entity in Palestine in 1922 and its link with the World Zionist Organization. What differs in the latter article is the historical delving into contemporary events shaping this organization, and outlining its actions and goals. Among other things, the Jewish Agency aimed at encouraging Jewish emigration to Palestine, buying land and encouraging agricultural settlement, and the spread of the Hebrew language in Palestine. These analyses led to the conclusion that the Jewish Agency was the de facto government for Zionist settlements.

From purely descriptive intelligence gathering to the historical, and finally to the more general and normative, the fourth article, on "Zionist terrorism,"[53] was a much longer article in the "Know your enemy" genre, with more focused conceptual discussions on what terrorism is and how to qualify Zionist or Israeli actions. "Facing the researcher in Zionist terrorism is a rare opportunity that does not present itself to any other researcher in terrorism whatever his identity and his influences because the leaders of Zionist terrorism have published prolifically and with great precision on the various terrorist organizations they belonged to, and the fundamental ideological dogmas on which they were built." Hence, "it is not an exaggeration to state that one cannot find in any political and military tradition any one people in the world with such a scary heritage that is Zionist terrorism."[54] Outlining the history of the other comes back to condemning his actions as harmful, sometimes by using the categories the enemy had used to condemn resistance.

The articles fleshed out their arguments one after another; history writing was no longer simple organizational description but the possibility

[50] al-'Ahd 181 (13/12/1987), 5.
[51] al-'Ahd 189 (5/2/1988), 13.
[52] al-'Ahd (2/4/1988), 12.
[53] al-'Ahd (29/4/1988), 12.
[54] Ibid.

to prove a line of conduct. From Weizmann's declarations, to the Balfour Declaration, to territorial incursions and so on, the writer brought to the reader's attention the various events that made up this qualification of Zionist actions as terrorist or as "out-of-tradition." The next "Know your enemy" article was practically the same in structure and was on "Contemporary Jewish Terrorist Organizations."[55]

Mirroring Western nomenclatures and strategies, the more Hizbullah was given certain labels, the more local intellectuals used these notions to retaliate and structure their understanding of the enemy.[56] Studying the Zionist "strategy" became fundamental, such as in an early article[57] that treated Israeli plans to gradually annex Jerusalem through reviewing all types of Israeli practices of forced emigration, military incursions, settlements, declarations of intent towards the fate of Jerusalem, etc.

Another noteworthy article of the period entitled "Lines on Zionist Fascism,"[58] in a section of the newspaper called Dirāsa (Study), shared a page with the "Know your enemy" column on "the Sefardim."[59] The study this time involved a full-blown account of ways to understand Zionist actions as akin to those of fascist organizations: It was "Zionist philosophy" that was in question. Building a racist state in present-day Palestine spreads Jewish/Zionist values, links the Jews of the world to Israel by convincing them of the vital importance of that state and encourages them to emigrate there without letting them integrate with the rest of the population. The rest of the article examined the educational system in Israel and how such ideas were spreading amongst the population and were nourished and protected by prevailing political, religious, and social institutions.

Hizbullah also tracked what was being said on the party and its resistance practices in Israeli media and other producers of information, a confirmation by the enemy that its efforts were effective. Over the next few years this developed into a sophisticated media prduction with the rise of al-Manar TV.[60] An early quotation was from a Hebrew University professor who also was the "defence minister of occupied territories affairs," Moshe Maoz. Maoz acknowledged in an interview with the "Hebrew radio" that the Islamic resistance was very successful, that its fighters were ready to die for their cause, and that "Muslim youth groups

---

[55] al-'Ahd (13/8/1988).
[56] And in this case, not only Israel but also the USA and other powers deemed to practice forms of occupation, such as the French in the early 1980s.
[57] al-'Ahd (14/5/1988), 12.
[58] al-'Ahd (18/6/1988), 9.
[59] Ibid.
[60] To my knowledge, Hizbullah is the only Lebanese party to have teams of Hebrew translators working from within the party for media organizations and research centers.

most certainly formed a group of utmost importance." In addition, Maoz allegedly acknowledged the success of "the Iranian model" and that, if no solution could be found, Islamic resurgence would inevitably expand building on this success. Constant scrutiny of what the Israelis say has continued. A noteworthy example was the multifaceted media campaign after the July 2006 war, tracing the defeat of Israeli troops through the statements of their generals, intelligence officials, and other politicians.

As we argued for previous cultural practices, earlier writing strategies have served as a template for later elaborations. Again, the only difference between today's styles of writing and previous ones is the institutionalization of knowledge that took place amongst the various parties concerned, and the way Hizbullah relied on these earlier techniques to systematize the process of writing about the Israelis. Conferences, talks, and television talk shows have multiplied over the years. Publications grouping different types of authors, at times not even related to Hizbullah, have played this performative role of presenting Hizbullah through specific fields of knowledge, as sponsored by Hizbullah-related research centers, publication houses, academics, and so on. Chapter 1 explained the Hizbullah-affiliated intellectual field and its development over time.

The more Israel became "known," the more it was demystified and perceived as vulnerable. It slowly lost its symbolic presence, because it was analyzable and "archivable" but most importantly because it could be argued that there was no space for its practices from a sociological perspective. Through the media exploitation of successful military practices, Israel stopped being perceived as an invincible actor. It was vulnerable and able to be defeated because its capacities were known, and, ultimately, its actions were predictable.

5 Confronting the State: Writing Space and Hizbullah's Politics of Legitimacy

Writing territory merges all previous attempts at archiving the past. Recapturing space involves not only fighting on the ground against the occupying forces but also proving the legitimacy of one's claim to that space, to link it in one way or another to a political entity that has some form of sanctifying[1] power, in this case, the modern state. Hizbullah emerged to fight to regain control of the South of Lebanon, but also faced the Lebanese army and the different militias in the southern suburbs of Beirut, a space with decades of social and political marginalization. Also, until the withdrawal of the Israeli army from South Lebanon in 2000, Hizbullah trained and developed in the more isolated regions of the Bekaa valley, especially its main town, Baalbek.

Hizbullah's representations of territory and its relations with the state are inextricably linked. The loss of South Lebanese territories to the Israeli occupier was squarely blamed on the state's policies of neglect. As will be seen below, articles written by Hizbullah-affiliated intellectuals always juxtaposed the problem of Israeli occupation to the Lebanese state's marginalization of South Lebanon. Importantly, for these intellectuals marginalization means lack of *knowledge*, or lack of writing and archiving on a particular entity. Before the emergence of Hizbullah, the south of Lebanon and Western Bekaa were not categorized or "statisticized" (in the sense of producing information about this geographical reality and drawing patterns from it) or marked as other more privileged regions in Lebanon have been. Moreover, the recent growth of a new spatial entity, the southern peripheral area of Beirut, Dahyeh, which brought together waves of migration from rural areas of the South and the Bekaa to settle closer to the capital, would become the focus of memorialization. This projection of the world as image and structure, as Timothy Mitchell would have it,[2] involves an empowering process where

---

[1] By "sanctifying" I mean the power that institutions such as the state have in imposing certain terms of speech as dominant ones. See for example Bourdieu, *Ce que parler veut dire.*
[2] Mitchell, "The Stage of Modernity."

groups or organizations create a duality between reality and representation of space as contested territory. The land becomes written, marked down: first, because of its thorny yet inevitable symbolic affiliation to a state (Lebanon), in itself a reproduction of previous writings; and secondly because it has been seized by the Israeli occupier, who is also involved in rewriting the identity of the land.

Thus, the politics of remembrance, which is at the heart of representations of territory, starts from a very present and urgent concern with writing the unwritten, digging out archival material that has not been proposed before as a consequence of state marginalization and the "normalization" of Israeli occupation. Resistance as project is thus presented throughout the different stages of history, in the various geographical locations of Hizbullah's constituency: the South of Lebanon under occupation; the Baalbek and Western Bekaa from which the resistance originated; and Dahyeh, the southern suburbs of Beirut, the space most active in the fight against a ruling regime perceived as pro-Israeli. Representations of the land produce narratives that suffuse stories of the resistance across time. Hizbullah-affiliated intellectuals read and write the land as a segment of the country and always strive to be united to the prevailing state, which is supposed to represent or have monopoly over the land. In so doing, and because the land has been occupied, this reclaiming process will involve questioning the nature of state rule and the role of the resistance as a project.

Writing Territory: From Reclaiming Dahyeh to Questioning State Authority

Finding a place for the stories of people and their actions, in the same way as outlining territory, enables the storyteller to finalize his plot. The actions of the resistance happen because of a usurpation of space, and this signals the presence of an enemy (Israel and the USA, for example) or of "guilty" actors (the Lebanese state and those having executive power in it). It is why resistance starts from a representation of territory.

In a newspaper such as al-'Ahd, any major commemoration aims not only at remembering the human legacy (Chapter 2) but also at marking a territorial presence. Titles suggesting the location of an event such as "In Beirut, the Bekaa, and in the South" point to the actual description of commemorations that took place on a particular week. This representation of space delineates the particular geography characterizing a part of the imagined geographical boundaries of the nation that the newspaper structures: Lebanese newspapers including al-'Ahd evince this ongoing sense of a particular targeted space as a represented whole. The space is the constituency that is being politicized. For example, a 1990 *al-'Ahd* article commenting on a recent demonstration has a revealing title: "Dahyeh's march: a human sea for the protection of the resistance." All the elements are there: territory, population, cause (or history).[3]

From the very first issues of *al-'Ahd*, Dahyeh was the geopolitical space where most of the questions of political legitimacy were lived out. In as early as the second issue there was an "investigation" of the social, economic, and political situation in Dahyeh (literally "the suburb" in Arabic) referring to the southern suburbs of Beirut, where Hizbullah is partly based. This early attempt is striking given that publication of the newspaper started in Baalbek at a time when the latter was cut off from the capital due to the war and security situation. In an interview with the author, Hizbullah-affiliated MP, and the founder and editor of *al-'Ahd*, Mohammad Raad tells the difficult story of those people in Dahyeh who provided the Baalbek-based team with analytical articles: delineating Dahyeh as a territory facing problems was essential in framing one of the main issues that puts into question the legitimacy of the state's official regime.

Al-'Ahd first appeared in 1984, in the midst of a conflict between what writers of that time have called *al-sulta* (the authorities) and "Islamists." The crisis of legitimacy took place over a perceived endangered territory, the South of Lebanon, where political conflict and a derived perception of legitimacy was read through this specific understanding of space. In his first book, published in 1994, Hassan Fadlallah, who became an MP for the Solidarity with the Resistance Coalition,[4] wrote that the conflict pitting "authorities" against "Islamists" reached its peak on 17 May 1983 as the government "signed an agreement with Israel, sponsored by Americans, ordering security, political and economic relations."[5] On that day, a demonstration of "*'ulamā'* and citizens that took place at Masjid Imām al-Riḍā'" in Bir al-Abed, a district of Dahyeh, quickly turned into a clash between the Lebanese army and demonstrators, resulting in several killed and many injured.

According to Fadlallah, a previous clash had taken place in March 1983, when "the army sent a force to set up training camps in Remayeh in the Bekaa, in a region where Islamic military groups were headquartered," a clear sign of then Lebanese president Amin Gemayel's intent on clamping down on any force outside its sovereignty, in a region that was considered at the time to be "Syrian territory."[6] Again in this case, Fadlallah understood this clash as the first time Hizbullah had to stake a

---

[3] *al-'Ahd* (20/1/1990), 2–3.
[4] This is Hizbullah's parliamentary coalition.
[5] Fadlallah, *al-Khayār al-ākhar*, 47.
[6] Ibid.

claim over territory. This happened because of a clash with the regime. More importantly, Fadlallah concludes that it was at the time of these clashes that the label "Hizbullah" first appeared in newspapers and other Lebanese media.[7] The necessity to give a name to the forces clashing with the authorities, especially after the Bekaa incident, arose from a need to identify territorial affiliation.[8] In other words, the name Hizbullah was born out of this initial confrontation with what was officially the legitimate authority, the state, forcing the latter to reconsider the nature of legitimate political practice.

The second and more important clash with the authorities came in August 1983, on the occasion of a commemoration of the disappearance of Imam Musa al-Sadr during a trip to Libya. Fadlallah explained that at that time "military forces succeeded in throwing the army out of Dahyeh." Fadlallah continued: "The war in Dahyeh was primitive and fast, weapons used were light, and it involved private people's arms, and from what was heard, everybody participated, even those not affiliated to a party, so much so that there was now a center in Beirut for military and political work that was not subjected to authorities and constantly threatened to be besieged by the army."[9]

Fadlallah's book al-Sīra al-zātiyya li-Hizbullāh (the autobiography of Hizbullah) was probably the first comprehensive attempt at writing the history of Hizbullah. It also had the first and probably the longest passage on the early confrontation with the authorities in the early 1980s, a passage most often overlooked by the literature on the history of Lebanon during the war era.[10] Although this period was covered by historians, media, and other producers of knowledge of all kinds, their concern was always with the fate of international players involved in Lebanon at that time, or with the actions of the Lebanese state and its struggle to restore some form of sovereignty. In other words, their writings articulated the concerns of the dominant player.

Fadlallah's take on the history of this period strikes the reader because of its alternative reading of the failure of the Israeli–Lebanese agreement of 17 May, the withdrawal of multinational forces,[11] and finally, the withdrawal of the Israeli army from Saida in 1985. But these ideas, which one finds ordered chronologically in this book, are already

---

[7] Ibid.

[8] This type of marking territorial affiliation was a common practice during the Lebanese wars of 1975–1990 given that the country was divided into separate militia-controlled geographies outside the actual control of the state.

[9] Fadlallah, al-Khayār al-ākhar, 51–52.

[10] One notable exception is Jaber, Hezbollah: Born with a Vengeance (New York: Columbia University Press, 1997).

[11] Multinational forces included contingents of the US, French, Italian, and British armies.

discussed in a similar way in early issues of *al-'Ahd*. In its second issue, for example, a front-page article outlined this concern that the authorities wanted to seize weapons in all areas of Lebanon so as to implement the "security plan," one of the controversial clauses of the 17 May Agreement with Israel. This second issue was published on 4 July 1984, several months after the Gemayel regime ordered the army to bomb certain parts of Dahyeh (in February), a war that quickly extended to West Beirut, "where Hizbullah forces, headed by Amal and the Progressive Party, penetrated into the Lebanese army barracks."[12]

Later on, the failure of the 17 May Agreement became the main date commemorated by Hizbullah in speeches and texts found in *al-'Ahd* throughout the 1980s, symbolizing the first demise of the prevailing "old" political order. The ultimate danger for Hizbullah was a possible rapprochement between the Lebanese state and the Israeli enemy, as that would put into question its very existence as a military force trying to liberate a territory. Resistance as a project would have no legitimacy if the state ratified the "security plan." The state's illegitimacy stemmed from its actions, which threatened to wipe out the very existence of a project that could stop the occupation.

Revealingly, throughout most of his book, Fadlallah is very open about the "Islamists" barring the way of the "authorities." The fact that this sentiment was not hidden was symptomatic of a feeling of righteousness inherent to an understanding of this confrontation. For Fadlallah, the authorities were obviously illegitimate, and all those practices in which "Islamists" were involved were tending toward restoring some form of political justice. Thus it is logical that the more these actions were explained and put out in the open, the more they gained credibility, because they were understood as reasonable. This would prompt the writer to simply write, in as much detail as possible, about the confrontation, as he saw it. But *al-'Ahd* had paved the way for this spate of justifications and descriptions of the conflict in this particular way – Fadlallah needed only to build upon this reservoir of writing. It was between 1983 and 1984 that the struggle with the Lebanese state and other state-related political entities reached its peak. The Lebanese state, the US, French, multinational forces, and other armed groups on Lebanese soil all posed a threat to Dahyeh.

Commenting on the battles of February 1984, Fadlallah stated that the Lebanese army was sponsored by the American army, which made "all kinds of operation of destruction (*'amaliyāt tadmīriyeh*)," and advised Amin Gemayel "to bomb Dahyeh."[13] Thus we read that the bombing

---

[12] Qassem, *Hizbullah*, 93.
[13] Fadlallah, *al-Khayār al-ākhar*, 53.

of Dahyeh happened at a time when the American army was positioned on the shores of Beirut facing Dahyeh. As a result of this, the sixth brigade of the Lebanese army, which was predominantly Shi'i, defected and joined Amal. In turn, Amal aligned with other opposition groups such as Jumblatt's PSP, transforming the conflict into one involving the confessional divides of West and East Beirut. The conflict had many turf-related undertones, sometimes not related to the resistance as it involved the rest of the Lebanese militias on the scene, and the political consequences of these events go well beyond the conflict that took place in Dahyeh. However, what is to be noted here is the reaction of Fadlallah and other Hizbullah writers to this event. Fadlallah and *al-'Ahd* writers during this period saw Gemayel's attack on Dahyeh as a Christian political threat (along with international allies) to the raison d'être of the resistance by calling into question the identity of the territory where Hizbullah was slowly laying the foundations of the militant organization.

In the second issue of *al-'Ahd*, an article[14] digs into Dahyeh's past, attempting to establish continuity in terms of what was done, and to study the "economic, historical, and military" reasons behind the "attack on Dahyeh." The article opened with a reminder of the confrontations that took place in 1983 in Bir al-Abed, which prompted a historical reflection over its causes. Dahyeh was placed on the Lebanese map through a specific understanding of its population: "one third of the Lebanese population (800,000) lives on less than 1/300 of Lebanese territories." This population can be differentiated through a specific culture, or social psychology as the author called it: "The socio-confessional make-up of the southern suburbs explains the social psychology of its inhabitants." Although there were Christian and Sunni (either Lebanese or Palestinian) minorities, the bulk of the population were Shi'i. In this case, the religious categorization is not just a social marker but conforms to a specific reading of history.

The author then explained the emergence of the area of Dahyeh. Before 1975 people had flocked from villages and rural areas to find employment in the city of Beirut, settling in its outskirts. Newcomers would look for people from their own regions, thus forming the different suburban pockets of Beirut according to confession, kinship, or geographical affiliations. The peculiar yet logical feature of the "refugees" (*muhajjarīn*) was that most of them were Shi'i. The rest of the article explained how Dahyeh as a space has been marginalized by state institutions, using all types of statistics and data to prove this point, and illustrating how state-allocated institutions supposed to deal with such questions have always been inoperative, both before and after 1975.

---

[14] *al-'Ahd* 2 (4/7/1984), 3.

A couple of years later, another interesting *al-'Ahd* article attempted to explain the concept of security and politics related to Dahyeh.[15] The article, in the style of an academic essay, started with two claims, one by Imam Ali bin Abi Talib and the other by Jacob Bronowski, who wrote *The Ascent of Man*. Imam Ali famously said: "Two unknown virtues: security and health!" and Bronowski argued that the "sedentarization" of humankind enabled people to focus on "the inside" rather than on "the outside," which in turn pushed humanity to look for a "just authority." Yet Lebanese political instances failed to deliver forms of security and were the source of "all instabilities." In 1988 an article on Dahyeh was subtitled "Generals of the army bombed it, gangs looted it and burnt what was left in houses."[16]

The relationship between this representation of space in the midst of the capital and the presence of the state would continue unfolding in the 1990s, after the implementation of the Taif Agreement, the end of the Lebanese wars, and the formation of a new government that brought a new political figure to the office of prime minister: Rafic Hariri. *Al-'Ahd* reported throughout the first years of the decade about the plans for the unification of Beirut, and made it clear that Hizbullah approved. Since the beginning of the war in 1975 Beirut had been divided into West and East sides, also labeled the Muslim and Christian sides respectively. Not one issue was published during this period without an opinion on the subject of the unification plans. The first step taken by Hariri's government after the cessation of hostilities was to lay down plans to rebuild the demolished city of Beirut along with other infrastructure, such as roads and bridges.

Problems arose when Hariri unveiled real-estate plans in Dahyeh itself, attracting the condemnation of Hizbullah and its media. Still a newcomer, Hariri encountered fierce opposition and heavy criticism in *al-'Ahd*. Fear of a takeover of Dahyeh, and the still-uneasy first contact with the newly established regime, led Hizbullah to a generally critical view of Hariri's politics. This is probably the most "anti-state" critique *al-'Ahd* or Hizbullah ever voiced, in terms of calling into question the socioeconomic policies of the new regime. For example, *al-'Ahd* published an article entitled "What does Hariri want from Dahyeh?" and asked "Does he want his real estate companies to take over?"[17] In the next issue, the question became: "What does Rafic Hariri want from Lebanon?"[18]

These clashes were brief as Hafez al-Assad's Syria eventually found a compromise, through which Hizbullah gained a free hand over the

[15] *al-'Ahd* (26/7/1986), 6.
[16] *al-'Ahd* (4/10/1988).
[17] *al-'Ahd* (5/2/1993), 10.
[18] *al-'Ahd* (27/3/1993), 10.

"security file" in the sense that it could continue its project of resistance against Israel while Hariri and his political coalition of entrepreneurs focused on running the economy. This is why Hizbullah gradually stopped criticizing Hariri's policies of post-war reconstruction; yet it also left Dahyeh as a no-state zone, and the major real-estate plans sweeping across the rest of the capital – and indeed, key parts of the country – would stop at its doors.

This conception of Dahyeh as a unique space in the capital still exists.[19] In the post-war era Dahyeh became the "Hizbullah land" of Beirut, security sensitive and isolated from the rest. Keeping the "Hariri plan" from one of the centers of the resistance promoted a representation of Dahyeh as isolated from the rest of the nation in the eyes of the different political groups and constituencies of the country, an image of Hizbullah's territory as run by "the state of Hizbullah," which resists assimilation with the state of Lebanon.

Years later, after the July 2006 war, it was a Hizbullah-related real-estate company that was responsible for the rebuilding of Dahyeh and parts of the South. Founded for that purpose in the aftermath of the war, Waad (literally "the promise"), an affiliate of Hizbullah's institution Jihād al-Binā' (see below), monopolized this process by replacing as many as 281 destroyed buildings, according to their website,[20] which surprisingly has a detailed historical survey of Dahyeh, its relation with the state of Lebanon, and the political stand it took throughout the history of the country's various ideological currents. "The southern suburb has a story," according to the website, and it started surprisingly early, in the summer of 1840, when Christians fled mountain areas following massacres perpetrated by Druze, and came to join "Shi'i quarters"; Shi'i helped them settle and feel secure again in 1960, it continues. This webpage's historical background focused mostly on the ideological debates that ripped apart the political groups of Lebanon in the 1950s and 1960s over whether Lebanon should be more aligned with the politics of its Arab neighbors, in the context of Gamal Abdel Nasser's pan-Arab politics from Egypt. Dahyeh supported pan-Arabism.

In effect, just as "outsiders" wrote about Dahyeh as the land of the marginalized, "locals" began to express themselves about Dahyeh. It is in this vein that the "subaltern speaks," as I proposed framing the issue in the introduction.[21] This search for a dissociated self is found through the

---

[19] For an interesting study on Dahyeh as a geographical space and the various politics that frame it see Mona Harb, *Le Hezbollah à Beyrouth 1985–2005: de la banlieue à la ville* (Paris: Karthala, 2010).

[20] See www.waad-rebuild.com/page.asp?id=22.

[21] I am drawing here from Spivak, "Can the Subaltern Speak?"

writing of history. All the early discursive attempts of *al-'Ahd*[22] found an echo in a long 2007 al-Manar documentary on the "contemporary history of Dahyeh." Made in a narrative style with voiceover, the documentary displayed an impressive array of photographic and video archives collected from the area, showing Dahyeh from the fall of the Ottoman Empire until the present day.[23] Again, it is noteworthy that these types of media material were never seen through other prevailing TV channels.

Territory and Occupation

The South of Lebanon experienced the first Israeli invasion in 1976, an event that significantly dramatized the marginalization of the region. This was exacerbated by the more permanent Israeli occupation of the South, up to the Litani river, in 1982. Hizbullah intellectual and political figures constantly repeat that this was the catalyst for the forming of the organization through the coalescing of local groups, religious and other militants with Iranian Revolutionary Guard training, logistics, and weapons.

Early on, *al-'Ahd*'s articles contained analyses of military acts of resistance against the Israeli army and its Lebanese proxy the SLA as Hizbullah-affiliated intellectuals proceeded to archive battles. Writers mentioned "The South" as a threatened space when the story involved occupation. The presence of the occupiers was analyzed in various ways. One early article,[24] which focused on the "Jewish greed for the waters of the Litani river," reiterated the problem by using relevant texts: "In the face of the denial of the Lebanese authority that some parties push for the idea that Israel does not have ambitions over water on Lebanese territory, it is necessary to come back to certain texts that express clearly the objectives and intentions of Israel in perpetually expanding." The first text used was the Bible, with excerpts from what Yahweh told Ibrahim: "We give you this land from Egypt's river to Euphrates's river." To be sure, this type of textual reference has often been given by Arabic writers and political actors ever since Zionism was first represented in different ways in the media. There are other biblical quotations that are then linked to current Zionist actions and political actors' declarations (for example,

---

[22] Some were mentioned above, but there are many more retrospectives occurring over the years of its publication.

[23] *Mawtini – My Homeland – The Story of a City and War – The Story of Beirut's Southern Suburbs* (Beirut: Dar al-Manar, 2008 [DVD]; also available at www.youtube.com/watch?v=YFR5mWLVdIY).

[24] *al-'Ahd* 9 (25/8/1984), 4.

Ben Gurion's promise related to the Litani river and the annexation of the South of Lebanon). It is in this sense that what was published in *al-'Ahd* could have been published word for word in any other pro-Palestinian or pro-Arab, if not any Middle Eastern, media device of that period.

Israel's expansionist practices were not just related to water concerns but more generally to the assimilation of territory. For Hizbullah, when Israelis occupy, they try to "normalize" this assimilation through a process that Hizbullah intellectuals have called "Judaification" (*tahwīd*). As seen in Chapter 3, Hizbullah-affiliated intellectuals' representations of Israel's "lack of tradition" narrowed down its Jewish culture in practice to the process of occupying and claiming a right to the territory of others.

Moreover, because occupation was the central act for the raison d'être of the resistance, most of Hizbullah's archiving efforts involved keeping a memory trace of territory. Early issues of *al-'Ahd* contained several articles on the annexation of villages (whether Palestinian or Lebanese). The interesting point here is the systematic work deployed in mapping this occupation process, listing numbers of homes destroyed in villages, the name of their owners, dates of occupation, and so on.[25] As will be illustrated below, it is through these practices that the political agenda of the resistance can be articulated to its fullest.

Although previous militant parties opposed to Israeli practices have all engaged in some of these ordering and recording techniques, none have matched the systematic nature of Hizbullah's work. Articles on military practices testify to this. They contain knowledge about the placement of military bases, strategic positions, and entry points in order to attack or defend. A first article of its kind in *al-'Ahd* described "liberated territories in Western Bekaa" through a "survey on the ground with the Islamic resistance." The article features a simple map of the area in question and the neighboring villages, and what seem to be the different roads reaching the region. The article is mostly rhetorical, focusing on the fight against Israel, the triumph accomplished by the Islamic resistance, and the coming victory.[26] It is in this issue that the front page features combatants planting the Iranian "Islamic Revolution" flag on top of a hill (see introduction).

A few issues later, a map featuring "an approximate sketch of the Israeli roads in Ramieh" accompanied a front-page article[27] about Israeli attempts at "Judaifying" (*tahwīd*) that village. In yet another issue[28] "a

---

[25] See for example *al-'Ahd* 173 (18/10/1987), 2, entitled "From 1923 to 1987: the annexation of 37 villages and 17542 dunam and the building of 3 settlements."
[26] *al-'Ahd* 131 (27/12/1986), 5.
[27] *al-'Ahd* 144 (28/3/1987), 1.
[28] *al-'Ahd* 176 (7/11/1987), 7.

fighter of the Islamic resistance explains the details of [an] offensive" with a map to illustrate. These first representations of the South through the prism of occupation were triggered by the military events taking place. Resisting occupation enables this marking, inscribing, recording, and detailing of territory through the battles that took place, the people who died, or were imprisoned, or simply incurred some form of injustice in the view of the Hizbullah-affiliated intellectual.

Moreover, the peculiarity of some of these intellectuals' concerns was around linking this representation of Israeli ambitions to reclaiming the South as a marginalized region. First of all, the stress is on how Israeli ambitions reveal the state's marginalization of the region in its darkest aspect. In three articles published in the first two years of al-'Ahd's publications, whenever Israeli ambitions are mentioned they are highlighted by emphasizing the state's neglect in the main title: "Israelis longed for it, and they wanted to swallow it: the wealth of the water that the state neglected for so long."[29] A few years later, another article was entitled "The Litani project, a signal of state neglect of the region of the South."[30]

Jabal Amil and the History of the Resistance

Paradoxically, as the focus turned to differentiating forms of politics, in the sense of new legitimizing devices, differentiating between "Islamic" understandings of history and the national or "secular" one initiated a process of writing history as localized in a particular territory with a clear definition of a population. Although it was not an imaginary that encompassed the rest of the territory of Lebanon, Hizbullah-affiliated intellectuals focused on particular sites such as Jabal Amil, or the South of Lebanon. Jabal Amil's history must be written as a site of perpetual effective resistance against invaders. Works on its history, although not lacking, were few, and since the birth of modern Lebanon only a few books have provided a history of the region from premodern to colonial times, until the establishment of the state of Lebanon.[31]

From the end of the 1980s, al-'Ahd's cultural pages were full of articles on Jabal Amil and its reclaimed illustrious history, specifically over its involvement in a general practice of resistance against foreign occupiers. In an early article of this kind, called "A look at the historical origins of the Islamic resistance,"[32] the author posed the problem in a peculiar way. His

---

[29] al-'Ahd 13 (22/9/1984), 6.
[30] al-'Ahd (27/5/1989), 7.
[31] One such reference is Muhammad Jabir al-Safa, Tārīkh Jabal 'Āmil (Beirut: Dar al-Nahar, 1981).
[32] al-'Ahd (25/2/1989), b. This article is part of a special "resistance" issue.

objective was to "know" more about the *umma*[33] of Jabal Amil, which has
stood up to enemies for decades, because this *umma* fought and continued fighting for a cause, unlike other communities, who fought for their
own interests. The cause, or even doctrine, that the *umma* abides by can
only be understood through the interstice of time, through the practice of
the many who came before and through their actions that contributed to
forming this way of "doing things." This doctrine is "Islam and its laws
(*sharī'atuhu*)". This *'aqīda* is apparent through the territorial presence of
mosques and *husayniyya*s that are found in every village of the South. The
author wrote that one of the main principles of Islam is the total rejection
of oppression, whether coming from a "Muslim" or a "secular" party;
"this is why the *umma* in Jabal Amil in particular and in Lebanon in
general has a long history of revolution and renaissances, whether
carrying Islamic or other flags in the face of the Ottoman authorities."[34]
Like attempts at writing the history of others (see Chapter 3), these
practices are a reaction to dominant narratives. One of those dominant
emphases is the focus on the Ottoman Empire as the oppressor, as
articulated by Christian historians. But in this case, the aim is to list the
various forms of resistance (of the Islamic as marking difference) that
resulted from that struggle against hegemony.

In order to mark down "Islamicity," the author pointed out that the
Ottoman Empire, although "Muslim" in character, was engaged in all
kinds of oppressive activities such as public executions, and named the
leading figure in the resistance against the French occupation, Sayyid Abd
al-Husayn Sharaf al-Din, a prominent Shi'i cleric. There were no real
details on Sharaf al-Din's involvement in the resistance[35] apart from
"being there" and "supporting," although one learns in the article[36]
that the French tried to arrest him before he could escape from his village.

Apart from Sharaf al-Din, there were two important characters of the
resistance against the French that find constant space in such texts: Sadeq
Hamzeh and Adham Khanjar. The author showed his amazement at how
"Maronite Lebanese history" considered them "bandits and *quttā' turuq*."
The Maronite state succeeded the French occupation forces as the primary enemy of Jabal Amil, and of Muslims in general, as they differentiated between Christians and Muslims in Lebanon "However, Muslims

---

[33] In this case, I think it could be best translated as "community."
[34] *al-'Ahd* (25/2/1989), b.
[35] Especially as most of what he wrote was related to Shi'i jurisprudential issues. See Sabrina
Mervin, *Un réformisme chiite, ulémas et lettrés du Jabal 'Āmil (actuel Liban-Sud) de la fin de
l'Empire ottoman à l'indépendance du Liban* (Paris, Beirut, and Damascus: Karala and
CERMOCIFEAD, 2000).
[36] *al-'Ahd* (25/2/1989), b.

confirmed this identity (*hawiyya*) of the land and the identity of the resistance in it," and the author here gives a list of what "marks" the Islamic character of the resistance (summarizing what we have been listing): the *shuhadā*ʾ (such as Raghib Harb and other clerics), its *isthishhādī*, its leaders, its Qur'anic slogans, its injured, and its "point of departure" (*muntalaqātiha*) such as *husayniyya*s and mosques. The history of the resistance is then partly this marking of territory by these "Islamic" rallying sites.

The article is also interesting because it directed its grievances solely at the Lebanese state without mentioning the Israeli occupation during this initial attempt at defining its Islamic character. Later articles of the sort would, first, go back earlier in history and, secondly, would contain a more systematic survey of the fight against the Israelis and Zionism as a political practice. And to echo the discussion in Chapter 2, history as resistance since the Israeli invasion of 1982 is marked by battles and people that testified about them. Thus, one reads[37] that the fight against the Israelis bears traces in Saida, the city of Nazih al-Qubrosli (one of the *istishhādī*), in Nabatiyeh, the city of Ibrahim Khadra, on "the road that stretches from Saida to Sur," what Israelis called "the valley of tears" because of the sheer number of victims who fell there. And while the cities of the South were to become symbols of the resistance, the villages also bear the flag: Jebsheet, Saksakiyeh, Halusiyeh, and so on. The rest of the article went into greater detail on the events that spanned from 1982 until the day on which it was written, in February 1989, on the occasion of Resistance Week. Names of battles that took place, movements of armies and the taking over of territory, new security situations, and so on, all come to form the resistance taking place in Jabal Amil.

A couple of months later, the next series of articles dealing with Jabal Amil's militant history went back much earlier in time and focused on events that took place during the French mandate period: the conference of Wadi al-Hujayr that took place on 24 April 1920 with the objective of organizing the resistance against the French occupation. This article is divided into three parts, spanning three consecutive *al-ʿAhd* publications. These articles are part of the cultural pages, and the emphasis this time is on the role of the clerics, most of all Sharaf al-Din, in resistance to the French mandate. The article presents the outcome of the conference as showing loyalty to a greater Syria, emphasizing several points made by Sharaf al-Din in his speech as reported by witnesses and the importance of the Shiʿi in shaping resistance against the French.[38]

[37] Ibid.
[38] *al-ʿAhd* 277 (14/10/1989), 7; *al-ʿAhd* 278 (21/10/1989), 8.

Two issues later[39] there was another round of articles on that early period, in this case focused on the resistance against the French as a symbol of resistance activities in the Middle East and North Africa. The author, Abou Hassan al-Amili (probably a pseudonym), started from a rather different angle, listing the number of acts of resistance against the French colonizers across North Africa (most of them having some Islamic imprint, whether territorial or not), and then discussing the one in Jabal Amil. Here the retrospective spans larger stretches of time, going back to the Crusaders, and the Lebanese feudal system (representations of which were discussed in Chapter 3). The Lebanese entity was a geographical center, Mount Lebanon, to which other regions were added later through the colonial practices of the French and the wish of Maronites to acquire political control. These (Islamic) regions such as the South, the Bekaa, and the north were condemned to be auxiliary to the central entity from the establishment of the state. One reads here that these regions were added for economic reasons to the "Maronite canton," confirming a colonial approach to the choice of territory. French colonialism and Maronite political privileges are thus inseparable.

The second part of the article went into detail over the different resistance efforts at the beginning of the twentieth century against the French presence in Jabal Amil. The picture on the top right-hand corner of the article showed the two popular fighters from the South with a little caption under it that reads: Adham Khanjar and Sadeq Hamzeh: *jihād 'Āmilī* (an Amili *jihād*).[40] This part of the article was mostly made up of the names of those who died fighting the French (*shuhadā'*, or martyrs).

Yet another article[41] on the occasion of the Resistance Week of 1990 focuses on the role of the *'ulamā'* in the resistance in Jabal Amil and traces the link between the past and the present from Sharaf al-Din to Raghib Harb, and Sheikh Obeid, who was kidnapped by the Israelis (see Chapter 2). In this article the author argued that "Islam" has been threatened from its inception by all forms of oppressive practices starting from the events that took place in Karbala and throughout the Islamic world. This is why "it is not strange that the Islamic resistance was rooted not just in Jabal Amil but in all parts of the Islamic world." The author then follows with a tentative listing of the attributes of a resistance movement of that sort.

In this article, one reads additional reported anecdotes on the life of Sharaf al-Din. Apart from organizing the Wadi al-Hujayr conference, he escaped an assassination attempt by throwing a French *'amīl* (collaborator) to the

[39] *al-'Ahd* 280 (5/11/1989), w; *al-'Ahd* 281 (12/11/1989), w.
[40] *Jihād* can mean struggle, fight, or effort.
[41] *al-'Ahd* 295 (16/2/1990), tah.

ground, and later traveled between Egypt and Palestine. We learn that the French subsequently took revenge by taking over his house in Sur for use as a military base, and burned his house in the village of Shhur. The articles continued tracing the role of certain clerics in contributing to resistance efforts against occupiers.

According to these authors, then, one cultural implication of French colonialism was this privileging of a "Maronite center" and the marginalization of an "Islamic periphery." This version of past events was read as a series of conspiracies targeting the Shi'i population of Jabal Amil. One such consequence was the expulsion of the inhabitants of what has been called "the seven villages," after the Israelis invaded them during the mandate period.[42] As the author of this al-'Ahd article argued,[43] the expulsions took place because of French efforts to normalize ties between Maronites and Zionists. These stories are typical anecdotes on political actors of the time that circulate within Lebanese society. After the withdrawal of the Israelis in 2000 from the south of Lebanon, one of the reasons why Hizbullah considered this step unfinished was the continued occupation of these villages along with the more famous case of the Shebaa farms. As will also be seen below, these villages would be catalogued during the 1990s in al-'Ahd as part of this cultural process of reclaiming Jabal Amil.

One later book published in 2005,[44] entitled al-Juzūr al-tārīkhiyya lil-muqāwama al-islāmīyya (The Historical Roots of the Islamic Resistance) by Muhammad Amin Kurani, mirrored in a synthetic way the attempts at grounding the idea of resistance in a historical continuum. Kurani briefly mapped out the types of militant practices against occupiers of the territory known as Jabal Amil and also in parts of Kiserwan and others, where Shi'i populations were present. In his preface Kurani pleads for a social history free from a concern with the fate of "kings and rulers, their situation, treasures, food and drinks." Moreover, he put the stress on the pious practices of Jabal Amil populations that made them socially conscious and non-elitist: they did not trade their religion (dīn) for a princely privilege (mansab imara), surely alluding to the practices of Bashir Chehab and other feudal elites of

---

[42] The seven villages are: Hunin, Qadas, Nabi Yusha, Salha, Tarbikha, al-Malikiya, and Abl al-Qimh. See Asher Kaufman, "Between Palestine and Lebanon: Seven Shi'i Villages as a Case Study of Boundaries, Identities, and Conflict," *Middle East Journal* 60:4 (2006): 685–706 for some information on the legal and historical controversies following the British mandate partitioning scheme of these villages.

[43] al-'Ahd 295 (16/2/1990), tah.

[44] Muhammad Amin Kurani, al-Juzūr al-tārīkhiya lil-muqāwama al-islāmīyya (Beirut: Dar al-Hadi, 2005).

Mount Lebanon.[45] The history of this resistance takes us back to 1516, from where the *mujāhidīn* (from *jāhada*, to work assiduously for a cause) are scattered across the centuries, through all forms of occupation from the time of the Crusaders until today. *Mujāhidīn* is the name given to Hizbullah fighters, specifically meaning the Islamic combatant. For example, Palestinian fighters were called *fidā'iyīn* (men of sacrifice). The Islamic imprint has always been there through the actions of a generalized resistance movement. The culture of resistance simply "is" because it has lived in places and through actions in the past.

It remains to be said that Hizbullah-affiliated intellectuals differentiated between several times or eras in order to address territorial issues and the legitimacy of the cause in the most effective way. The Islamic resistance of Hizbullah corresponds to a different time-frame – just as it is commemorated through its specific human legacy as seen in Chapter 2 – from that of earlier "Resistances" against occupiers. Sharaf al-Din, a clerical figure, is not commemorated by Hizbullah (except through the type of articles mentioned here).[46] As seen in Chapter 2, by remembering specific figures in an ordered way, Hizbullah differentiated its resistance project, which started in 1982, from previous movements, even though all could be thought of as being part of a chain of resistance movements. Official Hizbullah texts seldom mention events occurring before the creation of the modern state of Lebanon unless they serve as part of a very specific argument. This is partly explained by the fact that proper Islamic resistance commemoration starts from 1982 onwards, except for allusions to Musa al-Sadr's disappearance in Libya. The fact that Jabal Amil was at the forefront of resistance to the French occupation is of course mentioned, but figures such as Sharaf al-Din, Khanjar, or Hamzeh are never included in the ranks of *shuhadā'* celebrated in commemorations. In a sense, the centrality of the fight against Israel overshadows non-temporal definitions of space and "Islamicity" of a tradition outside the unfolding of actions in the present.

Reclaiming the South, Archiving the Villages

Al-'Ahd also published articles dedicated to describing the historical, economic, and social setting of villages of the south, focusing especially on the impact of Israeli occupation and resistance practices. The first of

---

[45] Ibid., 17. For example, Bashir Chehab is said to have converted to Christianity to gain political influence at a time when France and England were increasingly involved in the affairs of Mount Lebanon.

[46] Chapter 2 looked at that period of history that starts with *istishhādī*, clerics who had mobilizing power, along with other forms of military operations and how they were archived and remembered.

the kind came three years after the launching of the newspaper in 1987, focused on Aynata, a frontier village that came to play an important role in resistance activities.[47] The interesting aspect here is that the format of the article on Aynata was very similar to the one on the *shuhadā'* (see Chapter 2). The article started with an "Identity Card" box (*bitāqat hawiyya*):

Place:	[Aynata] falls on the demarcation line with the cancerous virus "Israel," 3 km from Palestine, and 45 km from Sur. One can reach it through three different routes, the first is the Sur–Jwaya–Bint Jbeil road, the second is Sur–Qana–Bint Jbeil, and the third the Sur–Naqura–Bint Jbeil road.
Identity:	Amili and activist Muslim village since Islam of the family of the Prophet (*ahl al-bayt*)[48] arrived more than 14 centuries ago.
Family situation:	raped by the Zionists since 1978.
Number of siblings:	10,000 exiled inside their own country.
Card number (*raqm sejel*):	25 *shahīd* and *shahīda* against the Turks and the French and the Zionists and the collaborators.
Judicial Record:[49]	sentenced to frustration (*qahr*) [and] deprivation (*hermān*) until the regime changes.

Occupation and the raising of religious consciousness: equated with resistance consciousness.[50]

The rest of the article mostly focused on specific operations that took place against Israeli occupation around the village of Aynata. Three years later, and over a two-year period, *al-'Ahd* published a long series of articles on the "162 villages and farms" occupied by Israel. Each issue contained a two-page article on a particular village or region. These articles were substantiated by interviews with local inhabitants, and information either derived from resistance efforts or independent research taken from other media.[51] The first in the series introduced the

---

[47] *al-'Ahd* (5/4/1987).
[48] A reference to the Shi'i Muslim currents.
[49] In Arabic *sejel 'adli*.
[50] Ibid.
[51] As confirmed by Mohammad Raad: interview with the author, June 2010.

area commonly called *al-sharīt al-muhtal* (the occupied line).[52] Beyond this new display of numbers and details on the villages and the geographical location in question, there is a particular way in which the area is defined: the articles are about 162 villages and farms that were "erased from the mother map" (*al-kharīta al-umm*), that were "lost twice, once when the enemy took over and the other when the state neglected them." The articles then propose to "go further south away from internal dissensions" in the hope of "recuperating a part of our identity (*zātina*) because the nation (*watan*) is one body, and if one part has concerns the other parts are prone to collapse, so what if that part is totally ripped off of that body."[53] This introductory article then lists all the villages and farms under Israeli occupation and gives the aim of starting a complete survey of each village "as land, people, history, territory, occupation and resistance," starting from the following week with Khiam, where the Israelis established their main prison in Lebanon.

History was the history of resistance, the history of the fight against the Israelis, the massacres that took place, the battles won, the numbers of houses demolished, and so on. The main difference is not just the increasing systematic character in the presentation of information but, first, the tense relationship with the state, and second, the urge to insert the existence of the movement into history as part of an imagined nation. Information about the economic, educational, and social situation of these villages up until the present day also became increasingly available. For example, the article on Khiam[54] started with a list of massacres and then went on to outline the different confessional makeup of the city by listing the names of all the families originating from there.[55] The next article, on Bint Jbeil and entitled "Bint Jbeil: the history of the resistance,"[56] started with an "old sheikh" from the village who could tell stories from the time of the French mandate to the present. The Bint Jbeil article was signed by Hadi Ibrahim, as were all subsequent articles. Again, the focus on a "history of resistance" can be found in the various directions the text takes. For example, the part on the economy of Bint Jbeil stresses the deterioration of affairs following the invasion of Palestine in 1948 by the Israelis, as trade was the main source of livelihood for that village. The Islamic markers follow the same rationale. The article on Ayta al-Shaab (among many others) focuses on the role of the *'ulamā'* in

[52] *al-'Ahd* (8/12/1990), 13.
[53] This organic conception of territory as belonging to a mother (Lebanese) nation, appears in many writings, not least Hassan Fadlallah's *Hizbullāh wal-dawla fī lubnān: al-ru'ya wal-masār* (Beirut: All Prints Distributors & Publishers, 2015).
[54] *al-'Ahd* (15/12/1990), 8–9.
[55] Originating somewhere means registered as being from that particular place as recorded in the Lebanese state's records.
[56] *al-'Ahd* (22/12/1990), 6–7.

the fight against the Israelis as early as 1948. We also learn minute details such as how the Israelis demolished the house of a certain Hajj Ali Lotfi accused of harboring resistance forces in 1969.[57]

These articles helped build the legitimacy of the resistance. In 2000 the Israeli army withdrew from most of the occupied territories of South Lebanon. At the time, Hizbullah retorted that the Shebaa farms, the hills of Kfarshuba, and the seven villages were all still under Israeli occupation and thus justified the continued existence of the Islamic resistance. Media and academics debated whether the party was looking for a pretext to continue its fight against Israel in order to legitimize the presence of its weapons. Shebaa and the Shebaa farms were occupied in 1967 during the second Israeli–Arab war, the seven villages were transferred to British mandate Palestine in 1924, and Kfarshuba was occupied by the Israelis in 1975 after repeated commando raids in the 1970s.[58] The Israeli army retreated from Kafarshuba village in 2000, but not from its hills, which strategically overlook Palestinian villages from the Golan Heights "up until Nablus." These villages and their interaction with the Israeli occupation produced a flurry of stories, but these writings helped to systematically classify them as sharing the same fate: being occupied and being part of Jabal Amil, especially the section that came to be called "the Occupied Belt" during the Israeli occupation. In light of this, I argue that the main point about Hizbullah's political agenda with regard to these territories is missed if one does not consider that whatever the true "intent" of Hizbullah's actions here, they developed as a direct consequence of the writing strategies and archiving practices of Hizbullah intellectuals.

Evidently, this territorial reclamation process, which not only predated the 2000 withdrawal but was actually part of the overall writing practices of the party since its debut, betrayed a systematic urge to archive, to legitimize, or sanctify what has been neglected, what has been left outside the bounds of state symbolic authority. The various arguments, metaphors, and writing styles articulated land as history and as resistance. Although the Shebaa farms are considered to be Lebanese and the seven villages Palestinian, as they predate the establishment of the modern state of Lebanon (1943) and are thus more easily referred to by Hizbullah's detractors as politically far-fetched, Hizbullah intellectuals consider both as part of their territorial heritage – as part of the imagined community of Jabal Amil.

---

[57] al-'Ahd (19/1/1991), 6.
[58] Kfarshuba has its own special article as part of the "Occupied Belt" series in al-'Ahd (5/10/1991), 10–11.

Indeed, Jabal Amil was imagined as the land of resistance without strictly defined borders in mind. The goal of reclaiming the location involved the systematic examination of all the land that is part of such an imaginary according to the various markers (language, confession, social status, and so on) and placing it in a temporal continuum through the writing of stories and histories. This is why Christian as well as Shi'i villages were included. For example, one could find as part of the series a long exposé on the extent to which al-Qulaya, a Maronite village, had a long history of differentiating itself from its environs and of being neglected.[59] Also, ten years before the withdrawal, and as part of the "Occupied Belt" series mentioned above, al-'Ahd had a special issue on Shebaa, as well as another on the Shebaa farms.[60] Each of the seven villages received a full two-page investigation with pictures of Lebanese identity cards (French mandate period) and tax payments by people registered in these villages. It is mostly after the year 2000 that media channels, intellectuals of all sorts, and political actors had to grapple with this as Hizbullah demanded that all these localities should be considered Lebanese territory. When writing about Hunin (one of the seven villages), Hadi Ibrahim remembered that the cleric Muhsin al-Amin had mentioned it in his book on Jabal Amil and that Ibn Jubayr, a medieval Arab geographer famous for his travels, mentioned Hunin as the main fortress and center of rule in Jabal Amil.

Two years later an interesting article on the seven villages carried the title "The foreigner gave it to the enemy, and the Lebanese state took back[61] its identity," written by Hanadi Muhammad and Saad Hamiyeh,[62] who argued that because the Lebanese state was territorially delineated on a confessional basis, new geographical boundaries left out certain villages – such as the seven villages – although they had initially been part of what was known as Jabal Amil. According to the article, they were handed over to the enemy in order to gain a strategic position in the region. The French authorities had initially included the villages in the newly drawn map of Lebanon, while keeping "the southern border open." The British, pressed by the Zionists, struck a deal with the French in order to get the villages as part of "Palestine," following the Sykes–Picot Agreement of 1916. The article displayed a picture of a French mandate

---

[59] al-'Ahd (6 Sha'bān 1412), 10–11.
[60] Israel would retreat from Shebaa village but not from the farms. These two locations seem to have been treated separately in common parlance, at least by Hizbullah and Israel. The al-'Ahd issue on the village of Shebaa is al-'Ahd (27 Ṣafar 1412), 14–15; on the Shebaa farms see al-'Ahd (4 Rabī' al-Awwal 1412), 12–13.
[61] In the sense of seizing it from the enemy.
[62] al-'Ahd (27/8/1993), 14–15.

"État du Grand Liban" identity card of one Hunin inhabitant, and told the story of the battles (and massacres) that allowed Zionists successively to take over the villages, encountering opposition in al-Malikiya, a symbolic "battle in the life of Muslims." What made these inhabitants Lebanese was the fact that they were recorded in a census carried out in 1921, and were clinging to Lebanese identity following a petition in 1922 presented by the mayor of Qadas, one of the villages. In fact, some people were able to get Lebanese nationality after a 1924 French mandate decree stipulating that "anyone who is of Turkish descent who lives on Lebanese territory on the 30th of August 1924 is Lebanese."[63]

Again, the crucial concern is with the identity of these villages and their attachment to a political entity. Representations of territory inevitably aimed at identification with the Lebanese state. Either the Lebanese state had neglected them, if not "disowned" them, or the enemy had attempted to snatch them, or both. Two words have been used to describe this process: *tahwīd* (Judaification) and *tatbī'* (normalization). The village of Adshit al-Qasir faced the danger of *tahwīd*. The subtitle of this article revealingly read: "The vanishing from the map of the nation."[64] Another article on Dayr Siryan was called "The struggle with normalization."[65] Normalization (or Judaification) in this sense symbolizes an acceptance of the status quo of occupation and the transformation of the territory from one "state of being" to another.

One should note that the stated goal of liberating Palestine, Lebanon, or any territory occupied by Israel followed the same logic: Their context induced an unavoidable confrontation with the Lebanese state, which had its own relationship to territory and history. The state of Lebanon attempted to produce clear boundaries, mostly reflecting colonial and post-colonial realities. Hizbullah's resistance project provided fresh writings on the concept of nationhood, which were constantly modified according to the militant practices on the ground. This urge to systematize understandings of territory was taking place against the backdrop of the absence/presence of the state and, along with various intellectual efforts to give it legitimacy, the delineation between Lebanon (reality) and Palestine (fantasy) became sharper with time, as the party engaged more directly with the multiple political developments. Indeed, nationalist movements across history have all in some way or another conformed to rationales of this kind. The interesting aspect in the case of Hizbullah is that the presence of the state and of a nationalistic imaginary

---

[63] Ibid.
[64] *al-'Ahd* (3/8/1991), 8.
[65] *al-'Ahd* (27/7/1991), 1.0

was prior to the formation of the organization. Hizbullah tries to recapture the state through this approach to territory, or at least what the state "should have been" for them. The same line of reasoning makes Hizbullah eternally wary of fully abandoning its organizational self-sufficiency to the benefit of the state.

Jihād al-Binā' Archives Space

Institutions were set up to replace the state's absence from parts of the territory. Jihād al-Binā' was created shortly after the Martyr's Association (see Chapter 2) in 1987, again mirroring Iranian institutions and signaling how central these institutions were to the formation of Hizbullah. The presence of such institutions enables a symbolic articulation of belonging to a space that has a specific political significance. Jihād al-Binā' rebuilds homes destroyed by Israeli (or other) military incursions. An article on Jihād al-Binā' around the time it was founded states that it targets rural areas as well as the southern suburbs where its first project was based, following the assassination attempt on Mohammad Hussein Fadlallah in Bir al-Abed, a car bomb that destroyed the buildings around Fadlallah's home. For example, the first activities of Jihād al-Binā' involved digging wells "in rural areas," according to this article. Its infrastructural work mostly focuses on the Bekaa and the part of the south that was not occupied by the Israeli army. But the article also shows that most of the work done happens to be in the Bekaa, a zone inaccessible not just to the Israelis but to the state. In effect, the Bekaa was the center of resistance training and all sorts of other activities, at a time when the south was mostly occupied.

Through this ongoing practice of rebuilding Jihād al-Binā' is able to chart territory through the same type of statistical or data production methods used by the Martyr's Association. In the midst of the run-up to the first parliamentary elections in which Hizbullah planned to participate in 1992, al-'Ahd published reports of Jihād al-Binā''s latest achievements; "700 work sites in 67 villages" was the title of a long and detailed article citing various villages (mostly from the Bekaa) that received aid and infrastructural help.[66]

Jihād al-Binā' also symbolizes the institutionalization, if not corporatization, of tasks in which Hizbullah was involved. If Hizbullah resembles a state within a state, it is a state that mirrors a corporation. If anything, Hizbullah as a "non-state actor" shows how certain social and political tasks can be carried out without traditional states and by emulating corporations. The more tasks are "corporatized," the more archiving processes create data and information that can be used for the politics of remembering.

[66] al-'Ahd (27/8/1993), 10–11.

The Bekaa and Baalbek as a Symptom of Nationalist Construction Priorities

An early *al-'Ahd* article showed that the first descriptions of villages came not from Jabal Amil but from Western Bekaa. As *al-'Ahd* interviews the family of a martyr, readers get the first rewriting of the history of a territory symbolizing resistance in its infancy. The title of the article is *"al-'Ahd* meets a group [the word used is *kawkabat*, meaning constellation, but also convoy] of families of martyrs from Mashghara."[67] The subtitle gives the names of the families being met and a summary of what they had to say. "The wife of martyr Nassar: the Jews described him as the strong guy (*za'īm*) of the resistance, the father of the martyr Sobh: I won't regret my son after you, O Nassar." These articles contained several different types of statements about social realities. In this case, for example, the writer(s) gave an interesting description of the martyrs' place of origin, Mashghara. Mashghara is a village in the Western Bekaa, falling outside of Israeli control, where Hizbullah began its military training. Most of the first fighters were actually from the area.

The abstract of the article on Mashghara started with the following sentence: "Islamic are the villages of Western Bekaa and it refuses all other denominations. Believing (*mu'mina*) they are and believing is their people and they refuse all other attributes (*sifāt*)." Then again we find a reference to heirs of the tradition, a recollection of past figures as the writer says of the Western Bekaa that "from Islam was its clay (*tinatuha*) and so it lasted and in the shade (*kanf*) of Islam it lived and so it grew. Others have tainted its chest with the martyred blood [blood that 'testified of' *shahida*] and killing/dying (*al-qatl*) was a habit to her and its dignity from God a testimony," referring to the sayings of Husayn son of Ali.[68]

These references become more salient when juxtaposed with the prevailing territorial appellations of the time. Mashghara, for example, is a confessionally mixed village, having both Christian and Muslim populations. A glance at what is published over the internet shows different writings of history: websites describe the city as a repository for Phoenician, Roman, and crusader ruins. The name Mashghara, according to a Wikipedia page on the subject, derives from *mashghar*, which in Phoenician means "a flow of water." The page does not mention an "Islamic" heritage, either with regard to historical episodes or even the legacy of the resistance. This is but a symptom of Christian – and especially Maronite – domination of writings of history, as discussed in

---

[67] *al-'Ahd* (2/8/1986), 6.
[68] This is drawn from the same saying of Zayn al-'Abidīn mentioned in Chapter 2, which is mentioned in most of Nasrallah's speeches.

Chapter 3. The *al-'Ahd* text achieves an ideological subversion of this narrative by suffusing the text with Islamic tropes. The text continues: "On the shoulders of Amila [Jabal Amil] and on its lap it [Mashghara] grew *tara 'ra 'at*", and other literary exercises develop: "Islam embraced Amila, then it embraced the land of Western Bekaa and passion increased … and lovers fused in the marvelous (*raw 'at*) experience of Islamic principles." The article then gives an account of the various interviews conducted. This gives an opportunity for interviewees to talk about their own impression of the martyr – to give life, so to speak, to the martyrs, most of the time employing the kinds of references previously outlined in this book.

The Bekaa, and especially the Western Bekaa (mostly occupied by Israel after 1982), is one of the most important regions for Hizbullah, given that it saw the birth of the organization and served as the main location for training from the early 1980s until the Israeli withdrawal in 2000. It allowed Hizbullah to form, train, and develop into the strong organization it is today, shielded from both the Israeli occupation and state interference. The main founders of Hizbullah, Abbas Moussawi and Sobhi Tufayli, were both from Baalbek, and, as Daher argues, Hizbullah was for a long time a Bekaa-based organization.[69] This is confirmed by Raad, who explained that *al-'Ahd* was for the first three years based in Baalbek before moving to Dahyeh, and managed to collect all its information through its correspondents' dangerous movements in Dahyeh, and even in the South.[70] This is partly why the first articles appearing in *al-'Ahd* about resistance-related themes were solely focused on Bekaa-based regions, fighters, or operations.

The centrality of the Bekaa, and especially the city of Baalbek, in setting up the Islamic resistance cannot be overstated, and it is noteworthy how this space was gradually overshadowed by the importance of the South. Even though the resistance owes its success to its origins in Western Bekaa regions, Jabal Amil gradually gained most of the attention through new (resistance-oriented) writings of history.

As a result, Western Bekaa and Baalbek did not receive the intellectual attention that Jabal Amil and Dahyeh gained in the quest for legitimacy through subverting prevailing writings of history and creating alternative narratives and imaginaries. Books written by Shi'i scholars on the Bekaa or Baalbek were mostly concerned with the *'asha 'ir* (clans, extended families), the tense relations between older tribal groupings and the interaction with newer ones.[71] In comparison, themes found in the

[69] See Daher, *Le Hezbollah*, 76–83.
[70] Mohammad Raad, interview with the author, June 2011.
[71] See for example Ghassan Tah, *Shī'at lubnān: al-'ashirat, al-hizb, al-dawla (Baalbak–al-Hermel namuzajan)* (Beirut: Dar al-Maarif al-Hikmiyya, 2005).

attempts at writing the history of Jabal Amil brought it to the forefront as a flourishing center of education and clerical fame, resistance culture, etc. For example, the article quoted earlier on Dahyeh and the concept of security contained a passage arguing that the Bekaa never had the religious revival that the South had experienced, and thus continued to be ruled by tribal formations.[72]

Moreover, when al-Manar TV started broadcasting video clips featuring footage of Lebanese regions, those featuring Baalbek were usually symbolized by images of Roman temple ruins, a dominant theme exported by Lebanese state cultural institutions and its affiliated artistic practices. During the period following the independence of Lebanon, Baalbek became famous as a national emblem due to the Roman ruins adjacent to the main city. For decades Lebanese would flock to the region for the annual arts festival, avoiding the main city.[73] At the symbolic level, the South as a marginalized space struggled to propose new forms of legitimacy, while the Bekaa-based discursive articulations simply espoused the prevailing one.

Yet some form of resistance to dominant discursive practices was still present in the Bekaa: During the summer of 2009 Hizbullah set up an exhibition to commemorate the July 2006 war in the entrance of the Roman site where tourists usually come throughout the year. Indeed, it paled in comparison to the usual exhibitions organized in Dahyeh (such as the "House of the Spider"), both in size and in quality, demonstrating again that the center of cultural practices was the southern suburbs of Beirut, even though the Bekaa had previously been the origin of the resistance as such.

These exhibitions' features are a trace of the resistance on the ground: Israeli weapons collected, the reproduction of operations rooms, offices, training areas, battles, and statistics of victories, lists of martyrs, pictures and videos of all sorts. Yet even at that level, a much more imposing exhibition was set up in Mleeta, a village in the South displaying an impressive array of Israeli military material collected throughout the years, especially after the war in July 2006. This "multi-media theme park" has welcomed more than 500,000 visitors since May 2010.[74]

---

[72] al-'Ahd 2 (4/7/1984), 3.

[73] See, for example, Christopher Stone, *Popular Culture and Nationalism in Lebanon: The Fairouz and Rahbani Nation* (London: Routledge, 2007) for a study of the importance of Baalbek as a site in the nationalistic constructions of the Rahbani brothers' theater. Many Hizbullah nationalist or pro-resistance songs have used similar idioms.

[74] *The Independent*, 15/08/2010, available at www.independent.co.uk/news/world/middle-east/hezbollah-theme-park-draws-the-crowds-2052895.html.

The ambiguous position of Baalbek and Western Bekaa in this reclaiming of space reveals the slow ascendancy of Jabal Amil as the main site of resistance, although Baalbek and Western Bekaa are considered to be the original sites from which resistance sprang, and Hasan Nasrallah constantly reminds his audiences of the centrality of this region. Ironically, Nasrallah, the first cleric from Jabal Amil to become secretary general, replaced Abbas Moussawi, and before him Sobhi Tufayli, both from Western Bekaa (respectively from Britel and al-Nabi Shayth).

The causes of the marginalization of the Western Bekaa and Baalbek, despite being the hinterland of resistance, seem logical enough. First, the region under occupation is the South. Second, it is true that Jabal Amil has a tradition of renowned clerics, and this phenomenon marries well with the Islamic imprint that Hizbullah wants to project. But what I suggest is more important is that Baalbek and Western Bekaa's unruly tribal formations are a challenge for Hizbullah's "modern" organization as a political party with systematic and meritocratic hierarchical structures. And whereas Hizbullah quickly prevailed over the South of Lebanon once the Israelis withdrew, the same cannot be said about Western Bekaa and Baalbek, where semi-autonomous armed clans still constitute a challenge to Hizbullah.

6   Confronting the State: Between Party and Community

In the mid-1980s the prominent Shi'i *marja' dīnī* (literally religious reference or example) Ayatollah Mohammad Hussein Fadlallah published a paper in the journal *al-Muntalaq* entitled "Who will lead the movement of change: the party of the community, or the community of the party?" Although rhetorical in its contours, his discussion of the question signaled a phenomenon that was crucial in understanding the ideological constructions of Hizbullah for the years to come as it aimed to define the causes to which the party of God owed its existence. The debate that Fadlallah opened up was symptomatic of a paradox faced by Hizbullah and the projected community from which it emerged. If change is understood as an overall social and cultural transformation, then the whole of the community should be involved in this activity. Fadlallah, other clerics, and like-minded laymen thought that social transformation was a concerted yet disseminated effort. Indeed, since the 1970s, and through the successive legacies of Musa al-Sadr, Mohammad Mahdi Shamseddine, Fadlallah, and others, the Shi'i community began to engage in social and political mobilizations of its own.[1] The prevailing atmosphere in the early 1980s was one of multiple political and social movements, parties, associations, committees, university groups, and so on. The state of Lebanon was gradually disintegrating, and militias had cantonized security in several areas of Beirut, Dahyeh being one.

But the Israeli invasion of 1982 precipitated the urgency of devising concrete plans to fight the enemy. The need for order, prioritizing, and most importantly narrowing down the content of the political project to particular demands involved among other things the formation of an organization. The direct cause for the formation of Hizbullah was the coalescing of several movements under the strategic intervention of the Pasdaran, who arrived in Baalbek in 1982 shortly after the invasion and

---

[1] As opposed to being diffused in various leftist or pan-Arabist political parties and organizations.

were received, as was mentioned earlier, by Sobhi Tufayli and Abbas Moussawi (who later became Hizbullah's first and second secretaries general respectively). The objective was to devise an organization that could fight occupation.[2] Over the years Hizbullah became a highly organized and secretive party while simultaneously acquiring legitimacy from popular mechanisms. Yet all along, there was an ironic conflict between the democratic nature of the political processes that led to the popularity of Hizbullah and the non-democratic, if not authoritarian, apparatus of how parties act on certain issues. When Fadlallah warned of this in his article, he was describing a problem that most modern political formations face, namely the particular dynamics of the constantly negotiated relationship between party and community in their quest for the state.[3]

For Fadlallah, the phenomenon of Hizbullah was different from "Western" political parties, as the former type of political formation emanated from the *umma* (the Islamic community) and kept an organic link to it. A political Islam is practiced every day in mosques where discussions take place alongside prayers and worship rituals. Unlike other political parties, Hizbullah's members have their "minds open to the intellectual and spiritual concerns of the people" and leaders have legitimacy to lead under the guidelines of the prevailing legal (i.e. Islamic) apparatuses.[4]

Fadlallah's argument is at times tortuous and frustratingly incomplete in trying to explain the difference between Hizbullah and other political parties, especially in terms of clarifying the difference between party–community relations and other secular party politics. But he does manifest the concern that a strong organic link should exist between Hizbullah's political practice and the demands of the community at large, a link that other political formations of the twentieth century had failed to maintain. The community is in symbiosis with the party through several institutional arrangements and is as important as the party in contributing to the process of change. The community is in a general cultural state-of-being linked to a political project, what the deputy president of Hizbullah, Naim Qassem, a student of Fadlallah, would later call *mujtamā' al-muqāwama* (the society of resistance).

[2] For a good description of these first organizational "moments" see Daher, *Le Hezbollah*, 76–87.

[3] On this, Antonio Gramsci's discussion of the function of modern political parties and their "natural progress to State power" is timeless. See Gramsci, *Prison Notebooks*, 152–154, especially his requirements for a political party to exist, which are strikingly similar to Fadlallah's discussion.

[4] Muhammad Hussein Fadlallah, "Man al-lazi yaqūd 'amaliyat al-taghīr hizb al-umma aw ummat al-hizb," in al-Haraka al-islāmīyya: humūm wa qadāya (Beirut: Dar al Malak, 2001), 71.

According to Fadlallah, if a party-like structure is to emerge from the community in order to produce the change needed, it must conform to certain basic principles. For example, secrecy may be necessary in the context of impending danger, but it has its limits.[5] An "Islamic education"[6] is imperative in order to avoid all forms of distancing from the community, a situation in which party members often find themselves, as they become "slaves to the party."[7] And although Fadlallah is clear on the "clerically led" character of such a movement, he goes so far as establishing the limits of the authority of the *walī al-faqīh*, which should be in line with "general Islamic political objectives."[8] These opinions delineating the credentials of *walī al-faqīh* were repeated often in the subsequent literature emanating from within and around the party.[9]

Fadlallah published his article in *al-Muntalaq* in 1985; the journal had been founded in 1976 by the Lebanese Association of Muslim Students (al-Ittiḥād al-Lubnānī lil-Talaba al-Muslimīn or al-Ittiḥād), of which several key future Hizbullah members such Mohammad Raad had been members[10]. As argued by Daher, even though al-Ittiḥād called for a socio-religious awakening, judging from the issues of *al-Muntalaq* of the period, it was neither specifically concerned with the Palestinian question nor was it advocating radical political change à la Iranian revolution.[11] This complacent social Islam seemed mostly concerned with a reworking of Muslim identity, social and pious practices in a turbulent period of weak state sovereignty. Al-Ittiḥād clearly contrasted with other social actors that championed radical revolutionary causes, such as Sadiq al-Moussawi, an Iranian cleric who arrived on the Lebanese scene in 1976, and who founded al-Haraka al-Islāmīyya (al-Haraka), which called for the toppling of the Maronite regime and the installation of an Islamic state, again in this case not concerned with fighting the Israelis. Although Hizbullah shared an outright rejection of the current confessional regime, it differed with al-Haraka's political ideals, instead focusing more on building military resistance against Israel.[12] The fate of al-Moussawi's movement was linked to

---

[5] Ibid., 90–91.

[6] Ibid., 85.

[7] Ibid., 86.

[8] Ibid., 82.

[9] For a detailed description of the role of the *walī al-faqīh* in Hizbullah see Daher, *Le Hezbollah*, 214–217.

[10] Future Hizbullah members came from three main organizations: Amal (or a faction of Amal known as Amal al-Islāmī); al-Daʿwa Party; and al-Ittiḥād, as well as various semi-independent groups in the south. See Daher, *Le Hezbollah*. Sankari adds Tajamuʿ lil-ʿUlamaʾ al-Muslimīn: see Sankari, *Fadlallah*, 194–198.

[11] Daher, *Le Hezbollah*, 57.

[12] In fact, al-Haraka was much more preoccupied with rallying "Muslims" against the regime than engaging in resistance efforts: ibid, 60. Also as explained in Chapter 3,

internal Iranian political disagreement over "exporting the revolution" to Lebanon. As Khomeini seemed to be more interested in the events unfolding in Iraq and favored a more focused "Lebanese" resistance against Israel, Hussein Ali Montazeri, al-Moussawi's patron, ended up losing to the more pragmatic faction of Ali Akbar Mohtashemi, the Iranian ambassador in Syria in the early 1980s. Mohtashemi sponsored the Pasdaran mission to Baalbek, which was aimed at training militants to fight Israeli forces.[13]

Hassan Fadlallah reinforced the claim that Hizbullah represented a different political line when he mapped al-Daʿwa Party's influence on Shiʿi political "infiltration" of Amal in the later 1970s and early 1980s.[14] Echoing Daher's work on the formative period, Fadlallah described al-Daʿwa and other Islamic groups as concerned with general "strategic" questions of political change affecting the identity of the community and not with "urgent political matters" (*ahdāth al-siyāsiya al-tāriʾa*),[15] something early autonomous resistance initiatives would focus on (such as the legacy of Raghib Harb). Fadlallah also stated that Amal was for a long time an umbrella organization for all those formations.[16]

In 1985 Hizbullah started spreading its resistance in the South, breaking out of its Bekaa-based isolation.[17] Fadlallah's article was written at a time when the resistance had assumed a more stable formation. A party was needed in order to produce change, but a party's political power had to be defined in clerical terms. It seems clear here that by this time Hizbullah had become a fully formed group distinguished from the other social and political initiatives that prevailed at the time of its formation. Was Fadlallah hoping that Hizbullah could be involved in much more than just military resistance? Was he trying to legally delineate the relationship between party and general community awakening? Either Fadlallah was too ambitious as to what Hizbullah, then still in its infancy, was able to do and maybe hoped to play a role in it, or he could foresee the development of a party and its relationship to the community and attempted to define its limits.

When Fadlallah was writing in the early 1980s, the climate was conducive to grand revolutionary projects, and his article signaled a strong hope for clerics at large and other "Islamicized" militants and intellectuals

---

Hizbullah's rejection of the confessional system seems to be linked to its representation of the Christian political other.

[13] For a discussion of Sadiq al-Moussawi's movement and its difference with the nascent Hizbullah see Daher, *Le Hezbollah*, 58–60.

[14] Ibid., 80–81.

[15] Ibid.

[16] Ibid.

[17] As the Israelis withdrew from Saida that year, Hizbullah slowly established itself as a force to be reckoned with: ibid., 104–108.

that Hizbullah would become the organizational and political catalyst of a generalized Islamic awakening (*sahwa islāmīyya*). As noted above, the multitude of militant and/or intellectual organizations, parties, committees and associations of all kinds were ripe for action, engaging in different types of social and cultural initiatives. By delimiting the scope of action of Hizbullah as a political party, Fadlallah may have been preparing the intellectual and juridical ground to link a general communitarian change to party-led political work, assigning to each field its responsibilities and limitations. His writings provided a cultural background in which Hizbullah made sense of its social mobilization through the use of the different Islamic tropes.[18] In effect, Fadlallah may have been, in this article in *al-Muntalaq*, the grand ideologue of the party that became known as Hizbullah.[19]

Yet Fadlallah was never institutionally linked to Hizbullah even though he was highly popular among the community.[20] And, from the mid-1990s, he gradually drifted away from the party. But he never condemned the legitimacy of the resistance project and the necessity for Hizbullah to carry it through. Instead, Fadlallah continued to play an important social and institutional role in the general shaping of religious and community ethics. Fadlallah, as Hizbullah MP Hassan Fadlallah would describe him, along with Mohammad Mahdi Shamseddine, labored at "the religious and cultural level with a social and institutional dimension (*tawajuhāt ijtimā'iyya wa mu'assasātiyya*)," unlike Musa al-Sadr, who worked at the "religious and social level with a political dimension (*tawajuhāt siyāsiyya*),"[21] thereby reinforcing Hizbullah's claim to al-Sadr's political legacy.

Fadlallah first distanced himself from Hizbullah after disagreeing on the legitimacy of Khamenei first as the successor of Khomeini as the *walī al-faq īh*, a position he thought could go to more prominent *'ālim* based in Iraq, and then in 1995, and second as the main religious *marja'* after the death of Abu al-Qassem al-Khu'i, who was one of the most prominent *marja'* alive after Khomeini. Fadlallah's point may have been to put primacy of religious knowledge ahead of regional political imperative, arguing either that the *walī al-faqīh* could come from any part of the Muslim world and was not restricted to an Iranian political position or even that *wilāyat al-faqīh* as an

---

[18] A proof of the cultural influence of Fadlallah on the early ideological production of Hizbullah is his Friday sermon, which was published weekly in the pages of *al-'Ahd*.

[19] There is also the attempt by Ali Kurani: *Ṭarīqat hizb allāh*.

[20] For a rich description of the relationship between Fadlallah and Hizbullah see Adham Saouli, "Intellectuals and Political Power in Social Movements: The Parallel Paths of Fadlallah and Hizbullah," *British Journal of Middle Eastern Studies* 41:1(2014), 97–116.

[21] Fadlallah, *Hizbullāh wal-dawla fī lubnān*, 84.

institution was not really needed after the death of Khomeini.[22] This contrasted with his declared allegiance to Khomeini's theory during the 1980s, even before most Shi'i jurists in Lebanon, Iraq, and Iran had accepted it.[23]

But to return to the main point of our discussion, Hizbullah first developed as a military organization dedicated to fighting occupation, and it remained relatively centered on this core purpose. Hizbullah's founders were disillusioned with the corrupt and inefficient dimension of "political work," and their focus was on how to form an organization that could fight Israel unencumbered by such activity. In this sense, when Hizbullah decided to engage in elections and then to participate in government later on in 2005, those decisions were geared at protecting the project of military resistance by having to gradually come to grasp, albeit prudently and conservatively, the realities of its political environment.

It is now safe to argue that Hizbullah was a significant departure from other, more radical and revolutionary, projects that were hatched in the early 1980s following the Islamic Revolution euphoria. It did benefit from and stayed heavily indebted to this cultural heritage, first in its reliance on it in the very early stages for mobilization and consolidation purposes, and second whenever it was asked to produce theory or theoretical formulations about its raison d'être. Gradually it became clear that alignment with Iran was dictated by political and security rationales, so much so that even when most "religious" and "social" imperatives were not there (as other social actors articulated it, namely MH Fadlallah) the bond remained resilient.

Most of Hizbullah's affiliated institutions that emerged over the years were dependent on or subservient to the primary purpose of resistance. Islamic practices were subordinate to the cause of armed struggle and not vice versa.[24] According to Hassan Fadlallah, the difference between Hizbullah and other parties in the 1980s was that the former was the only organization lacking a party-like structure and that it did not engage in "political work" (lam tumāriss 'amalan siyāsiyan).[25] Indeed, for Fadlallah, Hizbullah "worked in its early stages as a resistance and did not have other purposes outside this role."[26] As Daher notes, "the Secretary General of Hizbullah Hassan Nasrallah is primarily a military commander"[27] and the rest of Hizbullah's institutional infrastructure is subservient to the role of the military organization. In a revealing

[22] For a discussion of this see Saouli, "Intellectuals and Political Power," 115–116.
[23] Sankari, Fadlallah, 176.
[24] Daher, Le Hezbollah, 25.
[25] Fadlallah, Hizbullāh wal-dawla fī lubnān, 87.
[26] Ibid., 88.
[27] Daher, Le Hezbollah, 24.

interview with Mustafa Amin, Nasrallah explicitly stated: "We wanted a resistance, we did not come to create a political party."[28]

But how should this distinction between resistance and political party be read? First it means that Hizbullah is torn between the reappraisal of what political work means from an Islamic perspective as developed by Fadlallah and Kurani – that, to a certain extent, is al-Da'wa's legacy – and second that Hizbullah, born from the urgency of fighting occupation, was formed as a purely military organization unencumbered by such agendas. The calls for a particular type of work that stands between more conventional political party activities and broad social "Islamic" movements[29] was dropped for narrower military work. Yet it remained heavily indebted to al-Da'wa's legacy in using mosques, *husayniyya*s, *hawza*s, etc. as fields for social mobilization and recruitment. So the politics of Hizbullah are narrowly defined. The "party" that developed subsequently, especially in the 1990s, was dependent on this initial impetus and thus still struggles to define its raison d'être outside the resistance project.

If there is no party then there is no state project. Slogans exist because of cultural indebtedness and for mobilization purposes. The call for an Islamic state was a general slogan that "Islamists" used to question the legitimacy of the Lebanese state, which was dominated by Christian political elites. It does not mean that the slogan did not resonate in the hearts and minds of people at large, but in terms of it translating into a particular political strategy or vision, the ideological production of Hizbullah presents virtually nothing. And this is understandable given what has been explained above. As will be seen below, it also helps explain the role of the *walī al-faqīh* for Hizbullah, and the later gradual changes in its relationship with its immediate environment.

Yet Hizbullah soon recognized that it could not just remain a military organization, because first, it needed the political legitimizing clout of its environment, the empowering mechanisms of surrounding institutions (not least the state); and second, it was irrevocably involved in shaping the general affairs of its community, which it had already started doing at least for military mobilization purposes, fulfilling at least one of the imperatives outlined by MH Fadlallah. Hizbullah's "political work" gradually became an imperative in order to create forms of stability in its environment.

Thus, contrary to the argument that Hizbullah moved from the idea of an Islamic state to one of compromise and Lebanonization,[30] it seems fair to say that Hizbullah was a military organization with the objective of

---

[28] I am indebted to Aurélie Daher for pointing out this quotation: Amin, *al-Muqāwama fī lubnān*, 426.
[29] Kurani, *Ṭarīqat hizb allāh*, 15.
[30] See for this thesis Alagha, *The Shifts in Hizbullah's Ideology*.

fighting occupation, mostly unconcerned with politics or political projects, yet gradually came to develop party-like structures. Understanding
Hizbullah through either the Lebanonization or radical thesis depends
squarely on confusing Hizbullah slogans with the practical use of these
slogans by other prevailing cultural and political initiatives of the time.
In the early 1980s Hizbullah did propose political solutions to the prevailing civil war situation which involved representations of the state, but
they were at most rhetorical slogans, or just ideological templates of
general Shi'i discontent, with hazy political substance. What Hizbullah
struggled with in the 1980s became the main point of concern in the
subsequent years, and remains so. The relationship between a military
resistance, a party-led movement, and a state project came to coexist in
the presence of a political situation that was deemed to be eternally
unstable and unfit to protect the interests represented by the organization. In other words, instead of having a definite political project from its
beginnings, like many of its predecessors, Hizbullah found itself forced to
develop such a project only gradually in order to defend its military
organization, by accommodating with the confessional system as the
"natural" national formula (see Chapter 3).

At the core of Hizbullah's political work lies an unresolved tension
between the politics of military resistance and that of party-led politics
of statehood. MH Fadlallah's article signaled aspects of the dilemma in
which Hizbullah was placed. Hizbullah, which had started as a military
organization fighting occupation, emerged in an environment in need of
social and political change. Partly for mobilization purposes, or because
of the various convictions of its key members, but mostly because of the
imperative caused by being the leading power, Hizbullah became
involved in leading, to a certain extent, the process of change, while at
the same time prioritizing its core mission. Meanwhile, the community
itself kept reproducing and developing social practices that escaped the
influence of the party, given that even in the formative stages of the party
social change was visualized by different groups and actors in varying
ways and degrees, as seen above.[31]

---

[31] This is where I disagree to a certain extent with Harb and Deeb's analysis of Hizbullah
monopolizing cultural activities in Dahyeh and other Shi'i-dominated regions in
Lebanon. Hizbullah acts in these instances mainly to protect resistance activity (a point
mentioned by the authors, but not always pushed to its logical implications, in
Mona Harb and Lara Deeb, "Culture as History and Landscape: Hizbullah's Efforts to
Shape an Islamic Milieu in Lebanon," *Arab Studies Journal* 19:2 (2011), 10–41. They
also do mention "limited cultural control" (Mona Harb and Lara Deeb, *Leisurely Islam:
Negotiating Morality and Geography in Shi'i South Beirut* (Princeton: Princeton University
Press, 2013), 74–75).

Hizbullah developed its relationship with the state slowly, on terms that are still being negotiated, as it gradually came to understand what it is as a political entity. Ideological production that tries to define visions and purposes of the party can shed light on understanding this relationship between party and state. My main argument is that Hizbullah's attempt at theorizing the party involves a constant fallback to writing its own history, that is, the history of the resistance, which betrays an uneasy relationship with the idea of being a party. And in so doing, Hizbullah tells the story of its tumultuous relationship with the state. In the remainder of this chapter I will first discuss a few aspects of attempts at writing theory and then move to some of the writings that show Hizbullah's relationship with the state through interesting discussions of concepts of the nation.

Writing Hizbullah: Legitimizing Political Presence, from Theory to History?

As I have argued throughout this book, Hizbullah is engaged in a politics of remembrance, in an ongoing rearticulation of various events of the past and their implications for the understanding of land and people. Hizbullah has consistently archived events that made up its history. But these events consisted mostly of military achievements. Hizbullah-affiliated intellectuals moved over the years from recording a specific battle and the minute details of its unfolding to much grander historical writing on the resistance. There is a clear continuity of narration between the various articles found in the early issues of al-'Ahd and the most recent biographies of the party written by Hassan Fadlallah, whose writing we first encountered in Chapter 5. In between there is the foundational book written by Naim Qassem, who is, unsurprisingly for the only theorist of Hizbullah, a student of Mohammad Hussein Fadlallah.

Writing the history of the resistance starts by relating a particular experience of military operations. In 1988 a long article depicting one seemingly important battle that took place in Meydun is but an example of many accumulated texts that demonstrate the archival practices of Hizbullah. The importance of remembering the events of Meydun in 1991[32] lies in the fact that a newly appointed government was calling into question the necessity of the resistance – or indeed the existence of military groups other than the army. This article took as a witness (shahīd is the word used) the victory of Meydun as a proof of the righteousness of the resistance and why it should continue. The detailed description of the battle (al-malḥama) testified to the necessity of the resistance as a political

---

[32] al-'Ahd (10/5/1991), 9.

practice. Every martyr commemoration is an occasion to recall the legacy of the resistance, the latest battles, the various details of particular military operations. By the early 1990s Hizbullah's archival practices had devised very elaborate databases of these events, as seen in al-'Ahd, and as listed in the party's annual calendars.

These attempts at archiving the successes of the resistance piled up over the years and became a catalyst for writing the history of Hizbullah or the Islamic resistance. The major Hizbullah historian is Hassan Fadlallah. Revealingly, his books, which capture phases of Hizbullah's militant legacy, were written following major military events. His first book, al-Khayār al-ākhar, was written in 1994, after the Israelis launched the 1993 Operation Accountability attacks against Hizbullah. In 1997 Fadlallah wrote Harb al-irādāt after Operation Grapes of Wrath, which was another Israeli attempt at weakening Hizbullah's military capabilities. And yet again, the Israeli withdrawal of 2000 triggered a flurry of writing not just about the history of Hizbullah, amongst which was Fadlallah's book Sukūt al-wahm,[33] but also all kinds of retrospectives and studies about the fight against Israel. Writing history was indubitably important because of this necessity to archive the achievements of the resistance, the advances made on the ground, and the legitimacy acquired from it. The different Israeli wars became markers of Hizbullah's various stages: the invasion of 1982; the partial withdrawal of 1985; the 1993 and 1996 Israeli operations; the 2000 withdrawal; and finally the July 2006 war, all inscribing what Hizbullah became. Yet history writing was important because it was the only effective ideological device to explain what Hizbullah "is."

Hizbullah, the Party, and Beyond

At the time that MH Fadlallah was writing his 1985 article, several attempts at defining Hizbullah theoretically appeared in al-'Ahd, as well as independent book publications from the early period of its formation. The questions that were posed to define the movement would remain unanswered simply because it was never necessary to answer them, and instead, buoyed by the experience on the ground, the archiving of the human legacy, the history of the other, territory, and thus the memory of resistance practiced on the ground (especially in the sense of facing the Israeli occupier) later informed definitions of Hizbullah as the bearer of the resistance as a project. This project gained substance through the actions performed throughout time, the line of conduct to be transmitted,

---

[33] Hassan Fadlallah, Sukūt al-wahm (Beirut: Dar al-Hadi, 2001).

and ultimately the various promises fulfilled, and that would be poten-
tially fulfilled in the future (such as the liberation of Jerusalem).

The second issue of *al-'Ahd* published a small article that tried to explain
what lies behind the term Hizbullah, and what it represents as a cultural
and political organized force. This early 1984 anonymous text started with
the two Qur'anic verses that mention the term Hizbullah.[34] The author(s)
then argued that Hizbullah as a social movement was different from previous attempts at mobilizing because it is a "populist" movement that
"transcends tribal, organizational, or party-like formations."[35] This drew
the author(s) into an "Introduction to the concept of Hizbullah" to prove
that although the movement transcends all types of organizational frameworks, people's affiliation to it is "based on a clear political direction" that
follows a "legitimate mandate" (*wilāyat shar'iyya*). This subjection to the
wilāyat implies a hierarchical order of authority from the Prophet down to
clerics and other leaders in order to fulfill the norms of tradition.
So Hizbullah is neither a chaotic mass movement nor a narrow political
party. Rather, "it is a series of initiatives emanating from the people of the
umma in an organized way and under the umbrella of the legitimate
commitment (*al-iltizām al shar'ī*). In other words, Hizbullah is an "organized movement for the crowd of believers (*jamāhīr al-mu'mina*) under the
framework of the commitment to the *wilāyat al-faqīh*".

Wilāyat al-faqīh permits this ideological leap from conventional, sectarian, traditional, etc. to doctrinal, cause-driven, forms of allegiance. This is
an idea that comes back in Naim Qassem's book *Hizbullah*, which was
published almost two decades later.[36] More importantly, the article stresses
that if Hizbullah avoids chaos by aligning to *walī al-faqīh*, it enlarges its
room for maneuver. The article stresses that one key difference from other
Islamic movements of the time was that Hizbullah is not "a party organization that performs prayer and *zakāt* while they are on their knees, and
cannot participate in decision-making processes unless according to executive clear-cut and limited orders." How does allegiance to *walī al-faqīh*
permit this flexible political work? Daher has an excellent summary of the
organization implications of this in her book,[37] and here I am mostly
interested in its ideological undertones, specifically in the projection of
a particular understanding of community and state, as will be seen below.

This article was published a few months before the first Israeli withdrawal
in 1985, notably from Saida, an episode which saw the rise of Hizbullah as an
autonomous organization. These early formulations of the uniqueness of

[34] Sūrat al-Mā'ida, verse 56; Sūrat al-Mujādila, verse 22.
[35] *al-'Ahd* 2 (4/7/1984), 6.
[36] Qassem, *Hizbullah*, 33.
[37] Daher, *Le Hezbollah*, 214–220. Also Qassem, *Hizbullah*, 77–80.

"the party" of God as opposed to others can also be found in Ali Kurani's *Ṭarīqat hizb allāh fī al-'amal al-islāmī*, published sometime in this period. Kurani also stresses the non-party structure of Hizbullah and its difference from other Islamic organizations,[38] perhaps having al-Da'wa in mind, and he has a long discussion of Hasan al-Banna's Muslim Brotherhood, which he seems to have held in high esteem.[39] Kurani develops an intricate conceptualization of the "party of God" that is supposed to bring together any group that fights for the protection of Islam at a political level. Thus, there can only be one Hizbullah, or party of God, which unites (*yuwaḥed*) all similar types of organization in the world. In contrast, other parties are the "party of Satan" (*hizb al-shaytān*) because they are irremediably divided, not least through organizational differences and purposes.[40] This is why Kurani defines the party along "ideological lines," according to intellectual production, ideas, beliefs, and not "tribal, confessional and organizational" affiliations.

The contrast between these formulations and the political realities that shape the highly organized and hermetical gradual development of Hizbullah cannot be overstated. Yet these writings signal the ideological space in which Hizbullah-affiliated intellectuals have navigated ever since. Kurani, from al-Da'wa, who left the Lebanese scene for Qum, and MH Fadlallah, who attempted, as described above, to delimit Hizbullah as part of a larger social, religious, and political *sahwa* or *hāla islāmiyya*, ended up slightly outside this political project.

Yet there remained a necessity to articulate the cultural uniqueness of Hizbullah. The most notable example, published in the early 2000s, was by Naim Qassem, a cleric who since 1992 has been deputy secretary general of Hizbullah. Qassem's goal was much more ambitious than Fadlallah's. If the latter developed a simple narration of the events that made up Hizbullah's *vécu*, and added the various representations and points of view Hizbullah's leadership had taken in particular situations, reflecting his approach to theorizing the social field, Qassem incorporated a more doctrinal construction of what Hizbullah "is." Qassem's mission is at a juncture between writing history and laying down permanent foundations for the identity of the party. But the foundations he builds are still framed in a historical setting. Through his writings, Qassem emphasizes the particular qualities that render Hizbullah unique: remembering the practices of those concerned, such as piety, no fear of death, recruitment methods and ideals cultivated, as seen in previous chapters.

---

[38] Kurani, *Ṭarīqat hizb allāh*, 90–92.
[39] Ibid., 97.
[40] Ibid., 25.

Moreover, the Islamic character of these actions cannot be understood from "outside": it needs actual contextual existence. The "*jihād* spirit" is what is at stake, and defining *jihād* involves different writing strategies.[41] In this sense, Qassem is mostly interested in addressing the perceptions of "the West" and the latter's bewilderment in the face of acts of "Sacrifice, martyrdom, and *jihād*":[42] "Westerners who have agreed the reality of *jihād* have done so only due to the impossibility of negating it, but partial explanations still reign and the core reasons for *jihād* are still misunderstood." Indeed, Qassem seems to argue that Hizbullah is different at the level of its practices, as understanding its spirit involves living it, and living it implies being part of the group. So acts of *jihād* can never be understood by non-Hizbullah actors, yet it is this continual quest to understanding this phenomenon on the part of the other that Hizbullah's intellectuals aim at keeping active by writing history as the legacy of the resistance.

In most Hizbullah-related writings of the theoretical sort, there is an urge to define terms such as *jihād*. A 2007 paper co-authored by Hilal Khashan, a Political Studies professor at the American University of Beirut (AUB), and Ibrahim Moussawi, a former professor at AUB, former head of media relations of Hizbullah, and now editor at al-Manar TV, revolved around "Hizbullah's Jihad Concept." Accordingly, *jihād* for "the Lebanese Shiite community" has specific connotations (that are fleshed out and categorized in the paper), derived from the experience of that community. The conclusion taken from the abstract is revealing: "The study shows that Hizbullah has successfully developed a flexible and highly workable *jihād* concept that won it unrivaled acclaim from Lebanese Shiites whom it empowered after many years of political marginalization." The paper concludes that "Hizbullah has the institutional mechanism and the ideological flexibility to adapt its *jihād* concept in response to a rapidly changing regional and domestic political environment."[43] The paper goes over the history of the resistance and its various successes, and tries to find this "spirit" that Qassem talks about in the various experiences of resistance fighters and leaders, experiences that gave the party credibility and respect. The objective seems to be finding working concepts that explain a success deemed unique and legitimize a political legacy.

---

[41] Qassem, *Hizbullah*, 44.
[42] Ibid.
[43] Hilal Khashan and Ibrahim Moussawi, "Hizbullah's Jihad Concept," *Journal of Religion and Society* 9(2007), 1.

Resistance Writes the Nation and Confronts the State

In light of the institutional changes undergone since the 1990s, it became a necessity to direct the focus of the discussions on Hizbullah to the legitimacy of the resistance. Anything else became redundant. During a talk-show on al-Manar TV in June 2008, on "the Islamists between Resistance and state building," Ali Fayyad shifted the discussion from theoretical notions on Islamism(s) to a practical survey of the resistance's achievements in Lebanon. The contrast was all the more clear when Fayyad's counterpart on the show, the head of the Jordanian newspaper *al-Liwā'*, Bilal Hassan al-Tal, was discussing abstract understandings of Islamist agendas in Arab societies and their relation with the unpopular "secular" state.[44]

The picture Fayyad drew of Islamists in general and Hizbullah in particular is worth mentioning. First of all, he explained, "Islamists no longer prioritize treating Arab nationalism as a secular heretical idea that the West has sent to conspire against the Islamic world." If anything, Islamists are the new pan-Arabists and Hizbullah's secretary general, Hassan Nasrallah, is considered the new pan-Arab leader. Second, Islamists' relations with other political parties are not based on ideology but on their stand vis-à-vis the USA and Israel. The pragmatic line that Fayyad endorses is the culmination of the concerns voiced by writers on Hizbullah during the 1990s, sympathizers and opponents alike. But it is in relation to the state that Fayyad took a view straight out of liberalist textbooks: "At an early stage, the state should be able to provide adequate services to the people, to protect them, and protect independence. At a later stage, the state becomes the bearer of a message."

These enigmatic statements can be clarified if we look at Hassan Fadlallah's most recent book, *Hizbullah and the State in Lebanon*, which involves an unprecedented detailed historical account of the modern state and its relation with the various communities. Even more striking is a lengthy and intricate discussion of the relationship between nation and state. For Fadlallah, "the notion of nation (*watan*) remains constant despite [social and political] changes incurred, because it is linked to constant variables such as geography, human relations, social ties, and the only change possible involves the movement of inhabitants such as optional or forced exile."[45] According to Fadlallah states come and go, and it is the realm of the political that is always temporary or subject to change, while nations remain, because they are the embodiment of a particular quality of life, transmitted through habits and culture,

---

[44] "al-Kalima al-tayyiba," talk-show, al-Manar TV (1/6/2008).
[45] Fadlallah, *Hizbullāh wal-dawla fī lubnān*, 27.

which make up our sense of belonging.[46] But if the nation transcends the state, it is not at all clear from Fadlallah's text what it really is. Geography, human relations, and social ties are at best vague criteria for building national specificity, especially if we compare this language to nineteenth- and early twentieth-century nationalist intellectual discussions, which usually involve elaborate historical accounts of localized specificity. If anything, Fadlallah stops short of explaining more of this, rather providing an "Islamic" legitimization for the notion of nationhood by referencing several religious scholars, and even sayings of Imam Ali,[47] who argued for its importance.[48]

Nevertheless, Fadlallah does propose a Lebanese national specificity, even if implicitly. For instance, he mostly attributes the gradual weakening of once-popular leftist politics to the fact that the left did not have a state project that was organic to the natural situation of the Lebanese nation.[49] Is the national imaginary confessional then, or just made up of the various religions-as-communities that lived side by side in what became geographic Lebanon? If the national seems mostly to refer to a "living-together," an ethics of communal relationship, without this sense of a projected history that produces a Lebanese specificity, the main catalyst for the forging of this quality of life is the state. Indeed, Fadlallah seems to suggest that the process of national construction is still waiting for the state to take matters more seriously. Until now, in his opinion, the state has been doing the opposite. It has fostered divisions and has harmed the nation-building process. Behind this wrestling with fixing its relationship with the state lies a much deeper quest for political legitimacy and recognition that has always pervaded Hizbullah's discourse.

Several passages of the book seem to imply that historical state margin-alization meant that people had been denied the "right" to be "Lebanese." For Fadlallah, in the period from the birth of the modern state in the 1940s until the eve of the civil war the state had not put enough effort "in reinforcing national cohesion (al-llaḥma al-waṭanīyya) or to the construction of a state in the contemporary sense of the term."[50] As a consequence of this, when inhabitants of marginalized areas (Bekaa, the South, and Akkar) "chanted the presence of the state" the

[46] Ibid., 24–27.
[47] This is an interesting ḥadīth by Ali that Fadlallah chooses, as it emphasizes the pluralistic nature of statesmanship: "People are in need of a ruler (an amīr), righteous or licentious, under whose rule the believer would work, the infidel would enjoy life and the exalted would know God, fight the enemy and collect wealth. Livelihoods would then be sustained and the weak would be protected from the strong."
[48] Ibid., 17–23.
[49] Ibid., 67.
[50] Ibid., 68.

authorities "only showed [their] ugly face."[51] Apart from the state's anthropomorphic attributes signaling a longing for national recognition, there is an underlying tone to this writing, implying that the people from whom Hizbullah originated (namely the Shi'i community) believed in the "modernizing" and "civilizing" potential of the state. Fadlallah here quotes a letter that Sayyid Abd al-Husayn Sharaf al-Din wrote in 1948 (five years after independence) to Beshara al-Khuri, the first president of Lebanon, accusing the newly born state of not including Jabal Amil and the Bekaa in this "modernising" quest.[52]

Indeed, for Fadlallah, "the marginalizing of a large section of the nationals [muwātin] of this state, [who] felt in a constant state of exile. One of the ugly faces of the weak state is that while it is powerless in the face of its enemy, who escapes after hearing the first gunshots, it is, in contrast, forceful in dealing with its citizens when it suppresses any popular movement or when it closes the doors of political participation and exercises hegemony over the country."[53] The term muwātin used here has the ambiguous sense of the national and the citizen. This serves the purpose of emphasizing a quality of living together rather than defining a national specificity at a spiritual level. Most importantly, it also points to the centrality of the state in making "the national" possible in the first place.

So in a sense Fadlallah is clear that the national existed before the establishment of this state,[54] even if defined in open-ended terms that mostly involve an ideal of coexistence. But as much as the state plays an important role in transforming this quality of living together, it can also destroy it. In a sense, Hizbullah developed a type of nationalism born out of a frustrating relationship with the state and its poor attempts at modernizing. Writing the nation-as-citizenship requires a pragmatic approach to instrumentalizing the state and saving the relationships between the various groups under this state.

The state needs to adopt the proper imaginary, or sense of belonging – what Fadlallah in a Gramscian vein calls "culture" (thaqāfa). For a long time the state's culture was anathema to that of resistance. People joined leftist parties because they were the only ones willing to pursue a military resistance to Israel and because these were the only political groups confronting the politics of the state.[55] The state still needs to help write the nation by upholding the correct politics of citizenship. The culture of

---

[51] Ibid., 69.
[52] Ibid., 60 and 65.
[53] Ibid., 62.
[54] Fadlallah calls it al-hawiyya al-wataniyya, national identity, which he argues moved from being "united" to "confessionalized" over the course of the twentieth century. Ibid., 72.
[55] Ibid., 68–67.

resistance is definitely a starting point and should be a "national constant" (*thābit watanī*)[56]. But the problem for Fadlallah is that the state has rejected resistance as a legitimate course of action, putting into question its very culture, its *nahj* (See Chapter 3)[57]. This "state culture" is in line with its previous political legacy of a "weak state that is powerless in front of its enemy" and "forceful in dealing with its citizens."

Also, it is because the state was deemed illegitimate and bankrupt that one needed alternative sources of authority, i.e. states (such as Iran) that were in line with the "culture of resistance" that Hizbullah wanted to politicize. This is an important statement as it shows that resistance is a local project that aimed for institutional stability, which is why it went to Iran, and why the bond is still strong. Fadlallah argues that if Hizbullah's discourse sounded radical during the early 1980s it needed to be under-stood in relation to other discourses that were prevalent at the time, and in the absence of a disciplinary force (*nāzim al-ʿalāqa*) to regulate the rela-tionships between the various Lebanese factions.[58] It is the absence of a strong state that produced political divisions and led Hizbullah to align with *wilāyat al-faqīh*, which homogenized the political projects of the state "inside the framework of the Lebanese state."[59] Religious influence can bring order and security, and legal constraints.[60] According to Fadlallah, for Khamenei, groups need to abide by the law and decisions of a particular political system and society "even if the state is not Islamic."[61] This religious imperative can produce notions or "spirit" (*rūh*) of righteous (*sāliha*) citizenship (*muwātana*) as determined by reli-gious references (*marāji ʾ*)[62].

Thus, Hizbullah's relationship with Iran can only be understood through the prism of its loathing of the Lebanese state. There cannot be a viable political project with continuity over time through sole reliance on the current state of Lebanon. Fadlallah's book repeatedly stresses the stability and predictability provided by *walī al-faqīh*, but also *marāji ʿ* in general,[63] that modern states, especially the Lebanese type, cannot pro-vide. But this tortuous argumentative style, which places the actions of Hizbullah within the legitimizing orbit of the Lebanese state while at the same time critiquing the state for not delivering the basic institutional and political logistics that can produce such a project betrays not just

---

[56] Ibid., 109.
[57] Ibid., 91.
[58] Ibid., 116.
[59] Ibid., 40.
[60] Ibid., 33.
[61] Ibid., 34.
[62] Ibid.
[63] Ibid., 38–39.

Hizbullah's still uncertain and ongoing negotiated understanding of the state but its reluctance to define itself as a political party.

This treatment of the state helps resolve the mystery behind Hizbullah's affiliation to Iran and *wilāyat al-faqīh*. Fadlallah's book does seem to convey the idea that as long as Hizbullah still struggles to control or at least use the state for the kind of objectives that can be effective for their political presence this double allegiance remains important. The religious versus the national here seems to be almost reactive/defensive (on this point see Chapter 3), because the national has still not found its organic or socializing state. In contrast, from this perspective, Iran has provided all forms of technologies, institutional guidance and practices, organizational efficiency that permitted Hizbullah and its constituency to conduct the type of politics that address their grievances. Fadlallah's book, which was published in 2015, still shows the symptoms that existed at the formative stage of the party, that even though the state is no longer alienated from one segment of its "nationals," it has not yet stabilized and become the type of institution to which the party can "transfer." All the chapters of his book deal with the history of modern Lebanon by looking at this ever vanishing, weak, ambivalent, at times enemy state, and how Iran played a comforting, predictable, and stabilizing role that filled a political void.

An *al-'Ahd* article from 1990[64] discusses directly, during the commemoration of the Islamic revolution that year, the link between the Islamic revolution in Iran and the Islamic resistance. Interestingly, what starts as a discussion of this link develops into constant digressions about the achievements of the military resistance in Lebanon, and specifically discusses the fear that "the Zionist entity" experiences when the appellation "Islamic republic" or "Islamic resistance" is mentioned. What seems to matter here is the instrumentality of the link to the "real" cause: the fight against Israel.

Ibrahim Amin al-Sayyed, who was the Hizbullah spokesman during the 1980s until the election of Sobhi Tufayli as the first secretary general, had a famous "one-liner" to explain the relations between Hizbullah and Iran: "We never said that we are a part of Iran, we are Iran in Lebanon, and Lebanon in Iran."[65] The structure of this statement shows the ambivalent, unresolved nature of the relationship between the party and Iran. The Islamic revolution, the authority and politics of the *walī al-faqīh*, provided the "cultural tool-kit"[66] needed to produce Hizbullah's organizational efficiency. And in turn, Hizbullah's local experience and its

---

[64] *al-'Ahd* (10/2/1990), m.
[65] *al-Nahār* (5/3/1987).
[66] To use the expression of Ann Swidler in Swidler, "Culture in Action."

peculiar struggle against the state of Israel feeds into the general cultural framework started by the Iranian revolution.

This is one of the reasons why, despite the continued public criticism of these seemingly ambiguous shows of allegiance to the national and beyond, Hizbullah-affiliated intellectuals never shied away from producing all sorts of arguments defending the link between Iran and Hizbullah and the latter's official endorsement of *wilāyat al-faqīh*. A case in point would be Hassan Nasrallah's speeches, which never miss a chance to stress this resilient bond.

Hizbullah-affiliated intellectuals followed similar directions when conceptualizing religion in line with the gradual development of Hizbullah into a political party outlined above. In a paper presented at a seminar for the "Nationalist and Islamic Dialogue" held in Alexandria in 2007,[67] Fayyad argued for a separation between a "liberation program of the resistance" that is deemed to be "nationalist" and a "religious imperative" for a "conceptual key to understand the emergence of the resistance," as "the more the resistance was successful in its practices the more it became political." This marked a radical break between what is deemed religious and what is considered to be political. It is here that Fayyad and Qassem's very different concerns bring to the forefront different understandings of the resistance. That the resistance practices a "defensive Jihad"[68] is not really a point that needs to be researched. It is a given that the "doctrinal discourse of the resistance is a religious one." The religious is a cultural backbone for a more pragmatic realist if not strategic (to use Hizbullah appellations) and "nationalist approach" to politics.

One of the consequences of Fayyad's conceptual differentiations between the religious and the political is the separation between the *qawmī* and the *watanī*, two words usually translated as "nationalist,"[69] but that could in Fayyad's context be translated as the "communitarian" and the "nationalist" respectively. The community is the one of Muslims or Arabs and so on, or even the "regional," while the nation is the one of Lebanon. So for Fayyad: "Although the resistance moves according to Lebanese imperatives it aims to have an influence in the regional challenges," meaning under the imperative of the strong Westphalian state. Yet another consequence of this is a utilitarian notion of the state. It becomes a tool, a weapon for the resistance in its regional context. This

---

[67] Ali Fayyad, "al-Muqāwama: nahwa qawā'id nazariyya wa siyāsiya fī tajribat al-muq-āwama. Wijhat nazar islāmīyya," paper presented at the Nationalist and Islamic Dialogue conference, Alexandria, 9 January 2007.

[68] Ibid. In this text, Fayyad gives the most detailed definitions of what *jihād* should stand for through linguistic etymological arguments and Qur'anic references.

[69] Although there was a long debate in the early part of the twentieth century around the distinction between the two words.

is the state as the provider of security, goods, and services, and also the bearer of a message, that of the resistance.

Fayyad even disqualified the "ideological vision" of Hizbullah if it tried to impinge on the "liberation plan" (al-barnāmaj al-taḥrīrī),[70] which seemed to represent the political demands of the resistance. What Fayyad seems to mean here is that the "ideological," which is the list of religion-related references, can be understood separately from the actual political program of liberating territory or confronting Israel. This military work is substantiated by a more realist approach to politics. Even more revealing is that for Abdel Halim Fadlallah, who succeeded Fayyad as the head of Hizbullah's research center, Hizbullah has, simply, no ideology as other political parties have, but only a "vision" for fighting a "cause" (nazariyat nidāl),[71] echoing the statement issued by Fayyad with regard his "liberation plan."

In the same vein, for MP Hassan Fadlallah, "Hizbullah has a political vision (ru'ya fikriyya siyāsiyya) for social and state matters, and he presents this vision at times through theoretical and intellectual material (qālib), through studies and political documents, and sometimes through working programs and methods of work on the ground (adā' maydānī)."[72]

An interesting representation of the state and its relationship with the project of resistance was articulated by Husayn Rahhal, who has been the editor of al-Intiqād since 2009. During the opening remarks of a three-day conference in May 2006 on "The Culture of Resistance" (thaqāfat al-muq-āwama), which grouped intellectuals from different backgrounds together with Hizbullah officials, Rahhal used a historical perspective to compare different forms of resistance throughout time and their relations with their respective states. Rahhal's main interest was to defend the legitimacy of the political militant practices of a non-state actor. He noted that in France and Algeria resistance emerged from existing state structures, whereas Hizbullah not only had to struggle to be considered legitimate but also faced a highly divided society, which accounts for its particular "non-state" situation.[73] This is echoed by Fadlallah, who says that understanding the relations between resistance and state follows the French model.[74] Accordingly, the state is controlled by foreign forces, interest, or politics, and does not represent popular will. People are divided into different orientations (to which we need to add the confessional layer in the case of Lebanon).

---

[70] Ibid., 2.
[71] Abdel Halim Fadlallah, Head of the Center for Documentation and Archiving, Interview with Author, 13 May 2010.
[72] Fadlallah, Hizbullāh wal-dawla fī lubnān, 11.
[73] Rahhal in Thaqāfat al-muqāwama (Beirut: Dar al Hadi, 2006), 156.
[74] Fadlallah, Hizbullāh wal-dawla fī lubnān, 90–91.

Epilogue: Between the Open Letter and the Political Manifesto

The first official document ever issued by Hizbullah is its Open Letter to the Downtrodden of 1984, following the commemoration of Sheikh Raghib Harb's *shahāda*. Ever since then, Hizbullah has been pressured by pundits and political actors to rework its Open Letter, or at least to produce in writing an updated version of its political vision.[75] This became the objective of the Political Manifesto of 2009. Contrary to what has been said by pundits and the media at large, the most striking feature of this latter text is that there are no important differences between its major themes and those of the original Open Letter. The main difference lies in some of the language used, the omission of controversial slogans (such as the establishment of an Islamic state as a solution for Lebanon's political system), and, in general, the way the various "visions" of the party are presented.

It is important to note that, contrary to what other scholars have assumed, Hizbullah never called for an Islamic state.[76] It mentioned it as an ideal in its Open Letter, but qualified it as impossible. It is not that Hizbullah changed its political "ideology"; it never really worked for the establishment of such a state, and never actually seems to have intended to. One of the reasons for this is indeed the fact that Hizbullah was not really concerned with taking over or building the state. That is also because, as argued throughout this chapter, it never meant to be a political party, and only slowly came to adopt the type of politics used by such organizations. And yet a careful reading of the Open Letter shows the difference between Hizbullah and other Islamic political formations of the time, as it only prescribes an Islamic state if all the citizens of a state agree to it. Hizbullah seemed to rally around conventional Political Islam banners of the time in order to jump-start its resistance efforts. Most certainly, it shows that Hizbullah was not really concerned with the state or related type of politics as such.

The differences between the Open Letter and the Political Manifesto were a product of the different writing styles of the institutions issuing them: Whereas the Letter was written by a few leaders such as Moussawi, Tufayli, Nasrallah, and Raad, in 1984,[77] the Manifesto has known

---

[75] For example, Haytham Muzahem demanded that Hizbullah re-explain its political agenda: see Haytham Muzahem, "Hizbullāh wa ishkāliyāt al-tawfiq, bayna al-aydiyolōjia wal-wāqiʿ," *Shu'un al-awsat* 59 (February 1997).

[76] See Alagha, *The Shifts in Hizbullah's Ideology* and Hamzeh, *In the Path of Hizballah*.

[77] Abdel Halim Fadlallah, head of Center for Documentation and Research, interview with the author, May 2010.

endless drafts, and has been circulated back and forth between the various committees, units, and Hizbullah's research center before being finalized in 2009. Moreover, the Letter and the Manifesto have two different purposes that depend on the context in which they were issued. The Letter marks the first official media appearance of Hizbullah as a political group with a message. Thus, the first part deals with "Who we are, and what is our identity." In contrast, the Manifesto does not need such assurances, and builds directly on Hizbullah's legacy: the resistance. From one decade to another, the differences stood in the actions performed and how they legitimized the presence of the party.

And so whereas both the Open Letter and the Political Manifesto featured a direct condemnation of the "imperialist assault" on the region, the phrasing used was significantly different. In the Letter, the community (*al-umma*) of Hizbullah is "part of the community of Islam in the world that faces the imperialist threat." In contrast, as noted in the discussion of Fayyad and as fleshed out in the Manifesto, these threats do not put into question the very identity or culture of the people in this category, even though these threats still exist, and are probably greater at the time of writing. The Manifesto revealed this problem realistically, without too many existential references: states in the region faced a threat from the United States of America and its proxy, Israel, and the process of globalization is merely a front for a US military presence. Analyses in the first part of the Manifesto could come straight out of alter-globalization or leftist textbooks. Indeed, the condemnation of "American terrorism" and the "American project" on a global level probably took up the largest part of the Manifesto. But these themes are already present in the Open Letter, even if they were couched in a more apocalyptic rhetorical contour.

The section on Lebanon is also similar in both texts in the sense that the Manifesto reiterates Hizbullah's desire to have a just, legitimate state that represents Lebanon, except that in the Manifesto this claim is first backed by a reassurance that for Hizbullah, Lebanon belongs to all its citizens. The Manifesto repeated the Letter's condemnation of a federalization of Lebanon, and the prevailing confessional system, but unlike the Letter, omits to even mention Hizbullah's demand for an Islamic state, although the party had explained over the years that the question of an Islamic state is part of its "vision," but can only be established if the various constituencies of the country agree to it. The Manifesto then incorporated ideological constructions of the Fayyad type about the qualities of the state and what it should provide for its citizens.

As a result, the most striking aspect of the absence of an "Islamist rhetoric" is the Manifesto's discussion of "Lebanon and Islamic relations" (*lubnān wal-'alaqat al-islāmīyya*), which could well read as

"Lebanon as a state and its relation with other Islamic states, or environment." The discussion revolves around the need for countering the imperialist threat as a trigger of sectarian divisions (between Muslims and Christians, but mostly between Sunni and Shi'i Muslims). Iran is only mentioned insofar as it provides a model for successful resistance against Israel and the USA. And in keeping with the fight for the Palestinian cause, the chapter on hypothetical negotiations with the Zionist entity (a strongly condemned practice) reiterates that Jerusalem as a holy site for the Islamic environment remains a point of focus or objective in the fight against Israel and any form of occupation. At no point is there a redefinition or rearticulation of what being "Islamic" really means or boils down to; there is no mention of any form of loyalty to or affinity with the *wilāyat al-faqīh*, no need to develop why Hizbullah is different as an Islamic party, and so on. Indeed, the first and last articulation of these conceptual points took place in the early 1980s, and there was no need to change the template.

In brief, the template used in both documents remained largely unmodified, which is a striking illustration of the notion of ideology as template. What changed was the representation of the state, as the party of God was slowly empowered and institutionalized, learning from its practice on the ground, and developed its relationship with its political environment. What also changed was the accumulation of knowledge through the writing of history, or claiming of the past, here understood through the actions of the resistance. Last but not least, abiding by a state discourse empowered the resistance as practice (through the recalling of its past), and put aside the need to define the core "identity" of the political organization through other readings of history.

Conclusion

On 12 July 1985, a young man, barely in his twenties, named Hassan Nasrallah, stood up to give a speech in the locality of Kafarmelki in the South of Lebanon. On that day, Nasrallah developed a detailed historical sweep of the formation of Lebanon, the colonial mandate, the ups and downs of confessional politics, the origin and development of the Palestinian question, and various other issues that Lebanon then faced as a divided and weakened state.[1] Toward the beginning of his speech, Nasrallah said something quite intriguing. He reversed a then infamous slogan made by Abu Iyad, the deputy chief and head of intelligence for the PLO,[2] that the road to Jerusalem goes through Jounieh, a Christian-dominated area of Beirut. Abu Iyad was hinting that the Palestinians should control Lebanon in order to fight Israel. On this day in July 1985, Nasrallah may have had Abu Iyad in mind when he said: "It is not as was said that the road to Jerusalem goes through Lebanon but the road to Lebanon goes through Jerusalem." *Al-'Ahd*'s front-page editorial that week was entitled: "The road to Lebanon goes through Jerusalem."[3] In his speech, Nasrallah reiterated most of the ideas that recurred successively over two decades of the party's existence, and which have become much more resonant today: Ideas such as the need for a strong state in Lebanon, the importance of resolving the Palestinian issue in order to have lasting peace in the region, and also in Lebanon, between the various constituencies. These are the ideas for which Nasrallah has been famous in his speeches, especially since 2000. Yet he had first uttered them twenty years earlier. All the templates of this speech pointed to a set of ideas that, while they assumed different meanings according to different political contexts, remained basically unchanged.

[1] *al-'Ahd* (12/7/1985), 2.
[2] Abu Iyad's real name was Salah Khalaf. He was considered the Fatah second in command after Yasser Arafat. This statement was made sometime in September 1976 and was used by Christian elites as a proof that Palestinians had plans to control the country.
[3] Ibid., 1.

This book has argued that Hizbullah is engaged in a politics of remembrance that enables it to interact with its environment, make informed choices, and set specific agendas for future action. These practices involve a systematic archiving of the human legacy, as seen in Chapter 2, the Christian political other and his claims to history in Chapter 3, the Palestinian and other organizations that were involved in resistance practices in Chapter 4, their different representation of territory through particular readings of history in Chapter 5, and in Chapter 6 the displacement of theorizing about the party in favor of writing a history of resistance. The politics of remembering has enabled Hizbullah to develop and to defend the main project to which it owes its existence: resistance against Israel. The various intellectuals associated with the party drew from the archival power of the politics of remembering in order to construct and establish the "resistance-as-project." Hizbullah-affiliated intellectuals' writing practices show that their most important cultural development has been to focus on defining the scope and scale of the resistance, and those Islamic articulations of it were increasingly dependent on the necessity of salvaging that project. In so doing, they contributed to imagining the Lebanese nation.

I pointed out in Chapter 1 that by looking at its form, rather than focusing solely on its content, ideological production involves much more than systems of beliefs and theories. Texts, the main repository of ideology, may be considered as artifacts or traces of inscriptions (such as in the case of collecting writings of or about martyrs, as seen in Chapter 2), and their presence permits a specific archival usage conducive to the politics of remembering. Arguments made in the unfolding of texts and other cultural devices have a timeless property in the sense that, through assuming new meanings across time, they can be used in different ways, depending on the various contexts. Consequently, the elaboration of a style counts more than the actual meaning of a particular sentence at a given point in time. In Chapter 1 I proposed calling these constructions writing strategies in order to stress the importance of the rhetorical element, but also the importance of traces rather than some reified content abstracted from the actual text. These writing strategies constitute different ideological attempts at rendering Hizbullah's actions meaningful in varying contexts.

Importantly enough, texts serve as a trace of an ethical line of conduct, a tradition of "doing" that ties the community together and thus provides the cultural tools to imagine nations through writing history or the past. This tradition is developed through the interplay of events on the ground, such as military operations of the resistance, and the ideological production that gives coherence to this legacy and makes it communicable.

Hizbullah ideology, or what Hizbullah "is" in this sense, is the legacy of the resistance as a series of events, stories, people, and actions. Writing history is the most important discursive activity at the disposal of intellectuals around the party. Studying ideology in this sense does not just explain how Hizbullah helps imagine the nation or its communities in different ways, but also how the "Islamic" suffuses this imagination.

The referential aspect of these texts makes all these initiatives dependent on earlier literary elaborations, hence the central importance of *al-'Ahd*, the first media outlet that carried the various discursive articulations of Hizbullah leaders and intellectuals. Islamic references and tropes that were influenced by the changes occurring from one text to another depended on the performativity of these texts. Performativity here is understood as the role a text plays beyond the actual meaning derived from its content. It refers to its actual usage as an object. It does not mean that the content is not important, but that there is a more relevant dimension that goes beyond that aspect in terms of triggering a specific political action. In other words, it is through a specific use of that content that the text becomes politically relevant.

If this book has focused mostly on intellectual writings, as opposed to formal speeches, then the purpose was to describe the different human agencies and institutional contexts involved in forming and disseminating these texts. *Al-'Ahd* was instrumental in this regard as the earliest textual repository since the inception of the party. It saw most of those producers of knowledge contribute to it in one way or another before assuming different political and intellectual positions within or around Hizbullah. Most importantly, the presence of a periodical such as *al-'Ahd* permitted a repetitiveness of the weekly contributions that spanned nearly two decades, enabling a constant rearticulation and remembering of political history in response to varying contexts. In addition to *al-'Ahd*, various other media and publishing houses affiliated or sympathetic to the party have taken over, in different ways, the task of mapping out the relations between Hizbullah and its political environment: TV shows, newspaper articles, individual intellectual works, history books, political analyses, research and policy papers, contributions to conferences, and other audio-visual output.

The changes and developments observed at the level of this intellectual field within and around Hizbullah were a clear signal of the importance of such performativity when it came to use certain concepts crucial to the creation of difference between Hizbullah and other political formations. Through examining the different writing strategies of Hizbullah-affiliated intellectuals we have seen the polyvalent nature and use of certain concepts such as *wilāyat al-faqīh, jihād, shahīd, istishhādī*, and so on. Broadly, these concepts are what constitute "Islamic" references with regard to writing or any other process of inscribing. They are the words that usually constitute the different texts, and thus writing strategies that address particular political concerns. They are used in order to position Hizbullah in relation to a particular question raised by a political actor in place or a given situation.

The use of "Islamic" references is but a symptom of the institutional developments that took Hizbullah from a small militant organization to a fully fledged political party with military, legislative, and municipal wings and many affiliated committees and institutions. Yet they also point to the inherent tension between the centrality of the resistance project and the possibility of engaging the state, as modern political party formations usually do. An important aspect of Islamic references is the way they propose new imaginaries of communities by blending what have been characterized as secular and religious times, as explained in Chapter 2. The resistance was made up of a community of believers, and that was an experiential rather than a discursively intelligible phenomenon, as shown by the martyrs' artifacts, the storytelling (Chapter 2), and the arguments made by Qassem (Chapter 6).

Hizbullah's specific ideological trajectories are in reality a reflection of the organization's ongoing negotiated relationship with the Lebanese state. As explained in Chapter 6, as Hizbullah remains essentially a military organization, its political work centers on safeguarding this initial project, even if it has to take the concerns of its community to heart. This oscillation between resistance project and community concerns is what shapes its ambivalent representation of the state.

Another way I proposed to understand the practical implications of the various discursive articulations that tried to fix Islamic tropes in texts was that, depending on the political context, the Islamic character of the movement was defined in reaction to dominant political actors' claims. The rewriting of history has been crucial to crystallizing these claims. In Chapter 3 I argued that representations of Political Maronitism permitted Hizbullah-affiliated intellectuals to in turn reject and accept different notions of secularism. The initial virulent critique of secularism (*'ilmāniyya*), which was represented in the Lebanese context as an asymmetric form of power, a mere façade for Political Maronitism, decreased considerably, allowing the more acceptable concept of *muwātana*, or citizenship, to prevail in the various discussions on the subject. Citizenship under a pluralist state was represented as an invitation to coexistence between the different confessions of Lebanon. Chapter 3 described the various uses of the concept of *muwātana*, referring especially to Hizbullah's alliance with the Free Patriotic Movement, the largest Lebanese Christian political party. This process of addressing history as written by the other and delineating the presence of historical traditions permitted Hizbullah-affiliated intellectuals to judge possible partners.

This reclaiming of the past has found its most crucial use in a reclaiming of territory and a subsequent addressing of the relationship between resistance as a project and the state's legitimizing power. Chapter 4 mapped this last archival practice of territory, which subsequently led to changing representations of the state (Chapter 5). Above all, Chapter 6 showed the limits of the use of Islamic tropes and their subjection to the resistance project, especially after comparing Hizbullah's 1984 Open Letter to its latest 2009 Political Manifesto, and to the various theoretical and doctrinal writings in between.

Nasrallah's Speeches and the Future of Hizbullah's Ideological Production

Amidst this discursive field, Nasrallah's intellectual production emerges as a paradigm of speech writing and dissemination. His speeches are a synthesis of all those writing strategies outlined throughout this book, a synthesis of storytelling, recollection, and legitimacy building in the face of political entities such as the state, and the different constituencies represented by these political entities. First, these writing strategies, through the example of Nasrallah's speeches, signal the changing use of Islamic references as a symptom of the changing institutional structure of Hizbullah and its many and varied related organizations. It seems worth reiterating that the change is not ideological in the classical sense, but institutional. Second, they bear the mark of this politics of remembering that describes the legacy of the practices of the resistance through the commemorating of the martyrs, the leaders, the constituency that is supposed to represent the party, and the many other contributors who make the resistance project a political reality.

Nasrallah eventually became the secretary general of Hizbullah in 1992, and has been reelected to that post at every annual meeting of its Shura Council. From the 1990s, and through an impressive production of speeches for all sorts of occasions, Nasrallah's oratory skills have focused media attention on Hizbullah's cultural production. After the 2006 July war, for security reasons, and except for a few short live appearances, Nasrallah became an image behind a screen, speaking from an unknown location to escape Israeli or other assassination attempts. For the most important occasions that have state-related significance, such as the Day of the Liberation of the South, most political officials of the country gather around a huge TV screen at the Martyrs' Hall in Haret Hreik, an event broadcast live by most Lebanese television channels. In addition to that, as I showed in this book, a prolific industry of rearticulations of ideas around all these arguments and themes would develop, especially during the 1990s, and would find a renewed dynamism after the liberation of the South in 2000. Nasrallah's speeches occupy a particularly important place in that industry. Books were thematized, along with articles, academic or non-academic studies, commentaries, and critiques of Nasrallah's speeches. Ironically, there are no books authored by Nasrallah except a selection of some of his early Ashura week speeches.[4] As part of Hizbullah's production of discourse, Nasrallah's speeches need to be understood in the more general production of writings about Hizbullah, how the ideas he discusses are already structured by the ideological templates we have been mentioning throughout this book.

An illustration of that is not just the fact that Nasrallah's style and ideas were used and appropriated countless times in the different contexts of discursive production, but that two studies on his speeches were published by Dar al-Maarif al-Hikmiyya,[5] a publishing house that is close to the party. These studies categorize Nasrallah's writing style into different themes that help in turn to categorize the various ideologies as templates that can be used and reused. Most songs and videos on resistance-related themes would contain extracts of Nasrallah's speeches, and several party members would come to borrow not just his expressions but his argumentative style too. In this sense, Nicholas Noe's characterization that Nasrallah's speeches would become the main "voice of Hizbullah" is right to the point.[6] Nasrallah's speeches could be viewed as a synthesis of Hizbullah's various ideological constructions, or what I have called writing strategies.

This phenomenon probably has less to do with Nasrallah's now famous logical and analytical fashion of displaying his arguments, and moving from one "topic" to the other, than with the overall development of Hizbullah as an organization, as was explained in Chapter 1. The more Hizbullah underwent a process of institutionalization, the more different forms of discursive productions were confined to specific locations, in the hands of different organizations, groups, or

[4] Hassan Nasrallah, *Kitāb 'āshūrā'* (Beirut: Dar al-Safwa, 2000).
[5] Ali Majed, *al-Kitāb 'inda al-sayyid Hassan Nasrallah* (Beirut: Dar al-Maarif al-Hikmiyya, 2006); Ali Mahdi, *Āshūrā' wa kitāb al-muqāwama al-islāmiyya: al-sayyid Hassan Nasrallah namuzajan* (Beirut: Dar al-Maarif al-Hikmiyya, 2006).
[6] Nicholas Noe, *Voice of Hezbollah: The Statements of Sayyed Hassan Nasrallah* (London: Verso, 2007).

even ad hoc militants and other social actors. As was seen, first, publications such as *Baqiyatullah*, an offshoot of *al-'Ahd*'s cultural pages, testified to this branching out of cultural production. Second, there was the creation of a research center at the beginning of the 1990s, the Center for Documentation and Research, and a proliferation of media devices and committees producing art of all kinds. This contributed to create an increasingly specialized niche for the defense of the resistance-as-project by dissociating it from various themes that may not be directly related to the resistance and more so to general Islamic remembering practices (such as the commemoration of the return of the Mahdi or the birth of the Prophet).

Moreover, this growing institutional process brought together several intellectual fields, from actual "official" Hizbullah documents, to papers presented or interventions made at conferences, and TV talk-shows or interviews – all grouping Hizbullah-affiliated intellectuals with a larger intellectual field sympathetic to the resistance project. As was explained in Chapter 4, this prolific publication industry has become a self-feeding market that creates institutional promotions of all sorts, whether in research centers and foundations or university academic positions.

I also argued in Chapter 6 that Hizbullah's Political Manifesto is mostly concerned with a pragmatic articulation of the relations between a legitimized resistance and the existing state. Borrowing from the writing strategies of the 1982 Open Letter, the Political Manifesto drops the discursive articulations of a particular "Islamic" system or regime in order to defend what it had been, in fact, defending all along, namely the resistance-as-project. In effect, the only remaining overtly "Islamic" articulations of a vision for a society or community such as that prevalent in the writings of the deputy secretary general of Hizbullah, Naim Qassem, are still mostly aimed at legitimizing the concept of resistance through his *mujtamā' al-muqāwama* (society of resistance).

Consequently, formal or normative attempts at defining "what Hizbullah is" were slowly replaced by the defense of the resistance as a legitimate project. Any need to define what Hizbullah was as a "party" was supplanted by Qassem's idea of a "resistance community," in which Hizbullah became a mere reflection of collective will, with no additional agenda of its own. From doctrinal constructions that involved constant revisiting of history, Hizbullah has managed to negotiate its political presence in Lebanon and beyond through a thorough reworking of national narratives. In so doing, it has set new political frameworks within which Lebanese actors are to relate both to each other and to external enemies.

The Ideological Future

Central to this book is the notion that ideas are sticky, and tend to survive political changes. The birth of Hizbullah, in the midst of the Israeli occupation of South Lebanon, sparked a cultural repository of "resistance" that developed over the years with a few constants that it is hoped this book has outlined. What was said from 1984 onwards, as found in the early issues of *al-'Ahd*, is still very much salient today. As Nasrallah appears on TV almost weekly to voice the main views of the party on current concerns, he articulates a politics of remembrance that gives the organization coherence by using the past in different ways as a written template. Nasrallah is supported by a cohort of media outlets, cultural institutions, intellectuals, and political actors, who disseminate these templates and form an imagined community with slightly open boundaries, around the project of resistance. This is why consciousness of history feeds into a communitarian project. Consciousness of history should be viewed here as the ability of organizations to use the past and "the event," in order to produce political action.

Glossary of Arabic Terms

'ahd: promise; covenant
'ala al-'ahd: keeping the promise
'aqīda: doctrine; ideology
fāth: opening
ḥadīth: the Prophet's sayings
ḥizb: party
'ilmāniyya: secularism
istishhād: testimony; act of martyrdom, dying for a cause
istishhādī (pl. *istishhādiyyūn*):   martyr who dies for a cause by killing himself in a military operation
marja' (pl. *marāji'*):   literally, "reference": example, source of imitation
mujāhid (pl. *mujāhidīn*):   combatant, fighter; generally, someone who works hard at a task
muwāṭana: citizenship
nahj: method; approach; process
shahāda: martyrdom; testimony
shahīd (pl. *shuhadā'*):   martyr; witness
al-sulṭa: the authorities
'ulamā' (sing. *'ālim*):   religious scholars
walī al-faqīh: jurist–leader
waṭan: nation; homeland; country
wilāyat al-faqīh: juristic leadership
tahwīd: "Judaification," rendering something "Jewish"

Select Bibliography

Abisaab, R. J. "The Cleric as Organic Intellectual: Revolutionary Shi'ism in the Lebanese Hawzas." In H. E. Chehabi (ed.), *Distant Relations: Iran and Lebanon in the last 500 years*. London and New York: Centre for Lebanese Studies and I. B. Tauris, 2006.

Abukhalil, A. "Ideology and Practice of Hizballah in Lebanon: Islamization of Leninist Organizational Principles." *Middle Eastern Studies* 27, no. 3 (1991): 390–403.

Ajami, F. *The Vanished Imam: Musa al-Sadr and the Shia of Lebanon*. Ithaca: Cornell University Press, 1986.

Alagha, Joseph. *Hizbullah's Identity Construction*. Amsterdam: Amsterdam University Press, 2011.

  The Shifts in Hizbullah's Ideology: Religious Ideology, Political Ideology and Political Program. Leiden: ISIM/Amsterdam University Press, 2006.

Althusses, Louis. "Ideology and Ideological State Apparatuses." In *Lenin and Philosophy, and Other Essays*. New York: Monthly Review Press.

Anderson, Benedict. *Imagined Communities: Reflections on the Origin and Spread of Nationalism*. London and New York: Verso, 1983.

Arendt, Hannah. *The Human Condition*. Chicago: University of Chicago Press, 1958.

Asad, T. *Formations of the Secular: Christianity, Islam, Modernity*. Stanford: Stanford University Press, 1993, 2003.

  Genealogies of Religion: Discipline and Power in Christianity and Islam. Baltimore and London: Johns Hopkins University Press, 1993.

  On Suicide Bombing. New York: Columbia University Press, 2007.

Asadollahi, Masood. *al-Islāmiyyūn fī mujtamāʿ taʾaddudī*. Beirut: Arab Scientific Publishers, 2004.

Bayat, A. "Islamism and Social Movement Theory." *Third World Quarterly* 26, no. 5 (2005): 891–908.

Benjamin, Walter. *Illuminations*. New York: Schocken Books, 1968.

Beydoun, A. *Identité confessionnelle et temps social chez les historiens libanais contemporains*. Beirut: Librairie Orient, 1984.

Bourdieu, Pierre. *Ce que parler veut dire: l'économie des échanges linguistiques*. Paris: Fayard, 1982.

  Esquisse d'une théorie de la pratique, précédé de trois études d'ethnologie kabyle. Paris: Éditions du Seuil, 1972.

  Homo Academicus. Stanford: Stanford University Press, 1990.

Bourdieu, Pierre, and J. B. Thompson. *Language and Symbolic Power.* Cambridge, Mass.: Harvard University Press, 1991.

Brenner, Neil. "Foucault's New Functionalism." *Theory and Society* 23, no. 5 (1994): 679–709.

Brubaker, R., and F. Cooper. "Beyond Identity." *Theory and Society* 29 (2000): 1–47.

Carr, D. "Narrative and the Real World: An Argument for Continuity." *History and Theory* 25, no. 2 (1986): 117–131.

Chaib, K. "La représentation du martyr." In *Les mondes chiites et l'Iran.* Beirut: Karthala and IFPO, 2007.

Chalabi, Tamara. *The Shi'is of Jabal 'Amil and the New Lebanon: Community and Nation-State, 1918–1943.* New York: Palgrave Macmillan, 2006.

Chatterjee, P. *The Nation and its Fragments: Colonial and Post-Colonial History.* Princeton: Princeton University Press, 1993.

Comaroff, J. L., and J. L. Comaroff. *Of Revelation and Revolution,* volume II: *The Dialectics of Modernity on a South African Frontier.* Chicago: University of Chicago Press, 1997.

Daher, Aurélie. *Le Hezbollah: mobilisation et pouvoir.* Paris: Presses Universitaires de France, 2014.

Deeb, L. *An Enchanted Modern: Gender and Public Piety in Shi'i Lebanon.* Princeton: Princeton University Press, 2006.

"Living Ashura in Lebanon: Mourning Transformed to Sacrifice." *Comparative Studies of South Asia, Africa and the Middle East* 25, no. 1 (2005): 122–137.

Derrida, Jacques. *Dissemination.* London: Bloomsbury/Continuum International Publishing Group, 2004 [1972].

De la grammatologie. Paris: Éditions de Minuit, 1967.

Positions. Paris: Éditions de Minuit, 1972.

Eickelman, D. F, and J. Piscatori. *Muslim Politics.* Princeton: Princeton University Press, 2004.

Fadlallah, Hassan. *al-Khayār al-ākhar.* Beirut: Dar al-Hadi, 1994.

Harb al-irādāt. Beirut: Dar al-Hadi, 1997.

Sukūt al-wahm. Beirut: Dar al-Hadi, 2001.

Fadlallah, Muhammad Hussein. *al-Islām wa mantiq al-quwwa.* Beirut: Dar al-Malak, n.d.

"Man al-lazi yaqud amaliyat al-taghīr hizb al-umma aw ummat al-hizb." In *al-Haraka al-islāmīyya: humūm wa qadāya.* Beirut: Dar al-Malak, 2001.

Fayyad, Ali. "al-Muqāwama: nahwa qawā'id nazariyya wa siyāsiya fī tajribat al-muqāwama. Wijhat nazar islāmīyya." Paper presented at the "Nationalist and Islamic Dialogue" conference, Alexandria, 2007.

Nazariyyat al-sulṭa fī al-fikr al-siyāsī al-shī'ī al-mu'aser. Beirut: Center for Civilization for the Development of Islamic Thought, 2008.

Fayyad, Mona. "To be a Shiite Now." *al-Nahār.* Beirut, 8 August 2006. Available at www.10452lccc.com/hizbollah/fayad10.8.06english.htm.

Finnemore, M., and K. Sikkink. "Taking Stock: The Constructivist Research Program in International Relations and Comparative Politics." *Annual Review of Political Science* 4, no. 1 (2001): 391–416.

Foucault, Michel. *L'ordre du discours.* Paris: Gallimard, 1971.

Les mots et les choses. Paris: Gallimard, 1966.

Geertz, C. *The Interpretation of Cultures: Selected Essays.* New York: Basic Books, 1973.

Gerring, J. "Ideology: A Definitional Analysis." *Political Research Quarterly* 50, no. 4 (1997): 957–994.

Hamzeh, N. A. *In the Path of Hizballah.* Syracuse: Syracuse University Press, 2004.

"Lebanon's Hizbullah: From Islamic Revolution to Parliamentary Accommodation." *Third World Quarterly* 21, no. 5 (1997): 739–759.

Hanks, W. F. "Text and Textuality." *Annual Review of Anthropology* 18 (1989): 95–127.

Harb, Mona, and Reynoud Leenders. "Know thy Enemy: Hizbullah, 'Terrorism' and the Politics of Perception." *Third World Quarterly* 26, no. 1 (2005): 173–197.

Harik, J. P. *Hezbollah: The Changing Face of Terrorism.* London: I. B. Tauris, 2004.

Houri, Walid, and Rima Saber. "Filming Resistance: A Hezbollah Strategy." *Radical History Review*, no. 106 (2010): 70–85.

Idriss, Nisrine. *'Urss ayḥūl.* Beirut: Dar al-Hadi, 2001.

al-Islam wal-masihiyya: buḥūth fī nizām al-qiyām al-muʾāsira. Beirut: Dar al-Hadi, 2003.

Jaber, Hala. *Hezbollah: Born with a Vengeance.* New York: Columbia University Press, 1997.

Jumblatt, Kamal. "Le Liban et le monde Arabe (30/3/1949)." In *Les conférences du Cénacle.* Beirut: Cénacle Libanais (Michel Asmar), 1949.

Kawtharani, Wajih. *Bayna fiqh al-islāh al-Shīʿī wa wilāyat al-faqīh.* Beirut: Dar al-Nahar, 2007.

Kechichian, S. "The Many Faces of Violence and the Social Foundations of Suicide Bombings, Lebanon 1981–2000." Unpublished paper, 2007.

Kertzer, D. I. *Comrades and Christians: Religion and Political Struggle in Communist Italy.* Prospect Heights, Ill.: Wareland Press, 1980.

Politics and Symbols: The Italian Communist Party and the Fall of Communism. New Haven and London: Yale University Press, 1996.

Khalili, Laleh. "'Standing with my Brother': Hizbullah, Palestinians, and the Limits of Solidarity." *Comparative Studies in Society and History* 49, no. 2 (2007): 276–303.

Khashan, Hilal, and Ibrahim Moussawi. "Hizbullah's Jihad Concept." *Journal of Religion and Society* 9 (2007): 1–19.

Kramer, M. "Hezbollah: The Calculus of Jihad." In *Fundamentalisms and the State: Remaking Polities, Economies and Militance.* Chicago: University of Chicago Press, 1993.

"The Moral Logic of Hizbullah." In *Origins of Terrorism: Psychologies, Ideologies, Theologies, States of Mind.* Cambridge: Cambridge University Press, 1990.

"The Oracle of Hezbollah, Sayyid Muhammad Hussein Fadlallah." In *Spokesmen for the Despised: Fundamentalist Leaders of the Middle East.* Chicago: University of Chicago Press, 1997.

"Redeeming Jerusalem: The Pan-Islamic Premise of Hizballah." In *The Iranian Revolution and the Muslim World.* Boulder, Co: Westview Press, 1990.

Kurani, Ali. *Ṭarīqat hizb allāh fīl-ʿamal al-islāmī.* Beirut: Maktab al-Iʿlam al-Islāmī, 1986.

Kurani, Muhammad Amin. *al-Juzūr al-tārīkhiya lil-muqāwama al-islāmīyya*. Beirut: Dar al-Hadi, 2005.

Lears, J. T. J. "The Concept of Cultural Hegemony: Problems and Possibilities." *American Historical Review* 90, no. 3 (1985): 567–593.

Mahdi, Ali. *Āshūrā' wa kitāb al-muqāwama al-islāmīyya: al-sayyid Hassan Nasrallah namuzajan*. Beirut: Dar al-Maarif al-Hikmiyya, 2006.

Mahmood, Arwa. *Kital hizbullāh*. Beirut: Dar al-Amir, 2008.

Mahmood, Saba. *Politics of Piety: The Islamic Revival and the Feminist Subject*. Princeton: Princeton University Press, 2005.

Majed, Ali. *al-Kitāb 'inda al-sayyid Hassan Nasrallah*. Beirut: Dar al-Maarif al-Hikmiyya, 2006.

Makdisi, Ussama. *The Culture of Sectarianism: Community, History, and Violence in Nineteenth-Century Ottoman Lebanon*. Berkeley: University of California Press, 2000.

Mallat, Chibli. *The Renewal of Islamic Law: Muhammad Baqer as-Sadr, Najaf and the Shi'i International*. Cambridge: Cambridge University Press, 2003.

Manicas, Peter. *A History and Philosophy of the Social Sciences*. Oxford: Basil Blackwell, 1987.

Massad, J. A. *Colonial Effects: The Making of National Identity in Jordan*. New York: Columbia University Press, 2001.

Mawtini – My Homeland – The Story of a City and War – The Story of Beirut's Southern Suburbs. Documentary (DVD). Beirut: Dar al-Manar, 2008.

Mervin, S. "Les larmes et le sang des chiites: corps et pratiques rituelles lors des célébrations de 'ashûrâ' (Liban, Syrie)." *Revue des mondes musulmans et de la Méditerranée*, no. 113–114 (2006): 153–166.

Un réformisme chiite, ulémas et lettres du Jabal 'Âmil (actuel Liban-Sud) de la fin de l'Empire ottoman à l'indépendance du Liban. Paris, Beirut, and Damascus: Karthala and CERMOCIFEAD, 2000.

Messick, B. M. *The Calligraphic State: Textual Domination and History in a Muslim Society*. Berkeley and Los Angeles: University of California Press, 1993.

Mitchell, T. "The Stage of Modernity." In *Questions of Modernity*. Minneapolis and London: University of Minnesota Press, 1999.

Muzahem, Haytham. "Hizbullāh wa ishkāliyāt al-tawfiq, bayna al-aydiyolōjia wal-wāqi'." *Shu'un al-awsat*, no. 59 (February 1997): 61–67.

Nasrallah, Hassan. "al-Sayyed Hassan Nasrallah: al-sīra al-zatiyya." *al-Mustaqbal al-Arabi*, no. 331 (September 2006).

Kitāb 'āshūrā'. Beirut: Dar al-Safwa, 2000.

Nisan, Mordechai. *The Conscience of Lebanon: A Political Biography of Etienne Sakr (Abu-Arz)*. London: Frank Cass, 2003.

Noe, Nicholas. *Voice of Hezbollah: The Statements of Sayyed Hassan Nasrallah*. London: Verso, 2007.

Norton, A. R. *Amal and the Shi'a: Struggle for the Soul of Lebanon*. Austin: University of Texas Press, 1987.

Hizballah of Lebanon: Extremist Ideals vs. Mundane Politics. New York: Council on Foreign Relations (1999).

"Hizballah: From Radicalism to Pragmatism." *Middle East Policy* 5 (1998): 147–158.

Petran, T. *The Struggle over Lebanon*. New York: Monthly Review Press, 1987.
Picard, E. "The Lebanese Shi'a and Political Violence in Lebanon." In *The Legitimization of Violence*. London: United Nations Research Institute for Social Development, 1997.
Qanso, Wajih. *'A'imat ahl al-bayt wal-siyāsat*. Beirut: al-Mada, 2008.
Qassem, Naim. *Hizbullah: The Story from Within*. London: Saqi, 2005.
Mujtamā' al-muqāwama. Beirut: Dar al-Maarif al-Hikmiyya, 2008.
Rahhal, Hussain. *Muhammad Mahdi Shamseddine: dirāsāt fī ru'ah al-islahīyya*. Beirut: Center for Civilization for the Development of Islamic Thought, 2010.
Ranstorp, M. *Hizb'Allah in Lebanon: The Politics of the Western Hostage Crisis*. New York: St. Martin's Press, 1997.
"Hizbollah's Command Leadership: Its Structure, Decision-Making and Relationship with Iranian Clergy and Institutions." *Terrorism and Political Violence* 6, no. 3 (1994): 303–339.
"Terrorism in the Name of Religion." *Journal of International Affairs* 50, no. 1 (1996): 41–62.
"The Strategy and Tactics of Hizballah's Current 'Lebanonization Process'." *Mediterranean Politics* 3, no. 1 (1998): 103–134.
Rosiny, S. *Shia's Publishing in Lebanon: With Special Reference to Islamic and Islamist Publications*. Berlin: Das Arabische Buch, 2000.
Saad-Ghorayeb, A. "Factors Conducive to the Politicization of the Lebanese Shi'a and the Emergence of Hizbu'llah." *Journal of Islamic Studies* 14, no. 3 (2003): 273–307.
Hizbullah: Politics and Religion. London: Pluto Press, 2002.
Saafan, Hassan. *Ususs 'ilm al-ijtimā'*. Beirut: Dar al-Nahda al-'Arabiyya, 1975.
al-Safa, Muhammad Jabir. *Tārīkh Jabal 'Āmil*. Beirut: Dar al-Nahar, 1981.
Sankari, Jamal. *Fadlallah: The Making of a Radical Shi'ite Leader*. Beirut: al-Saqi, 2005.
Sfeir, J. *L'exil palestinien au Liban: le temps des origines (1947–1952)*. Paris: Karthala Editions, 2008.
Shaery-Eisenlohr, R. *Shi'ite Lebanon: Transnational Religion and the Making of National Identities*. New York: Columbia University Press, 2008.
Sharara, Walid. *Dawlat Hizbullāh: Lubnān mujtamā' an Islāmīyyan*. Beirut: Dar al-Nahar, 1998.
Spivak, G. C. "Can the Subaltern Speak?" In *Marxism and the Interpretation of Culture*. Urbana: University of Illinois Press, 1988.
Swidler, A. "Culture in Action: Symbols and Strategies." *American Sociological Review* 51, no. 2 (1986): 273–286.
Tah, Ghassan. *Shī'at lubnān: al-'ashirat, al-hizb, al-dawla (Baalbak–al-Hermel namuzajan)*. Beirut: Dar al-Maarif al-Hikmia, 2005.
Volk, Lucia. *Memorials and Martyrs in Modern Lebanon*. Bloomington: Indiana University Press, 2010.
Wedeen, Lisa. "Conceptualizing Culture: Possibilities for Political Science." *American Political Science Review* 96, no. 4 (2002): 713–728.
Peripheral Visions: Publics, Power, and Performance in Yemen. Chicago: Chicago University Press, 2008.

Weiss, M. "The Cultural Politics of Shi'a Modernism: Morality and Gender in Early 20th-Century Lebanon." *International Journal of Middle East Studies* 39, no. 2 (2007): 249–270.

Other Sources

Newspapers

al-'Ahd
Baqiyatullah
al-Intiqād
al-Nahār
al-Safīr

Television Broadcasts

Hassan Nasrallah's speeches
al-Manar TV clips

Websites

www.alintiqad.com
www.muqawama.org

Interviews

Anonymous communist fighter, South of Lebanon (Summer 2007)
Employee at Athār al-Shuhadā' (July 2009)
Abdel Halim Fadlallah (May 2010)
Ali Fayyad (June 2009)
Ibrahim Moussawi (July 2010)
Muhammad Raad (June 2010)

Index

Other Books in the Series

For EU product safety concerns, contact us at Calle de José Abascal, 56–1°, 28003 Madrid, Spain or eugpsr@cambridge.org.

www.ingramcontent.com/pod-product-compliance
Ingram Content Group UK Ltd.
Pitfield, Milton Keynes, MK11 3LW, UK
UKHW020827130526
470833UK00021B/338